essentials

EXCEL 2000
advanced

J. BURDEANE ORRIS
COLLEGE OF BUSINESS ADMINISTRATION, BUTLER UNIVERSITY

Prentice
Hall

A division of Pearson Education
Upper Saddle River, NJ 07458

Excel 2000 Essentials Advanced

International Standard Book Number: 1-58076-303-0

Library of Congress Catalog Card Number: 99-60066

Printed in the United States of America

First Printing: July 1999

03 02 01 00 4 3 2 1

Interpretation of the printing code: the rightmost double-digit number is the year of the book's printing; the rightmost single-digit number, the number of the book's printing. For example, a printing code of 00-1 shows that the first printing of the book occurred in 2000.

Trademark Acknowledgments

Screens reproduced in the book were created using Collage Plus from Inner Media, Inc., Hollis, NH.

Excel 2000 Essentials Advanced is based on **Microsoft Excel 2000**.

Publisher:
Robert Linsky

Executive Editor:
Sunthar Visuvalingam

Series Editors:
Marianne Fox
Larry Metzelaar

Operations Manager:
Christine Moos

Director of Product Marketing:
Susan Kindel

Acquisitions Editor:
Sunthar Visuvalingam

Development Editor:
Joyce Nielsen

Technical Editors:
Jan Snyder and Asit Patel

Software Coordinator:
Angela Denny

Book Designer:
Louisa Klucznik

Design Usability Consultant:
Elizabeth Keyes

Project Editor:
Sherri Fugit

Copy Editor:
Cynthia Fields

Proofreaders:
Terri Edwards, Donna Martin, Heather Talbot

Indexer:
Becky Hornyak

Layout Technician:
Cheryl Lynch

Team Coordinator:
Melody Layne

Usability Testers:
Lynda Fields
Fox Consulting

Amy Wierenga
College of Business (Economics) Administration, Butler University

Lakshmy Sivaratnam M.Sc.
University of Missouri-Kansas City

About the Author

J. Burdeane ("Deane") Orris earned a Ph.D. in Organizational Behavior with a minor in statistics and computer science from the University of Illinois at Urbana/Champaign. For 28 years he has taught statistics and computer courses in the College of Business Administration at Butler University. In 1964, he wrote his first FORTRAN program, and by the late 1970s, he was building microcomputers from kits. In 1979, he wrote *Microstat,* which was one of the first statistics programs for personal computers. The program has evolved through several versions and has recently been published as *MegaStat,* an Excel add-in consisting of more than 4,000 lines of Excel VBA code.

Dedication

I would like to dedicate this book to my wife, Barbara, whose help and support made it possible.

Acknowledgments

Although the author is solely responsible for its content, this book and the *Essentials* series as a whole have been shaped by the combined experience, perspectives, and input of the entire authoring, editorial, and design team. We are grateful to the Series Editors, **Larry Metzelaar** and **Marianne Fox**, and to the College of Business Administration at Butler University, for hosting the listserv on which the implications and value of every series element were thoroughly discussed and finalized even as this book was being written. They also hosted a November 98 seminar for the *AIM* authors and coordinated much of the usability testing at the Butler campus. I acknowledge **Robb Linsky** (Publisher, Que Education and Training) for having provided the initial direction and for having allowed the Essentials 2000 team to shape this edition as we saw fit. You, the reader, are the greatest beneficiary of this ongoing online collaborative effort.

Chuck Stewart adapted the original Que E&T *Essentials* series for corporate training. In early 1998, however, he began revamping the *Office 2000 Essentials* pedagogy to better serve academic needs exclusively. He enlisted the services of Series Editors Metzelaar and Fox because of their extensive background in courseware development, many years of classroom teaching, and innovative pedagogy. Early discussion with the Series Editors revealed the need for the three new types of end-of-chapter exercises you find in the *Office 2000 Essentials*. Chuck continued to provide ideas and feedback on the listserv long after handing over the executive editorship to Sunthar. Together, they completely overhauled the *Essentials* series, paying particular attention to pedagogy, content, and design issues.

Sunthar Visuvalingam took over as Executive Editor for the *Essentials* series in October 1998. He stepped into a process already in full swing and moved quickly to ensure "a level of collaboration rarely seen in academic publishing." He performed admirably the daunting task of coordinating an army of widely dispersed authors, editors, designers, and usability testers. Among the keywords that characterize his crucial role in forging a well-knit "learning team" are decisive leadership, effective communication, shared vision, continuous pedagogical and procedural innovation, infectious enthusiasm, dogged project and quality management, active solicitation of feedback, collective problem-solving, transparent decision-making, developmental mentoring, reliability, flexibility, and dedication. Having made his indelible mark on the *Essentials* series, he stayed on to shepherd the transition of the series to Alex.

Linda Bird (AIM Series Editor and author of both *PowerPoint Essentials* books) and **Robert Ferrett** (co-author of *Office Essentials*, all three *Access Essentials* books, and of the related *Learn* series) made significant contributions to enhancing the concept and details of the new series. A newcomer to the series but not to educational publishing, **Keith Mulbery** seized increasing ownership of *Essentials* and undertook the initiative of presenting the series at the April 1999 National Business Education Association Convention.

Alex von Rosenberg, Executive Editor, manages the Computer Applications publishing program at Prentice Hall (PH). The PH team has been instrumental in ensuring a smooth transition of the *Essentials* series. Alex has been ably assisted in this transition by **Susan Rifkin**, Managing Editor; **Leanne Nieglos**, Assistant Editor; **Jennifer Surich**, Editorial Assistant; **Nancy Evans**, Director of Strategic Marketing; **Kris King**, Senior Marketing Manager; and **Nancy Welcher**, Media Project Manager.

Operations Manager **Christine Moos** and Senior Editor **Karen Walsh** worked hard with Sunthar and Alex to allow authors maximum flexibility to produce a quality product, while trying to maintain a tight editorial and production schedule. They had the unenviable task of keeping the book processes rolling while managing the complex process of transitioning the series to Prentice Hall. Book Designer **Louisa Klucznik** and Consultant **Elizabeth Keyes** spared no efforts in making every detail of the new design attractive, usable, consistent, and appropriate to the *Essentials* pedagogy. **Joyce Nielsen**, **Jan Snyder**, **Asit Patel**, **Nancy Sixsmith**, and **Susan Hobbs**—freelancers who had worked on earlier editions of the *Essentials* and the related *Learn* series in various editorial capacities—helped ensure continuity in procedures and conventions. **Tim Tate**, **Sherri Fugit, Melody Layne,** and **Cindy Fields** also asked sharp questions along the way and thereby helped us refine and crystallize the editorial conventions for the *Essentials*.

I am grateful to Sunthar Visuvalingam for bringing me into this project and to Marianne Fox and Larry Metzelaar for their guidance, support, and manuscript reviews. The manuscript was tech-edited twice for accuracy, before development by Asit Patel, then again very thoroughly after author review by Jan Snyder. I would especially like to thank Joyce Nielsen, my development editor, for her many late night sessions patiently editing my manuscripts. She caught and fixed many inaccuracies, reshot figures, and did much to polish up the presentation. I thank Sherri Fugit, Project Editor; Cindy Fields, Copy Editor, as well as the usability testers—Lynda Fields, Amy Wierenga, and Lakshmy Sivaratnam—for their feedback and suggestions.

Contents at a Glance

Table of Contents

Introduction

Essentials courseware from Prentice Hall is anchored in the practical and professional needs of all types of students. This edition of the *Office 2000 Essentials* has been completely revamped as the result of painstaking usability research by the publisher, authors, editors, and students. Practically every detail—by way of pedagogy, content, presentation, and design—was the object of continuous online (and offline) discussion among the entire team.

The *Essentials* series has been conceived around a "learning-by-doing" approach that encourages you to grasp application-related concepts as you expand your skills through hands-on tutorials. As such, it consists of modular lessons that are built around a series of numbered step-by-step procedures that are clear, concise, and easy to review. Explicatory material is interwoven before each lesson and between the steps. Additional features, tips, pitfalls, and other related information are provided at exactly the place where you would most expect them. They are easily recognizable elements that stand out from the main flow of the tutorial. We've even designed our icons to match the Microsoft Office theme. Likewise, the end-of-chapter exercises have been carefully graded from the routine Checking Concepts and Terms to tasks in the Discovery Zone that gently prod you into extending what you've learned into areas beyond the explicit scope of the lessons proper. Below, you'll find out more about the rationale behind each book element and how to use each to your maximum benefit.

How to Use This Book

Typically, each *Essentials* book is divided into seven or eight projects, concerning topics such as Designing Forms, Creating Macros, Integrating Applications, and Creating Hyperlinks. A project covers one area (or a few closely related areas) of application functionality. Each project is then divided into eight or nine lessons related to that topic. For example, a project about recording macros is divided into lessons explaining how to prepare to record a macro, record the macro and use the macro. Each lesson presents a specific task or closely related set of tasks in a manageable chunk that's easy to assimilate and retain.

Each element in *Excel 2000 Essentials Advanced* is designed to maximize your learning experience. Here's a list of the *Essentials* project elements and a description of how each element can help you:

- **Project Objectives.** Starting with an objective gives you short-term, attainable goals. Using project objectives that closely match the titles of the step-by-step tutorials breaks down the possibly overwhelming prospect of learning several new features of Excel into small, attainable, bite-sized tasks. Look over the objectives on the opening page of the project before you begin, and review them after completing the project to identify the main goals for each project.
- **Key Terms.** This book includes a limited number of useful vocabulary words and definitions, such as ***Macro***, ***Function Palette***, ***Hyperlink***, and ***OLE***. Key terms introduced in each project are listed in alphabetical order immediately after the objectives on the opening page of the project. These key terms are shown in bold italic and are defined during their first use within the text. Definitions of key terms are also included in the glossary.

- **Why Would I Do This?** You are studying Excel to accomplish useful tasks in the real world. This brief section tells you why these tasks or procedures are important. What can you do with the knowledge? How can these application features be applied to everyday tasks?
- **Visual Summary.** This opening section graphically illustrates the concepts and features you will learn in the project. One or more figures, with ample callouts, show the final result of completing the project. This road map to your destination keeps you motivated as you work through the individual steps of each task.
- **Lessons.** Each lesson contains one or more tasks that correspond to an objective on the opening page of the project. A lesson consists of step-by-step tutorials, their associated data files, screenshots, and the special notes described below. Though each lesson often builds on the previous one, the lessons (and the exercises) have been made as modular as possible. For example, you can skip tasks that you've already mastered and begin a later lesson using a data file provided specifically for its task(s).
- **Step-by-Step Tutorial.** The lessons consist of numbered, bolded step-by-step instructions that show you how to perform the procedures in a clear, concise, and direct manner. These hands-on tutorials, which are the "essentials" of each project, let you "learn by doing." Regular paragraphs between the steps clarify the results of each step. Also, screenshots are introduced after key steps for you to check against the results on your monitor. To review the lesson, you can easily scan the bold, numbered steps. Quick (or impatient!) learners may likewise ignore the intervening paragraphs.
- **Need to Know.** These sidebars provide essential tips for performing the task and using the application more effectively. You can easily recognize them by their distinctive icon and bolded headings. It's well worth the effort to review these crucial notes again after completing the project.

- **Nice to Know.** Nice to Know comments provide extra tips, shortcuts, alternative ways to complete a process, and special hints about using the software. You may safely ignore these for the moment to focus on the main task at hand, or you may pause to learn and appreciate these tidbits. Here you'll find neat tricks and special insights that you can use to impress your friends and co-workers!

- **If You Have Problems...** These short troubleshooting notes help you anticipate or solve common problems quickly and effectively. Even if you do not encounter the problem at this time, make a mental note of it so that you know where to look when you find yourself (or others) in the same difficulty.
- **Summary.** This provides a brief recap of the tasks learned in the project. The summary will guide you to places where you can expand your knowledge, which might include references to specific Help topics or the Prentice Hall *Essentials* Web site (http://www.prenhall.com/essentials).

- **Checking Concepts and Terms.** This section offers optional True/False, Multiple Choice, and Discussion Questions designed to check your comprehension and assess retention. If you need to refresh your memory, the relevant lesson number is provided after each True/False and Multiple Choice question. For example, [L5] directs you to review Lesson 5 for the answer. Lesson numbers might also be provided for other types of exercises, but only where relevant.

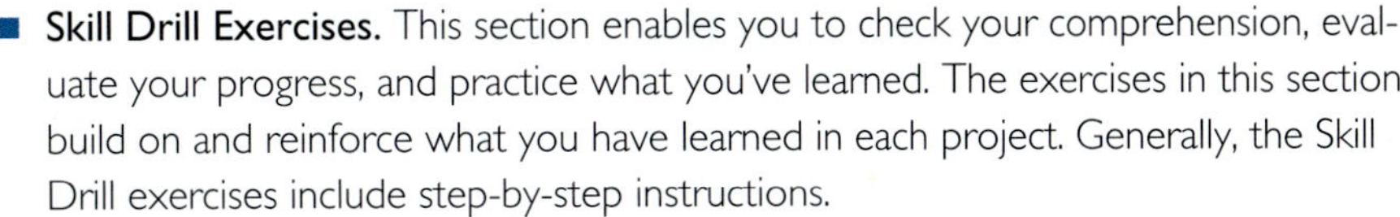

- **Skill Drill Exercises.** This section enables you to check your comprehension, evaluate your progress, and practice what you've learned. The exercises in this section build on and reinforce what you have learned in each project. Generally, the Skill Drill exercises include step-by-step instructions.

- **Challenge Exercises.** This section provides exercises that expand on or relate to the skills practiced in the project. Each exercise provides a brief narrative introduction followed by instructions. Although the instructions are often written in a step-by-step format, the steps are not as detailed as those in the Skill Drill section. Providing less specific steps helps you learn to think on your own. These exercises foster "near transfer" of learning.

- **Discovery Zone Exercises.** These exercises require advanced knowledge of project topics or application of skills from multiple lessons. Additionally, these exercises might require you to research topics in Help or on the Web to complete them. This self-directed method of learning new skills emulates real-world experience. We provide the cues; you do the exploring!

- **Learning to Learn.** Throughout this book, you'll find lessons, exercises, and other elements highlighted by this icon. For the most part, they involve using or exploring the built-in Help system or Web-based Help also accessible from the application. However, their significance is much deeper. Microsoft Office has become so rich in features catering to such diverse needs that it's no longer possible to anticipate and teach you everything you might need to know. It's becoming increasingly important, as you learn from this book, that you also "learn to learn" on your own. These elements help you identify related, perhaps more specialized, tasks or questions and show you how to discover the right procedures or answers by exploiting the many resources already within the application.
- **Task Guide.** The Task Guide that follows the last project lists all the procedures and shortcuts you will have learned in the book. It can be used in two complementary ways to enhance your learning experience. You can refer to it while progressing through the book in order to refresh your memory on procedures learned in a previous lesson. And you can keep it as a handy real-world reference while using the application for your daily work.
- **Glossary.** Here you'll find the definitions—collected in one place—of all the key terms defined throughout the book and listed on the opening page of each project. Use it to refresh your memory.

Typeface Conventions Used in This Book

We have used the following conventions throughout this book to make it easier for you to understand the material:

- Key terms appear in ***bold italic*** the first time they are defined in a project.
- Text that you type, as well as text that appears on your computer screen as a warning, confirmation, or general information, appears in a special `monospace` typeface.
- Hotkeys, the underlined keys onscreen that activate commands and options, are also underlined in this book. Hotkeys offer a quick way to bring up frequently used commands.

How to Use the CD-ROM

The CD-ROM accompanying this book contains all the data files for you to use as you work through the step-by-step tutorials, Skill Drill, Challenge, and Discovery Zone exercises provided at the end of each project. The CD contains separate parallel folders for each project. The filenames correspond to the filenames called for in the textbook. Here is how the files are named: The first three characters represent the software and the book level (such as XL3 for *Excel 2000 Essentials Advanced*). The last four digits indicate the project number and the file number within the project. For example, the first file used in Project 1 would be 0101. Therefore, the complete name for the first file in *Excel 2000 Essentials Advanced* is XL3-0101.

Files on a CD-ROM are Read-Only; they cannot be modified. In order to use the provided data files while working through this book, they must first be transferred to a read-write medium where you may modify them. Because classroom and lab rules governing the use of storage media vary from school to school, this book assumes the standard procedure of working with the file(s) on a 3.5-inch floppy.

A word of caution about using floppy disks. As you use a data file, it will increase in size or automatically generate temporary work files, so you should make sure your disk remains at least one-third empty to provide the needed extra space. Moreover, using a floppy for your work disk is slower than working off a hard drive; also, you'll need several floppies to hold all the files on the CD.

- **Saving to a 3.5-inch floppy disk.** For security or space reasons, many labs do not allow you to save to the hard drive at all. The *Excel 2000 Essentials Advanced* book shows you how to open a file from the CD-ROM and save it with a different name to a 3.5-inch floppy disk. This is the most portable solution because you can take your files with you easily from the classroom to the lab and back home to complete your exercises.
- **Copying to a 3.5-inch floppy disk.** Instead of opening and saving each data file individually as you start to work on it, you can also copy one or more files to the floppy disk.

  First select the files on the CD that you want to copy and ensure that their combined size (shown on the status bar of the Explorer window) will fit into a 1.44-MB floppy. Right-click on the selection with your mouse; choose Send To on the context menu that appears, then 3 1/2 Floppy on the submenu. After copying, select the copied files on the floppy and right-click the selection with the mouse again. This time choose Properties, choose the General tab on the Properties dialog box that appears, and then uncheck the Read-Only attribute at the bottom of this page. Because the original files on the CD-ROM were Read-Only, the files were copied with this attribute turned on. You can rename files copied in this manner after you have turned off the Read-Only attribute.

  Although you can use the same method to copy the entire CD contents to a large-capacity drive, it is much simpler to use the installation routine in the CD-ROM for the purpose. This will automatically remove the Read-Only attribute while transferring the files.
- **Installing to a hard drive or Zip drive.** The CD-ROM contains an installation routine that automatically copies all the contents to a local or networked hard drive, or to a removable large-capacity drive (for example, an Iomega Zip drive). If you are working in the classroom, your instructor has probably already installed the files to the hard drive and can tell you where the files are located. You'll be asked to save or copy the file(s) you need to your personal work area on the hard drive or to a floppy work disk.

Otherwise, run the installation routine yourself to transfer all the files to the hard drive (for example, if you are working at home) or to your personal Zip drive. You may then work directly and more efficiently off these high-capacity drives.

CD-ROM Installation Routine

If you have been instructed to install the files on a lab computer or if you are installing them on your home computer, simply insert the CD-ROM into the CD-ROM drive. When the installation screen appears, follow these steps:

1. From the installation screen, click the Install button.
2. The Welcome dialog box is displayed. Click the Next button.
3. The Readme.txt appears. The Readme.txt gives you important information regarding the installation. Make sure you use the scrollbar to view the entire Readme.txt file. When you are finished reading the Readme.txt, click the Next button.
4. The Select Destination Directory is displayed. Unless you are told otherwise by your instructor, the default location is recommended. Click Next.
5. The Ready to Install screen appears. Click Next to begin the installation.

   A directory will be created on your hard drive where the student files will be installed.
6. A dialog box appears confirming that the installation is complete.

The installation of the student data files allows you to access them from the Start menu programs. To access the student data files from the Start menu, click Start, click Programs, and then click the *Essentials* title you installed from the list of programs. The student data files are in subfolders arranged by project.

Uninstalling the Student Data Files

When you have completed the course, you might decide you don't need the student data files anymore. If that's the case, you have the ability to uninstall them. The following steps walk you through the process:

1. Click on the Start menu and then click Programs.
2. Click the *Essentials* title that you installed.
3. Click Uninstall.
4. Click one of the Uninstall methods listed:
   - Automatic—This method deletes all files in the directory and all shortcuts created.
   - Custom—This method allows you to select the files you want to delete.
5. Click Next.
6. The Perform Uninstall dialog box appears. Click Finish. The Student data files and their folders will be deleted.

The *Annotated Instructor's Manual*

The *Annotated Instructor's Manual (AIM)* is a printed copy of the student workbook—complete with marginal annotations and detailed guidelines, including a curriculum guide that helps the instructor use this book and teach the software more effectively. The *AIM* also includes a Resource CD-ROM with additional support files for the instructor; suggested solution files that show how students' files should look at the end of a tutorial; answers to test questions; PowerPoint presentations to augment your instruction; additional test questions and answers, and additional Skill Drill, Challenge, and Discovery Zone exercises. Instructors should contact Prentice Hall for their complimentary *AIM*. Prentice Hall can be reached via phone at 1-800-333-7945, or via the Internet at http://www.prenhall.com.

Project 1

Designing Onscreen Forms

Objectives

In this project, you learn how to

- **Add a Check Box to a Worksheet**
- **Add an Option Button to a Worksheet**
- **Add a Combo Box and Link to a List**
- **Add a Spinner Control to a Worksheet**
- **Enhance a Form**
- **Protect a Form**
- **Save a Form as a Template**
- **Use a Template Form**

Key terms introduced in this project include

- check box
- combo box
- controls
- linked object
- onscreen forms
- option button
- spinner
- template

Why Would I Do This?

Onscreen forms eliminate the need to re-enter the same information repeatedly, and they can be filled in and printed or transmitted electronically whenever necessary. Onscreen forms can be created in other Microsoft software, including Word and Access, but if you need to both collect information and perform calculations, you should create the form in Excel.

Before you start creating your form, it is wise to draft a rough copy on paper to use as a guide. Your forms can be as simple or as sophisticated as you choose. You can create *controls* such as check boxes, option buttons, or combo boxes. These controls are similar in functionality and appearance to those found in dialog boxes. Controls can be linked to allow a choice from the combo box to activate a particular cell in your worksheet. This linking option helps to reduce errors in data entry and save time. After you have created your basic form, you can enhance it with borders, shading, and color for a more professional appearance.

Visual Summary

Your data for creating an onscreen form in this project is provided as a worksheet from the Millennium Computer Supply Company. You use Excel's Forms toolbar to format the objects, add controls, protect some portions of the form from user changes, and save the form as a template.

Figure 1.1 shows a completed form using some of the control options which will be discussed in this lesson. Figure 1.1 also reflects enhancement features, which will be covered in Lesson 5.

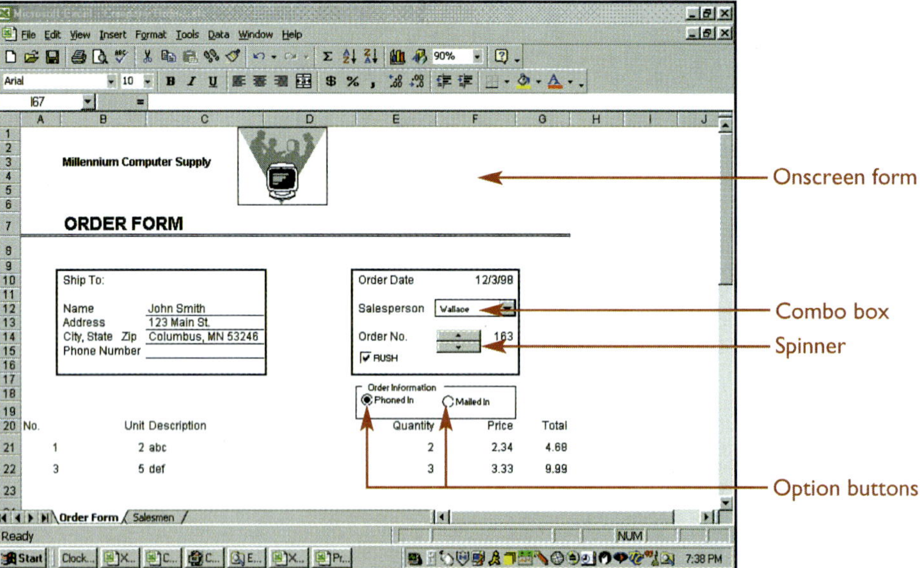

Figure 1.1
This completed form uses multiple control options.

Lesson 1: Adding a Check Box to a Worksheet

All the tools you need to create a form are on the Forms toolbar. With this toolbar you can add controls to your form. Controls are data entry devices. The first control you are going to use is the check box. A ***check box*** is a Forms control that allows the user to make an either/or choice, such as yes or no, or true or false. Clicking the box toggles a check mark to select or deselect the box.

To Add a Check Box to a Worksheet

1. **Open the XL3-0101 workbook and save it as `Company Orders`.**
2. **Activate the Order Form worksheet.**
3. **Select View, Toolbars, Forms.**
   The Forms toolbar displays. Figure 1.2 shows the Forms toolbar with all the button names labeled.

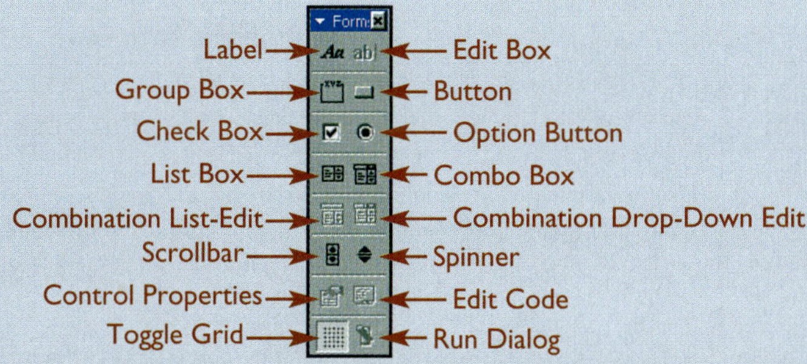

Figure 1.2
The Forms toolbar contains buttons for adding controls and editing forms.

You should be able to drag the toolbar around your worksheet so that it is not in your way as you create your form. You drag a toolbar by clicking and holding the title bar of the toolbar and moving it to another location. If the toolbar is docked along one edge of the screen, you can drag it by clicking and holding the "handle" that is on the left or top end of the toolbar.

4. **Click the Check Box button on the Forms toolbar.**
   The mouse pointer changes to a small cross.
5. **Place the mouse pointer on the upper-left corner of cell E15. Hold down the mouse button and drag to draw a box approximately the size of the cell. Release the mouse button.**

   Aligning Objects
   If you hold the Alt key while drawing, moving, or sizing a box (or any object), the borders of the box line up exactly with the underlying worksheet cells.

6. **Change the label currently in the cell to `RUSH` by clicking inside the box, deleting the `Check Box` label, and typing `RUSH` (see Figure 1.3).**

continues ▶

To Add a Check Box to a Worksheet (continued)

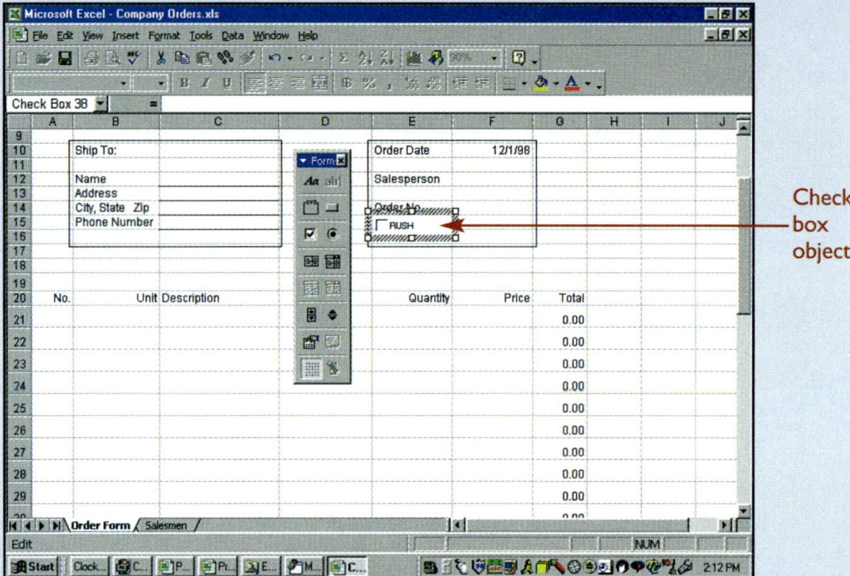

Figure 1.3
The check box produces a check mark when clicked.

7 Click another cell in the worksheet to deselect the box.

You may have difficulty seeing the box you have created. This is corrected when you complete the formatting later. To see the box now, click in the cell and a check mark appears. To remove the check mark, just click the cell again.

You have completed the first lesson. Save your changes but leave the workbook open and go on to Lesson 2.

Adjusting Boxes
In order to resize, move, or delete the box you have just created, hold down Ctrl and click the left mouse button over the border of the box. Handles (white boxes around the border of the cell) can be used to move, resize, or delete the check box. This is the method you'll use to alter a box created from the Forms toolbar.

Special Control Buttons
The Edit Box, Combination List-Edit, and Combination Drop-Down Edit controls on the Forms toolbar can be used only with charts or dialog boxes, and cannot be used on a worksheet. If a Forms toolbar button is not active, Excel will not respond when you try to select the button.

Lesson 2: Adding an Option Button to a Worksheet

The check box control was a simple either/or option. In this lesson you are adding an option button. An ***option button*** is a Forms control device that is useful where there are a limited number of data choices and only one can be selected; for example, Pick-up or Delivery.

Option buttons work as a group. Individual option buttons constitute a group no matter where they are created on the worksheet and allow only one option to be chosen. You can also create option buttons within group boxes. This allows you to have multiple option groups within a worksheet. If you want to group option buttons, you must first create a group box and then add the option buttons to that group.

To Add an Option Button to a Worksheet

1. **Display the Order Form worksheet in the Company Orders workbook.**

2. **Click the Group Box button on the Forms toolbar.**
   The mouse pointer now appears as a small cross.

3. **Place the mouse pointer on the upper-left corner of cell E18. Hold down the left button and drag to the lower-right corner of cell F19. Release the mouse button.**
   You have now created a Group Box in cells E18:F19. Handles appear on the border, as shown in Figure 1.4.

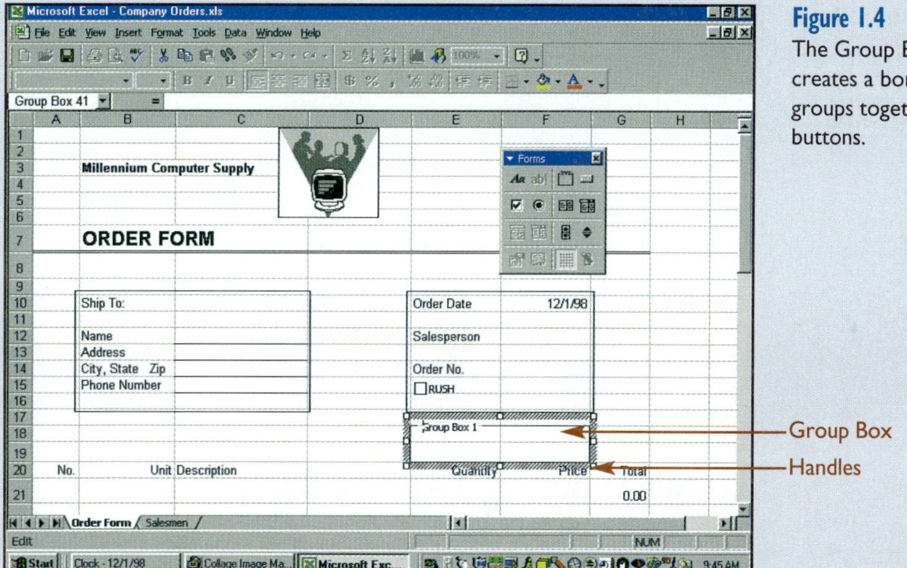

Figure 1.4
The Group Box button creates a border that groups together option buttons.

4. **Click inside the control, delete the current label, and type `Order Information`.**

5. **Click the Option button on the Forms toolbar.**

6. **Place the mouse pointer on the upper-left corner of the Group Box. Hold down the left mouse button and drag the mouse to create a box the size of cell E19. Release the mouse button.**
   You have now created an option button in cell E19. You can see the button and the label `Option Button` in the box (see Figure 1.5).

continues ▶

To Add an Option Button to a Worksheet (continued)

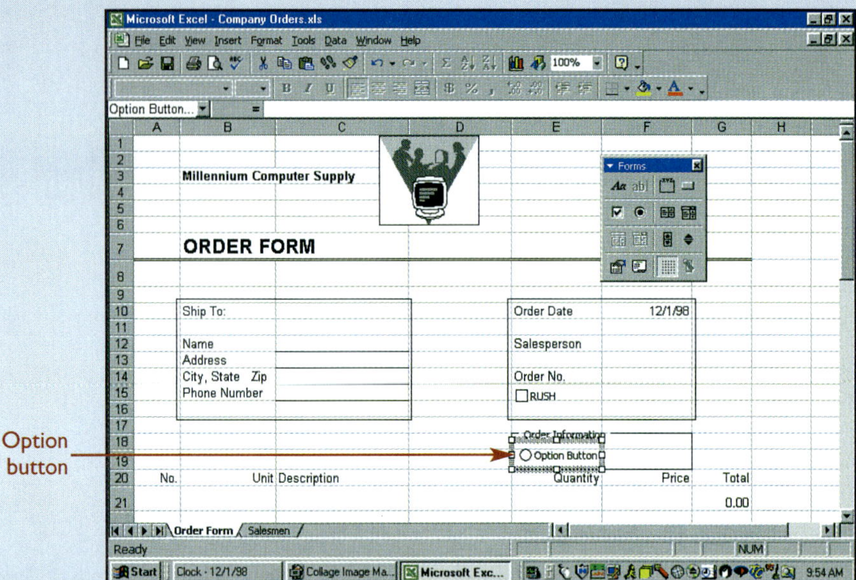

Figure 1.5
Option buttons are used to select one option from a list of two or more choices.

7. **Click inside the box, delete the `Option Button` label and type `Phoned In`.**
8. **Click the Option button on the Forms toolbar.**
9. **Place the mouse pointer on the upper-left corner of cell F19 and drag the mouse to draw a box the size of the cell. Release the mouse button.**
10. **Click inside the box, delete the current label, and type `Mailed In`.**
11. **Click another cell on the worksheet to deselect the box.**
    You have now created a Group Box with two option buttons. Save your changes, keep the workbook open, and go on to Lesson 3.

Lesson 3: Adding a Combo Box and Linking to a List

Option buttons are a good control device when the user has only two or three possible choices. For form items with more than three possible choices, a combo box is less confusing and enables the user to see all of the available choices. A ***combo box*** control displays all of the options and may be appropriate when no single selection is likely to be dominant. To create a combo box, first draw the box and then link it to the list that will be displayed in the box. A ***linked object*** is an object that appears to be in one file when it is actually in another file or on another worksheet.

To Add a Combo Box and Link to a List

1. **Display the Order Form worksheet in the Company Orders workbook.**
2. **Click the Combo Box button on the Forms toolbar.**

3 Place the mouse pointer on the upper-left corner of cell F12. Hold down the left mouse button and drag the mouse to draw a box the size of the cell. Release the mouse button.

4 With the combo box still selected, click the Control Properties button on the Forms toolbar.

You should now see the Format Control dialog box for the combo box control. This box gives you options for the control you have chosen. For a combo box, the dialog box asks you to determine the data control limits.

5 Select the Control tab, if necessary. Click in the text box labeled Input range (see Figure 1.6).

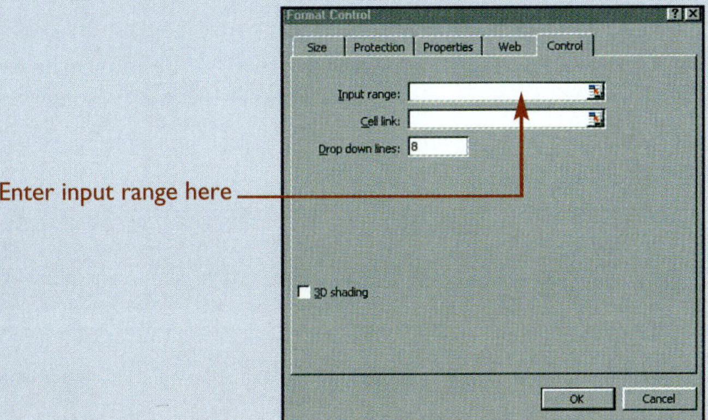

Figure 1.6
The combo box lets you create a drop-down list containing text.

6 While the dialog box remains open, click in the Input range box, and then click on the Salesmen sheet tab of your workbook.

This tab should reveal a worksheet listing the last names of all of Millennium Computer Supply's salespeople. They are listed in cells A2:A6.

7 Select cells A2:A6.

8 Click OK and then click another cell on the worksheet to deselect the box.

When you click the drop-down arrow, the combo box reveals a list of the salespeople. Clicking on a name selects that name for the form box.

Save the changes you have made, keep the workbook open, and go on to Lesson 4.

Another Way to Define the Range

An alternative method of selecting text in existing worksheet cells is to type the range of cells in the Input range text box. If you are not already in the Salesmen worksheet, the entry would be `Salesmen!A2:A6`. It is faster and more accurate to point to the range, however. The range in this box represents the information shown on your drop-down list.

Lesson 4: Adding a Spinner Control to a Worksheet

A *spinner* is a control that is used to increase or decrease the numerical amount that can be placed in a linked cell. The spinner symbol is a two-headed arrow. This control allows you to quickly select a number instead of typing the number.

To Add a Spinner Control to a Worksheet

1. **Display the Order Form worksheet in the Company Orders workbook.**

2. **Click the Spinner button on the Forms toolbar.**

3. **Place the mouse pointer on the upper-left corner of cell F14. Hold down the left mouse button and drag the mouse to draw a box over cells F14 and to the center of F15. Release the mouse button.**

   You have now created the spinner control in cells F14 and F15. The spinner should be displayed with handles, as shown in Figure 1.7.

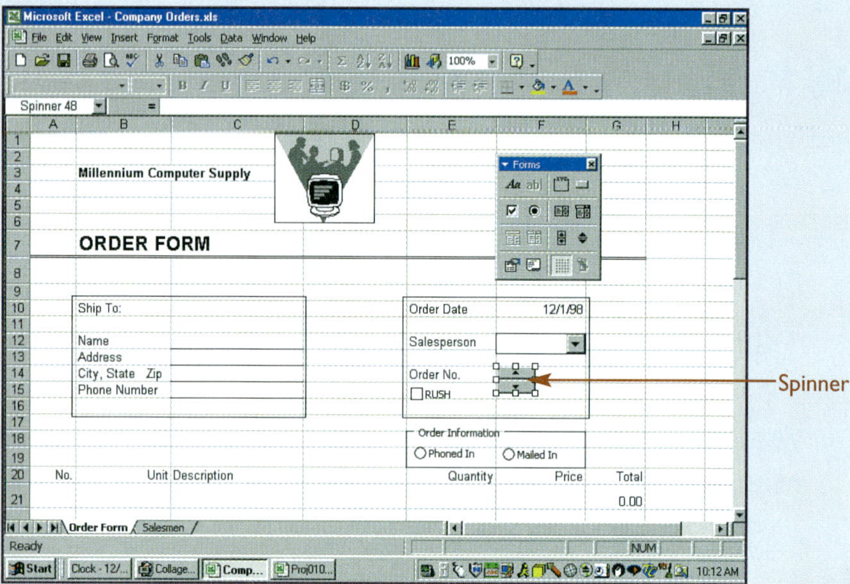

Figure 1.7 The spinner is drawn on the worksheet.

4. **Click the Control Properties button on the Forms toolbar.**

   The Format Control dialog box for the spinner control appears (see Figure 1.8).

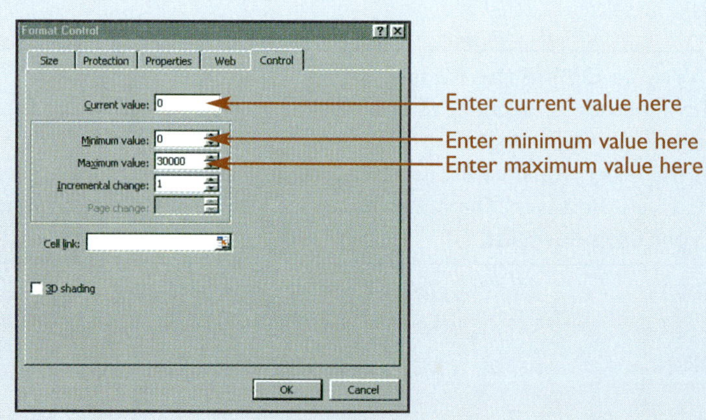

Figure 1.8 The Format Control dialog box is used to set the control's parameters.

5. **Select the Control tab, if necessary.**

6. **Type `100` in the text box labeled Current value.**
   100 is the starting number for the order forms.

7. **Type `100` in the text box labeled Minimum value.**
   This prevents the order form numbers from going below 100.

8. **Type `1000` in the text box labeled Maximum value.**
   This prevents the order form number from exceeding 1000.

9. **Type `F14` in the text box labeled Cell link.**
   The order form number displayed in cell F14 can be changed in increments of one by clicking the up or down arrows in the spinner control.

10. **Click OK and then click another cell in the worksheet to deselect the spinner.**
    The current value of `100` appears in cell F14. Save the changes to the workbook, keep it open, and go on to Lesson 5.

Adjusting the Spinner Control Increment
If you want to change the increment to a number other than 1, type the increment you want to use in the Incremental change text box of the Format Control dialog box. However, for this lesson, leave the increment set at 1.

Lesson 5: Enhancing a Form

If the form you are creating is going to be printed, you may want to give it a more professional look. This can be done by adding borders, shading, or a 3D appearance; or by choosing to have some of the control values or formulas hidden.

In this lesson you use formatting techniques to create a form that is easier to use and more closely resembles a paper form.

To Enhance a Form

1. **Display the Order Form worksheet in the Company Orders workbook.**

2. **Click the Toggle Grid button on the Forms toolbar.**
   The worksheet gridlines disappear. This improves the appearance of the form, and makes the text and controls easier to read.

3. **Click the border that surrounds the rectangle in cells B10:C16, and then press Shift while you click the border surrounding the rectangle in cells E10:F16.**
   You have now selected both objects.

continues ▶

To Enhance a Form (continued)

4 Select Format, AutoShape.
The Format AutoShape dialog box appears. You can also display this dialog box by right-clicking the selected control object and selecting Format AutoShape from the shortcut menu.

5 Select the Colors and Lines tab, shown in Figure 1.9.

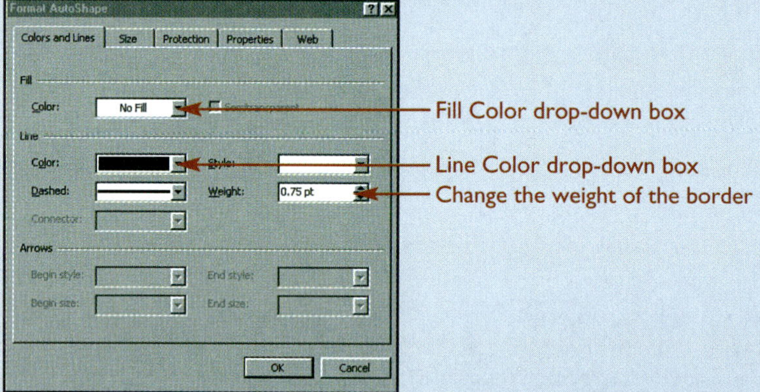

Figure 1.9
The Format AutoShape dialog box allows you to add visual effects to your form.

6 Select No Fill in the Fill Color drop-down box.
This creates a white background in your control box. If you wanted to view or print your form in color, you could select one of the color options.

7 Select Automatic in the Line Color drop-down box.
This places a black border around your control box. If you wanted to view or print your form in color, then you would select a color option.

8 Select 1.5 pt in the Line Weight spin box.

9 Click OK, and then click another cell in the worksheet to deselect the boxes.
A thicker border now surrounds the two boxes.

Cells G21:G38 of the worksheet contain formulas that multiply the quantity by the price per item and display the total cost. Cell G39 contains the SUM function to total the order. When no data is entered in the form, zeros are displayed in the formula cells. You are now going to remove these zeros from the display so the cells appear to be blank.

10 Select Tools, Options, then click the View tab (see Figure 1.10).

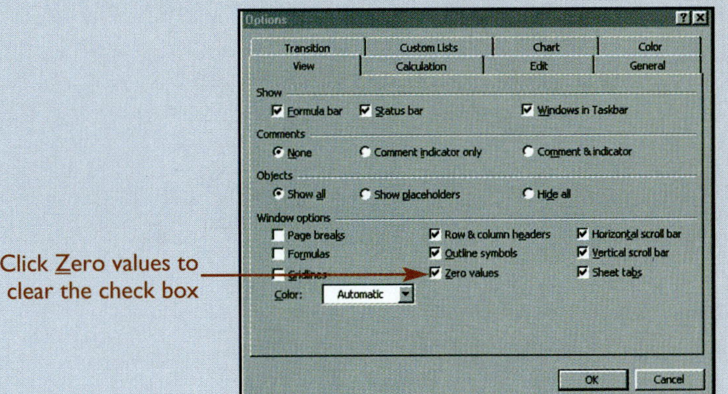

Figure 1.10
Use the View tab of the Options dialog box if you want to hide the zeros throughout the worksheet.

11. **Uncheck Zero values, and then click OK.**
12. **Click the Print Preview button on the Standard toolbar to see how your completed form will look when printed.**
13. **Click the Close button to exit Preview mode, and then close the Forms toolbar.**
    The form is now complete. Save the changes, keep the workbook open, and go on to Lesson 6.

Lesson 6: Protecting a Form

To prevent the format and formulas of your form from being changed by another user, Microsoft Excel provides a protection feature on the Forms toolbar. As with any other protected worksheet, when protection is activated, the form cannot be edited. In order for your form to serve its data collection function, you must unlock the data entry cells before you activate the protection feature.

To Protect a Form

1. **Display the Order Form worksheet in the Company Orders workbook.**
2. **Select the range C10:C15.**
3. **Hold down the Ctrl key and select the range F11:F15.**
4. **Continue holding down the Ctrl key and select the range A21:F38.**
   All three ranges will be selected simultaneously.
5. **Choose Format, Cells, and then click the Protection tab.**
6. **Click the Locked check box to remove the check mark, and then click OK.**
   This allows the selected cells to be changed by the user. You can now protect the rest of the form.

continues ▶

To Protect a Form (continued)

7 Select Tools, Protection, Protect Sheet.

The Protect Sheet dialog box appears (see Figure 1.11).

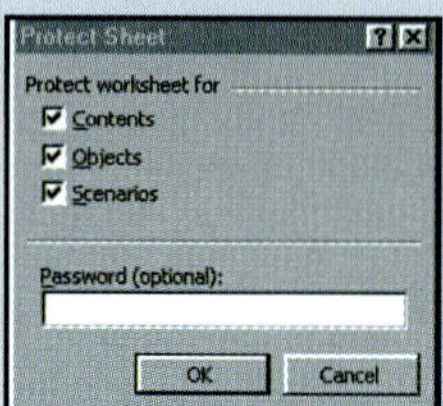

Figure 1.11
Use the Protect Sheet dialog box to select or deselect the protection feature.

8 Click OK to select the default settings (all of the boxes will be checked).

You have now protected all of the form except those areas you previously unlocked. You can assign a password by filling in the Password text box, but a password is not required to protect the form. You may now test your protection feature.

9 Click cell B18 and press the Del key.

You should see an alert box notifying you that the cell is protected and cannot be changed (see Figure 1.12). If the Office Assistant is enabled, you will see a help bubble instead of an alert dialog box.

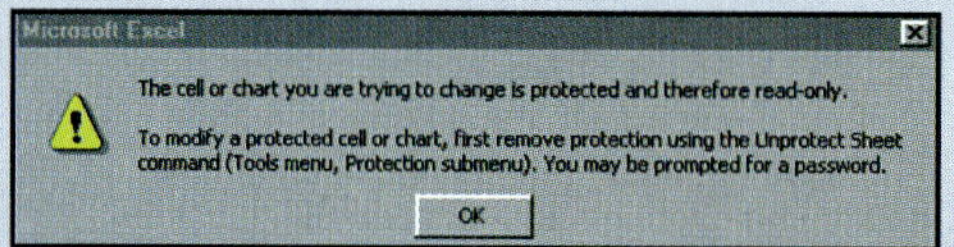

Figure 1.12
The alert box warns you when you have attempted to change a protected cell.

10 Click OK.

Save the changes you have made to the workbook and go on to Lesson 7.

Lesson 7: Saving a Form as a Template

Now that your form is complete and protected, you can save it as a template. A ***template*** is a document with features such as boilerplate text, styles, and Form controls that will be applied to any document created from the template. Saving your form as a template is a way of having it easily accessible to users for data entry while still protecting the contents and format of the document. When Excel saves a form as a template, it gives the file an .xlt extension and treats it as it would a workbook.

To Save a Form as a Template

1 Display the Order Form worksheet in the Company Orders workbook. Select File, Save As.

2 Type `Order Form` in the File name text box.

3 Click the arrow beside the Save as type drop-down list box, and select Template (*.xlt).

As shown in Figure 1.13, available file types are in the drop-down list.

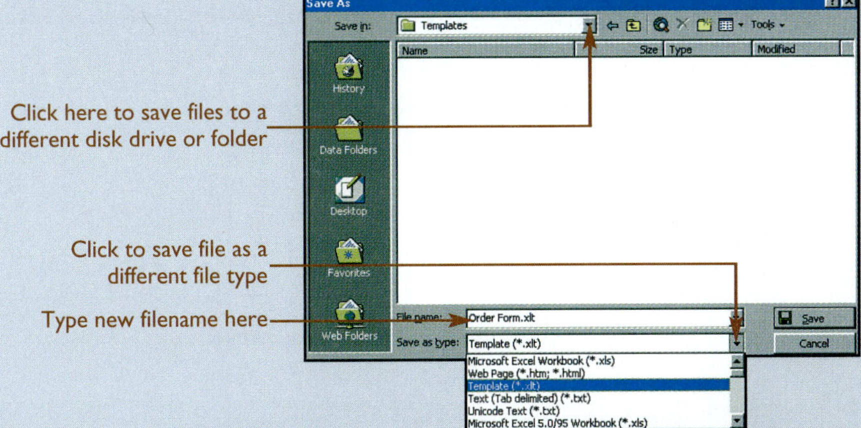

Figure 1.13
The Save As dialog box enables you to name the template, change the file type, and specify a disk drive and folder.

4 In the Save in drop-down list, save your file to a 3 1/2 floppy disk, zip drive, hard disk, or network drive, as appropriate.

Normally Excel would save your template to the Templates folder on the hard drive, but because you may be working in a lab setting, save your template to a 3 1/2 inch floppy disk. You can also save the file to a Zip drive or network drive if appropriate. If you have questions about where to save your template, consult your instructor.

5 Click the Save button.

6 Click File, Close to close the template.

Using Built-in Templates

When you select Template in the Save as type drop-down list, Excel automatically displays the Templates folder located on the hard drive as a subfolder of the Windows folders (usually `C:\Windows\Application Data\Microsoft\Templates`). A listing of available template files is shown. A template must be saved to the Templates folder in order to be accessed from the File, New command.

Lesson 8: Using a Template Form

To use your new form, open your template by using the File, New command, and select your template. Your template is now opened as a new Excel workbook. Data can be entered and the completed form saved as a Microsoft Excel workbook, while the template remains intact and available for use again.

To Use a Template Form

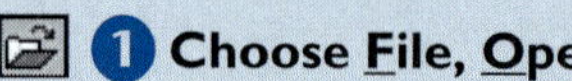

1. **Choose File, Open.**
   The Open dialog box appears.

2. **Select 3 1/2 Floppy A: from the Look in drop-down list.**
   Normally you would access your template with the File, New command. The General tab displays all available templates. To use a template saved to a location other than the Templates folder, you can open the template and then save it as an Excel workbook.

3. **Select Templates (*.xlt) from the Files of type drop-down list (see Figure 1.14).**

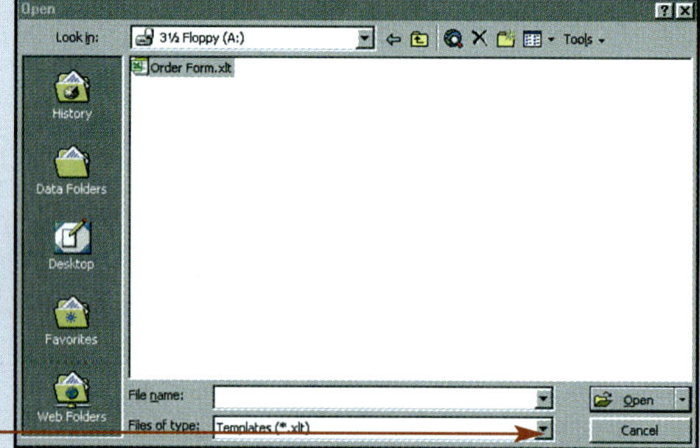

Figure 1.14
The Open dialog box displays the Order Form template.

4. **Double-click the Order Form file.**
   The template is open, ready to save as a new workbook before entering data.

5. **Choose File, Save As.**

6. **Select Microsoft Excel Workbook (*.xls) from the Save as type drop-down list.**
   Keep the name `Order Form` as the name of the new workbook.

7. **Click Save.**
   Your form should now be displayed and ready for data entry.

8. **In cells C12:C15, enter the following data:**

   ```
   Memex Corporation
   5151 Smith Road
   Columbus, OH 42330
   614-555-0122
   ```

9. **In the Salesperson drop-down list (in cell F12), select Jones.**

10. **Click the RUSH check box in cell E15.**

11. **Change the order number to 104.**

12. **Click the Phoned In option button.**

13. **As shown in Figure 1.15, complete the data entry for row 21 with the following information (skip cell D21):**

Cell	Entry
A21	`101`
B21	`50-pack`

C21 `3.5 inch formatted disks`

E21 `5`

F21 `10.99`

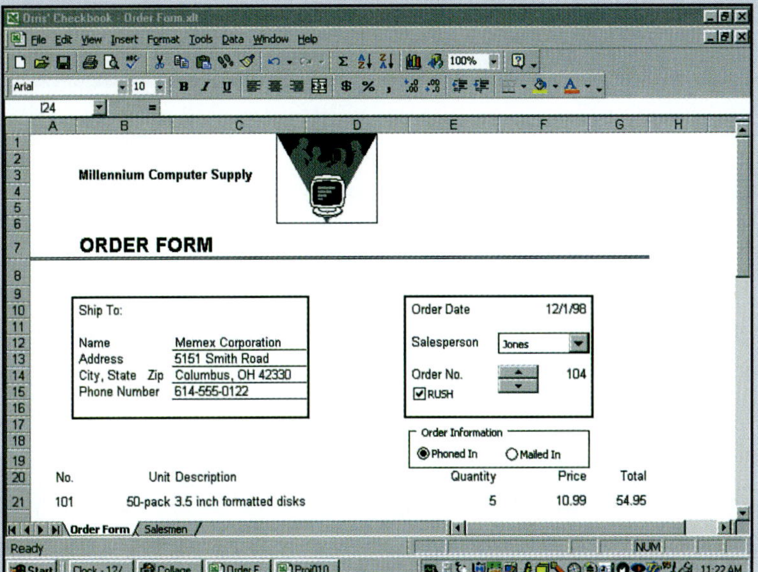

Figure 1.15
You can use a template to create a workbook to fill out a form.

⑭ **Click the Save button and close the file.**

Protecting Built-in Templates
When a template is saved on the hard drive, Excel automatically opens a copy when it is accessed from the File, New command. This temporary or copy name will be something like Order Form1 or Order Form2. When you are ready to save the filled in template, the dialog box displays the temporary name and it is automatically specified as an Excel workbook. These precautions should help prevent any accidental damage to your template.

Freezing Panes
If you want to see the header information while scrolling through the worksheet, you can click in the appropriate cell and freeze the pane by choosing Window, Freeze Panes.

Summary

In this project, you learned how to create onscreen forms in Excel worksheets. From the Forms toolbar you were able to insert a variety of controls to simplify data entry. By using the enhancement features, you were able to give your onscreen form a professional appearance. This project also explained the concept of a template and how to save and use your form as a template.

You can increase your proficiency with Excel forms by experimenting with the Forms toolbar options—including the scroll option, which was not covered in the Project lessons—and by taking time to review Excel's built-in templates. Remember to use the Help menu if you encounter a problem while creating a form.

Checking Concepts and Terms 

True/False

For each of the following, check *T* or *F* to indicate whether the statement is true or false.

__T __F **1.** Controls created from the Excel Forms toolbar cannot be formatted. [L4]

__T __F **2.** A form that collects information for calculations is best created in Excel. [Why]

__T __F **3.** Data entry cells need to be unlocked before a form is protected. [L6]

__T __F **4.** A template is assigned an .xlt extension. [L7]

__T __F **5.** You must assign a password in order to protect a form. [L6]

__T __F **6.** An option button is always associated with a group. [L2]

__T __F **7.** The Print Preview button is found on the Forms toolbar. [L5]

__T __F **8.** A combo box is really a drop-down list box. [L3]

__T __F **9.** Locking a cell prevents it from being edited. [L6]

__T __F **10.** Once a form has been protected it can never be changed. [L6]

Multiple Choice

Circle the letter of the correct answer for each of the following.

1. The best control option for a data entry cell with three or more selections is ______________. [L3]

a. an option button

b. a check box

c. a text box

d. a combo box

2. A control can be formatted in which of the following ways? [L5]

a. colors and patterns

b. shading

c. 3D

d. all of the above

3. When you want to unprotect an area of a form to make changes, first select the cells and then choose which of the following? [L6]

a. Format, Cells, Protection tab

b. Tools, Protection, Unprotect

c. Format, Sheet, Hide

d. Tools, Options

4. The control properties for a combo box include [L3]

a. input range

b. cell link

c. drop-down lines

d. all of the above

5. Which button on the Forms toolbar is used to link a control to a worksheet cell? [L3]

a. Edit Box

b. Combo Box

c. Create Button

d. Control Properties

6. You must specify which of the following values when creating a spinner? [L4]

a. maximum value

b. current value

c. minimum value

d. all of the above

7. To protect a form you would select [L6]

a. Tools, Options, Protect

b. Tools, Protection, Protect Sheet

c. Format, Controls, Protect

d. none of the above

8. To set a workbook so it doesn't display cells that contain zeros, you would select [L5]

a. Tools, Options, View, Zero values

b. Format, Number, Zeros

c. File, Display, Format

d. Tools, Format, Zeros

9. Why would you want to create a template file? [L8]

a. to avoid errors

b. to save space

c. to have a model file

d. none of the above

10. If you wanted to change the color of a box you had drawn around controls, you would use [L5]

a. Format, Cells

b. Insert, Line, Color

c. Format, Autoshape

d. Change, Line, Color

Discussion Questions

You have just gone to work for a new health club and they have asked you to design a member registration form that will both collect member data and calculate their monthly membership fee based on the services they select. All members must pay the base membership fee. Refer to Figure 1.16 for a list of services and fees. Members will receive a copy of the form as a receipt.

1. Discuss what type of member data would be appropriate to include and what type of control should be used for each item. Consider the reason each control was chosen, for example, ease of data entry, error reduction, and so on.

2. How will the Services and Fees information be incorporated into the form? What formulas will be used?

3. What control options will be most appropriate for the Services and Fees information and why?

4. Based on the information provided at the beginning of the Discussion section, what information besides member data and Services and Fees should be added to the form?

5. Should the form be enhanced? If so, why and what enhancements would you choose?

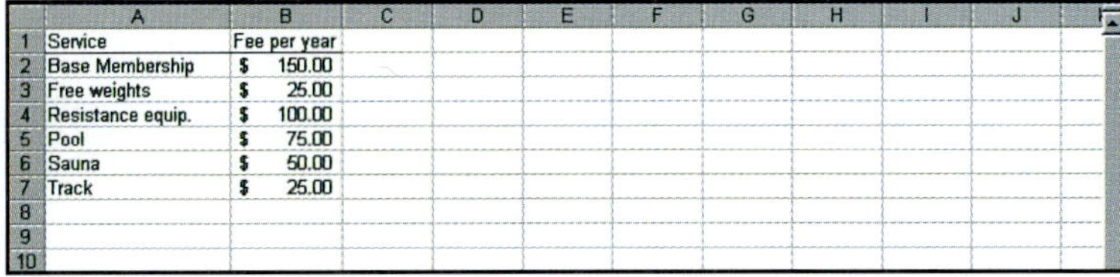

	A	B
1	Service	Fee per year
2	Base Membership	$ 150.00
3	Free weights	$ 25.00
4	Resistance equip.	$ 100.00
5	Pool	$ 75.00
6	Sauna	$ 50.00
7	Track	$ 25.00

Figure 1.16
Health club services and fees.

Skill Drill 

Skill Drill exercises reinforce project skills. Each skill reinforced is the same, or nearly the same, as a skill presented in the project. Detailed instructions are provided in a step-by-step format.

Your company has created an onscreen form for requesting computer assistance but you want to make the data entry easier. Work through the following exercises to practice your skills with forms.

1. Adding Check Boxes to a Worksheet

Your company has created an onscreen form for requesting computer assistance, but you want to make the data entry easier.

1. Open the XL3-0102 file and save it as Work Order.
2. Display the Form worksheet.
3. Use the Forms toolbar to create a check box in cell B14. Label it `Hardware`.
4. Use the Forms toolbar to create a check box in cell C14. Label it `Software`.
5. Save your changes and keep the workbook open.

2. Adding a List Box to a Worksheet

You are now going to add a combo box with a drop-down list of all the departments that request computer assistance.

1. Display the Form worksheet in the Work Order workbook.
2. Use the Forms toolbar to create a list box in cells B8:B10. Create a box that is the full width of the column.
3. Format the list box by adding an input range. The input range for the control is cells A2:A6 in the Data worksheet of this workbook. If necessary, resize the list box to completely display the five departments.
4. Save your work and keep the workbook open.

3. Adding Option Buttons to a Worksheet

You are now going to add an option button to identify the hardware type.

1. Display the Form worksheet in the Work Order workbook.
2. Use the Forms toolbar to create a group box in cells B16:C17. Label the group box `Hardware Type`.
3. Create three option buttons in the group box and label them `PC`, `Modem`, and `Printer`.
4. Save your changes and keep the workbook open.

4. Enhancing a Form

You are going to enhance your form to resemble a paper form by changing the weight of the border.

1. Display the Form worksheet in the Work Order workbook.
2. Select the two rectangle objects in cells C4:D4 and C11:D11.
3. Format the borders of the two rectangles; choose the sixth style option (2 1/4 pt) from the Style drop-down list in the Format AutoShape dialog box.
4. Remove the gridlines from the form.
5. Preview the form.
6. Save your changes, but keep the workbook open.

5. Testing a Form

Fill in your form as a test before releasing it for general use.

1. In the Form worksheet of the Work Order workbook, click cell B6 and type your name.
2. In cell B8, choose Finance from the list box.
3. Type `Immediate` in cell E8.
4. Select the Software check box and deselect the Hardware check box.
5. Click cell B18 and type a project description.
6. Preview the form.
7. Save your form as a new file named Work1.

6. Changing a Form

Often you want to make changes or fine-tune a form after it is finished. Any of the form objects can be moved and/or changed.

1. In the Work1 file, click on the group box to select it.
2. Hold down the Ctrl and ⇧Shift keys, and click on the three option buttons in the group box.
3. Click on the selected items and drag them so that the upper-left corner of the selection is in cell D15.
4. Rename the option buttons as `Computer`, `Scanner`, and `Network`. If necessary, resize the group box and option buttons so you can see the new labels.
5. Save the form and close it.

Challenge 

Challenge exercises expand on or are somewhat related to skills presented in the lessons. Each exercise provides a brief narrative introduction followed by instructions in a numbered step format that are not as detailed as those in the Skill Drill section.

Each exercise is independent of the others, so that you may complete the exercises in any order. Be sure to save the workbook after completing each exercise. If you need a paper copy of the completed exercise, enter your name centered in a header before printing.

1. Using Drawing Tools with Forms

When you created forms in the previous exercises, you probably found it was difficult to align and space objects. The form controls are also drawing objects, so you can use the Drawing toolbar to work with them.

1. Open XL3-0103, and save it as Challenge-A.
2. Display the Form worksheet.
3. Choose View, Toolbars, Drawing.
4. Press and hold down Ctrl and ⇧Shift, and then click all of the option boxes in the Select a region group to select them.
5. On the Drawing toolbar, choose Draw, Align or Distribute, Align Left.
6. On the Drawing toolbar, choose Draw, Align or Distribute, Distribute Vertically.
7. Save your changes, but leave the workbook open for the next exercise.

2. Creating Dynamic Lists

Sometimes you want the contents of a list box to change based on another selection. In this example we want the list box to show cities from various regions.

1. Display the DataList worksheet from the Challenge-A workbook from the previous exercise.
2. Click the drop-down arrow beside the Name box and examine the named ranges. Note that there is a name for each region, and Region5 represents all regions combined.

   Any name could have been used but they all have to have the same root name and be numbered sequentially starting at one.

   The SelectedRegion named cell will be used to store the number of the selected option button.

3. Select the Form worksheet, and right-click the first option button. Select Format Control from the shortcut menu.
4. In the Format Control dialog box, click the Control tab and then type `SelectedRegion` in the Cell link box. Click OK.

   Because the option buttons are in a group box, all of them will now have the same cell link. Check a couple of them.
5. Choose Insert, Name, Define.
6. In the Define Name dialog box, type `RegionList` in the Names in workbook box, and in the Refers to box, type the following formula (and then click OK):
   `=INDIRECT("Region"&SelectedRegion)`

   Make sure you type it exactly like this; include the "=" sign and do not use any spaces. The expression uses the concatenation operator "&" that you will learn about in Project 3. This formula defines the region name by appending the appropriate number to the root name Region.

   Note that RegionList is like a named cell, but it does not refer to a cell and its contents are not visible anywhere in the workbook.
7. Select the Form worksheet and right-click the list box. Select Format Control from the shortcut menu.
8. In the Format Control dialog box, click the Control tab, and type `RegionList` as the Input range. Then type `SelectedCity` as the Cell link. Click OK.

   When you select a city, the number of the city is placed in the SelectedCity named cell in the DataList worksheet. In the next exercise you will see how to use the number to extract the correct name and place it on the Form worksheet.
9. Save your changes, but leave the workbook open for the next exercise.

3. Extracting an Item from a List

When you specify a cell link for a list box, the cell address of the item is stored in the cell, not the text of the item. In this exercise you will see how to extract the actual item.

1. Display the Form worksheet of the Challenge-A workbook.
2. Select cell C20 and type `=INDEX(RegionList,SelectedCity)`.

   The INDEX function uses the number SelectedCity named cell to find the appropriate item in the currently defined list in RegionList.
3. Save your changes and close the workbook.

4. Adaptive List Sizing

One problem with lists is that they often change in size over time. This means you have to keep editing the Input range box for a list box or a combo box. In this exercise you will see a way to have a list automatically change as the contents of the list change.

1. Open the Company Orders workbook and save it as Challenge-B.
2. Select the Order Form worksheet.
3. If the workbook is still protected, remove the protection with Tools, Protection, Unprotect Sheet.
4. Choose Insert, Name, Define.

5. In the Define Name dialog box, type `SalesmenList` in the Names in workbook box, and in the Refers to box, type:

```
=OFFSET(Salesmen!$A$1,1,0,COUNTA(OFFSET(Salesmen!$A$1,1,0,999,1)),1)
```

   Click ADD and click OK.

   It is not critical to understand how this works, but as a challenge, look it up in Help. The important thing to remember if you want to use this technique elsewhere is to replace `Salesmen!$A$1` with the cell reference immediately above the list. The `999` in the formula refers to maximum list size and could be changed.

   Remember that this technique will also work with list boxes as well as combo boxes.

6. Right-click the list box. Select Format Control from the pop-up menu. In the Format Control box type `SalesmenList` as the Input range. Click OK.
7. Add and remove some names from the list box and note how it works. If your list becomes larger than the number of drop-down lines specified in the Format Control dialog box, a scrollbar will appear.
8. Save and close the workbook.

Discovery Zone

Discovery Zone exercises require advanced knowledge of topics presented in *Essentials* lessons, application of skills from multiple lessons, or self-directed learning of new skills. Each exercise is independent of the others, so you may complete the exercises in any order.

1. Using the Control Toolbox as an Alternative Method of Creating Forms

Choose View, Toolbars, Control Toolbox to open the Control Toolbox toolbar. This toolbar looks very similar to the Forms toolbar. It is designed for attaching Visual Basic code to form controls, but it can also do all of the functions of the Forms toolbar and some others. Take some time to experiment with the controls, and think about how you might use them in other applications.

2. Viewing Your Worksheet with Internet Explorer

Open Microsoft Internet Explorer 5.0 (or the browser of your choice), and use the Open command to open one of the worksheets you created above. Your browser changes to look almost like Excel. You can use any of the controls and perform many worksheet operations. This means that if you put a worksheet on a server, anyone could have access to it without downloading it. You'll learn more about this topic in Project 8.

3. Emailing a Workbook

Open one of your workbooks with Excel. Choose File, Send To, Mail Recipient (as Attachment). If you are connected to the Internet, your email program will load, and you can send a message and your workbook as an attachment. Send the workbook to yourself as a test. If you have trouble, use Excel's Help system to find more information.

Project 2

Project 2

Automating Tasks with Macros

Objectives

In this project, you learn how to

- **Prepare to Record a Macro**
- **Record a Macro**
- **Play a Macro**
- **Record a Macro in a Personal Macro Workbook**
- **Play a Macro from the Personal Macro Workbook**
- **Unhide and Edit the Personal Macro Workbook**
- **Create a Macro Button in a Workbook**
- **Add a Macro Button to a Toolbar**

Key terms introduced in this project include

- macro
- macro button
- Personal Macro Workbook
- Visual Basic Editor
- Visual Basic for Applications (VBA)

Why Would I Do This?

A *macro* is a way of consolidating multiple commands or keystrokes. When a particular function or task is performed frequently, using a macro to perform that function with a single keystroke or a button can be a real timesaver as well as being more accurate. A macro can be created for something as simple as typing a very long company name, to something as complex as creating a chart.

When a macro you've recorded is played back, it is as if an invisible typist were rapidly entering keystrokes. Some early macro recorders literally did just that—recorded keystrokes and played them back on command. However, Excel handles macros differently. Because all Microsoft Office programs are "object-oriented," the macro recorder does not look at your keystrokes, but instead looks at the result of your keystrokes and creates a subroutine in a language known as ***Visual Basic for Applications (VBA),*** which gives the same result as your keystrokes.

Macros are viewed and edited using the ***Visual Basic Editor***. You may want to "fine-tune" the macro code or delete lines that resulted from incorrect keystrokes. The Visual Basic Editor is also used to create programs from "scratch." This is how many add-in programs, such as Data Analysis Tools, are created.

Visual Summary

Figure 2.1 shows a worksheet with a macro button. This macro button will transfer the selected row of data to the Completed worksheet, eliminating the need for the user to re-enter all the data. Figure 2.2 shows the VBA programming code used by Excel to create a macro. These subjects will be dealt with in detail in the following lessons.

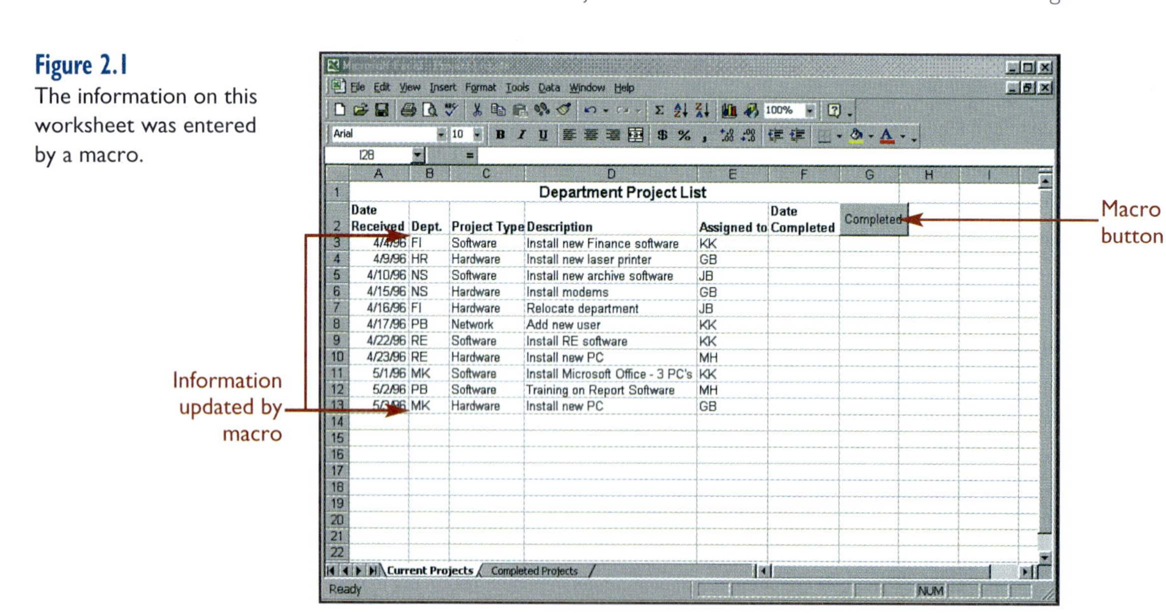

Date Received	Dept.	Project Type	Description	Assigned to	Date Completed
4/4/96	FI	Software	Install new Finance software	KK	
4/9/96	HR	Hardware	Install new laser printer	GB	
4/10/96	NS	Software	Install new archive software	JB	
4/15/96	NS	Hardware	Install modems	GB	
4/16/96	FI	Hardware	Relocate department	JB	
4/17/96	PB	Network	Add new user	KK	
4/22/96	RE	Software	Install RE software	KK	
4/23/96	RE	Hardware	Install new PC	MH	
5/1/96	MK	Software	Install Microsoft Office - 3 PC's	KK	
5/2/96	PB	Software	Training on Report Software	MH	
5/3/96	MK	Hardware	Install new PC	GB	

Figure 2.1
The information on this worksheet was entered by a macro.

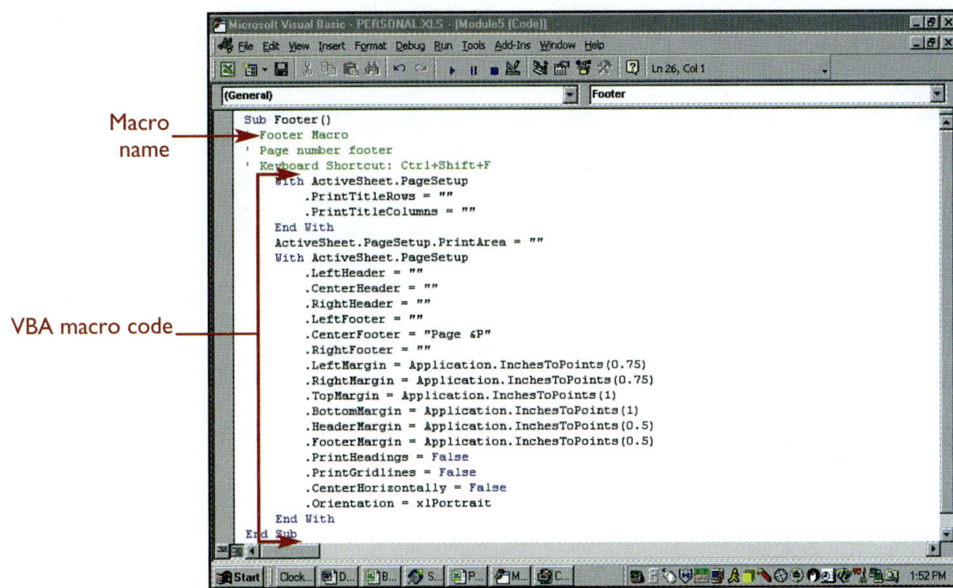

Figure 2.2
The Visual Basic Editor reveals the VBA code for a macro.

Lesson 1: Preparing to Record a Macro

Before you can record a macro, you need to decide what to name the macro and where to store it. In this lesson, you create a macro that records the closure date of a project and then transfers the project from the Current Projects worksheet to the Completed Projects worksheet.

To Prepare to Record a Macro

1. **Open the XL3-0201 file, and save it as Project List.**
   This workbook contains two worksheets, named Current Projects and Completed Projects.

2. **Type `4/8/98` in cell F4 of the Current Projects worksheet and press ↵Enter.**
   You have now indicated that the project in row 4 has been completed.

3. **Select row 4 by clicking on the row heading.**
   You need to select the row you want to transfer before recording the macro, because the row number will change with the completion of different projects.

4. **Using the Office Assistant, type the query: `How do I record a macro?` Then click Search.**
   Explore some of the resulting Help topics, and then close the Help window.

5. **Select Tools, Macro, Record New Macro.**
   The Record Macro dialog box appears, as shown in Figure 2.3.

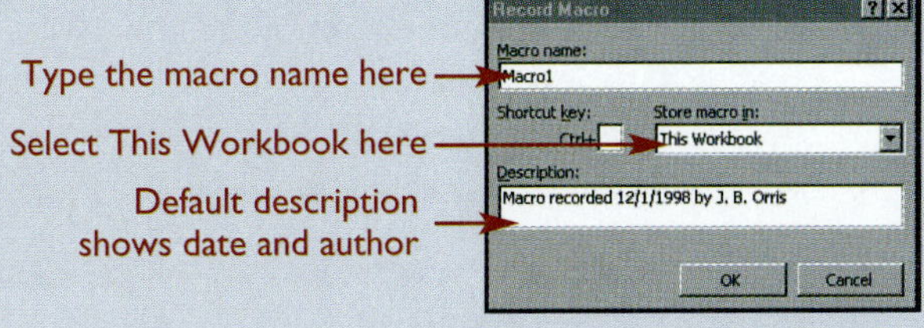

Figure 2.3
In the Record Macro dialog box, you enter a name and other options for the procedure you are about to record.

continues ▶

To Prepare to Record a Macro (continued)

6 Select the Macro name text box and type `Completed`.

You name your macro before you record it. If you fail to name the macro, Microsoft Excel gives it a default name of Macro1, then Macro2, and so on.

Assigning Shortcut Keys to Macros

You can assign a shortcut key to your macro that can be an upper- or lowercase letter. To do so, type a letter in the Shortcut key text box. To run a macro using this shortcut key, press and hold Ctrl and then press the letter you assigned to the macro. If your shortcut key is an uppercase letter, press and hold both Ctrl and ⇧Shift with the appropriate key.

7 In the Store macro in text box, select This Workbook from the drop-down list.

If you choose, you may enter a description of the macro in the Description text box. If you do not enter a description, the current date and author's name are entered as defaults.

8 Click OK.

The macro recorder is now on. You should see the `Recording` message at the bottom of your Excel screen and a Stop Recording toolbar onscreen (see Figure 2.4).

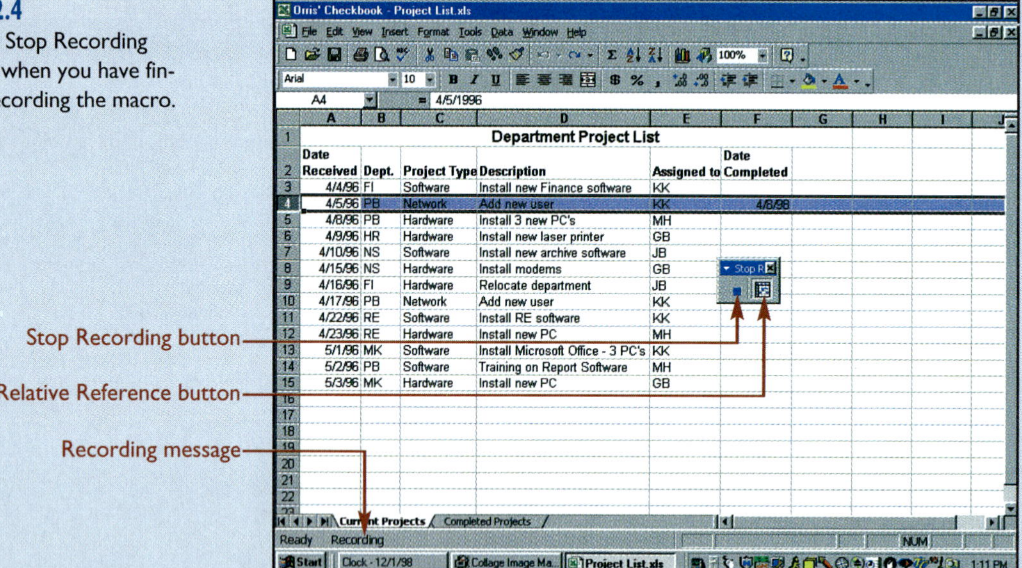

Figure 2.4
Use the Stop Recording toolbar when you have finished recording the macro.

9 Click the Relative Reference button on the Stop Recording toolbar.

The Relative Reference button allows you to play the macro anywhere on the worksheet. An absolute reference ties the macro to a particular cell. If you are creating a series of macros, the default reference will be the reference you chose for the previous macro. For the first macro, the Excel default setting will be the absolute reference.

You are now ready to record your macro. Keep the Project List workbook open for the next lesson.

Lesson 2: Recording a Macro

Now that you have established a name and destination for your macro, you can begin the recording process. The steps to be recorded are copying the selected range in the Current Projects worksheet to the Clipboard, pasting it into the Completed Projects worksheet, and deleting the selected range from the Current Projects worksheet.

To Record a Macro

1. **Display the Current Projects worksheet of the Project List workbook, with row 4 selected.**
2. **Make certain that the status bar shows `Recording`.**
3. **Click the Copy button on the Standard toolbar.**
   This copies row 4 to the Clipboard. A marquee appears around row 4.
4. **Click the Completed Projects sheet tab.**
   This is now the active sheet.
5. **Press Ctrl+Home.**
   Cell A1 is now the active cell.
6. **Press End and then press ↓ twice.**
   With these keystrokes, you check to ensure that the active cell is the first blank cell below the data. The active cell is now cell A5, the first cell in the blank row below the data.
7. **Click the Paste button on the Standard toolbar.**
   This pastes the selected data from row 4 of the Current Projects worksheet to row 5 (the first blank row) of the Completed Projects worksheet.
8. **Press ↓ and then click the Current Projects sheet tab.**
   This deselects the pasted row and returns the active cell to the Current Projects worksheet. Row 4 should still be selected.
9. **Select Edit, Delete.**
   This deletes row 4 from the Current Projects worksheet, since the information is now recorded in the Completed Projects worksheet.
10. **Click elsewhere on the worksheet to deselect row 4.**
11. **Click the Stop Recording button on the Stop Recording toolbar.**
    Save your changes, leave the Project List workbook open, and go on to Lesson 3.

Lesson 3: Playing a Macro

After a macro has been recorded, you can run (or play) it whenever you want to. To run the macro, you can either use the Tools, Macro command or the shortcut key, if you assigned one to the macro.

To Play a Macro

1 Display the Current Projects worksheet in the Project List workbook, type `4/13/98` in cell F7, and then press ↵Enter.

You have now updated the Department Project List to show that the project in row 7 was completed on 4/13/98.

2 Click the row 7 heading.

You may now use your macro to complete the transfer of the project to the Completed Projects worksheet. (Although you selected row 4 when you first created the macro, you can run the macro with any row selected.)

3 Select Tools, Macro, Macros.

The name of the macro you created (`Completed`) appears in the Macro dialog box, as shown in Figure 2.5.

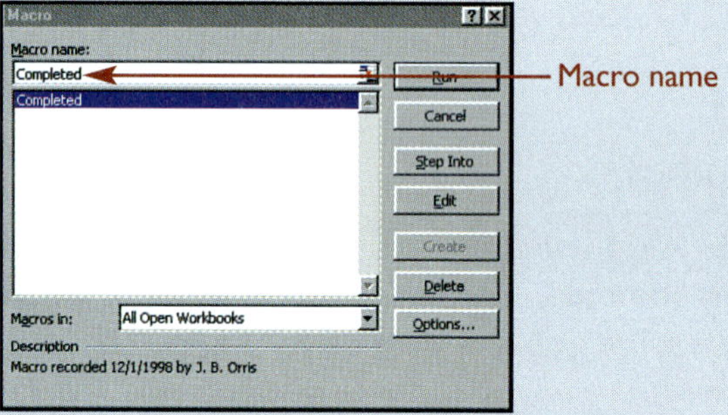

Figure 2.5
The Macro dialog box enables you to select and execute macros.

4 Click on `Completed` in the Macro name list, and then click Run.

Remember that `Completed` was the name given to your macro. The macro now performs its designated task and returns to the Current Projects worksheet. You should note that a macro may also be deleted from the Macro dialog box. Simply select the macro you want to delete and click on the Delete button.

5 Click the Completed Projects sheet tab.

You should see that the last completed project is the one transferred to the worksheet from row 4 of the Current Projects worksheet (see Figure 2.6).

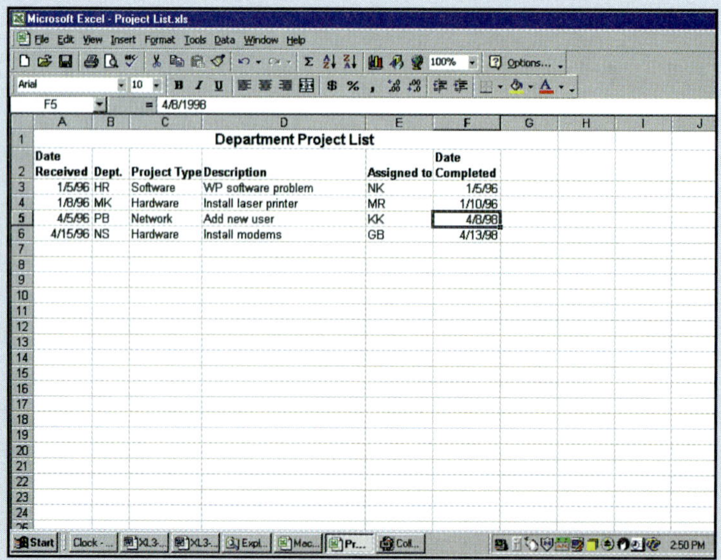

Date Received	Dept.	Project Type	Description	Assigned to	Date Completed
1/5/96	HR	Software	WP software problem	NK	1/5/96
1/8/96	MK	Hardware	Install laser printer	MR	1/10/96
4/5/96	PB	Network	Add new user	KK	4/8/98
4/15/96	NS	Hardware	Install modems	GB	4/13/98

Figure 2.6
The Completed Projects worksheet is now updated.

Save your changes, keep the Project List workbook open, and go on to Lesson 4.

Viewing a Macro's VBA Code
If you want to see the VBA code generated by any macro, you may select the macro name from the list box (in the Macro dialog box) and click the Edit button. This action loads the Visual Basic Editor. To watch the macro run step-by-step, you would instead select the Step Into button in the Macro dialog box and then press F8 to see each line as it executes. Choose File, Close and Return to Microsoft Excel (or press Alt+Q) when you're done with the Visual Basic Editor.

Lesson 4: Recording a Macro in a Personal Macro Workbook

It is possible to create macros that can be used with any workbook. The macro you created in Lesson 2 was for use with one specific workbook, so it was saved in a module sheet for that workbook. Now you want to create a macro that can be used in any workbook and save it to your Personal Macro Workbook. A ***Personal Macro Workbook*** is a Microsoft Excel file designed to contain macros that are intended to be available to all workbooks. Macros created for specific workbooks may also be saved to your Personal Macro Workbook if you find it more convenient to store all of your macros in one location.

To Record a Macro in a Personal Macro Workbook

1. **Choose File, New to open a new workbook.**
2. **Select Tools, Macro, Record New Macro.**
3. **Select the Macro name text box, type `Footer`, and press Tab.**
   Microsoft Excel will warn you if you have typed in a name that has already been used. You may then rename the current macro or the previous macro.
4. **Type the uppercase letter F in the Shortcut key text box and press Tab.**
5. **Click on the arrow beside the Store macro in box and select Personal Macro Workbook from the drop-down list. Press Tab.**

   If you are unable to save the macro to the Personal Macro Workbook, it may be because you are using a network system which protects this file. If this is the case, save the macro to This Workbook.

6. **Type `Page number footer` in the Description text box.**
7. **Click OK.**
   The Stop Recording toolbar should be displayed and the status bar should show the word `Recording`.

continues ▶

To Record a Macro in a Personal Macro Workbook (continued)

8. **Verify that the Relative Reference button on the Stop Recording toolbar has been pressed. (It may still be active from Lesson 2.)**

9. **Select File, Page Setup, and click the Header/Footer tab in the Page Setup dialog box (see Figure 2.7).**

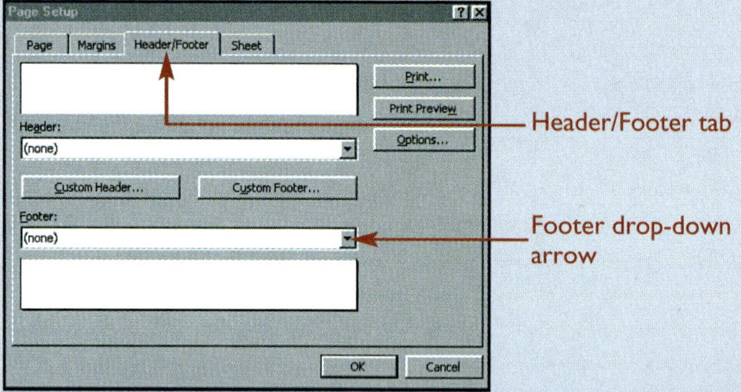

Figure 2.7
You add page numbers in the Header/Footer tab of the Page Setup dialog box.

10. **Click the Footer drop-down arrow.**

11. **Select Page 1 from the drop-down list, and then click OK to close the dialog box.**

12. **Click the Stop Recording button.**

    You have finished recording the macro and may close the workbook without saving the changes, because your macro is saved in your Personal Macro Workbook. The next lesson will show you how to play this macro.

Lesson 5: Playing a Macro from the Personal Macro Workbook

You have created a macro to insert a page number into a footer. This was saved to your Personal Macro Workbook because it is a macro that you may want to use in several different workbooks. You may play the macro from your Personal Macro Workbook, or if you assigned a shortcut key, you may use the shortcut key within any workbook.

To Play a Macro from the Personal Macro Workbook

1. **Display the Current Projects worksheet from the Project List workbook.**

2. **Click the Print Preview button.**

   This allows you to view the worksheet without a page number displayed in the footer.

3. **Click the Close button.**

4 Press and hold the Ctrl and ⇧Shift keys, and then type the letter F.
This plays your macro in the open workbook.

> If you receive an error message, `Ambiguous name detected`, it means that more than one copy of your macro has been detected in the Personal Macro Workbook. You can delete the duplicate by following the steps in Lesson 6.

5 Click the Print Preview button.
You should now see the worksheet with a page number in the footer.

6 Click the Close button.
Save the changes you have made, keep the Project List workbook open, and go on to Lesson 6.

Lesson 6: Unhiding and Editing the Personal Macro Workbook

Your Personal Macro Workbook is always open in Excel—it just isn't visible. This lesson shows how to unhide the Personal Macro Workbook and view the Visual Basic code it contains. It is necessary to unhide the workbook in order to edit or delete a macro stored there.

To Unhide and Edit the Personal Macro Workbook

1 In the Project List workbook, select Window, Unhide.
The Unhide dialog box appears, as shown in Figure 2.8.

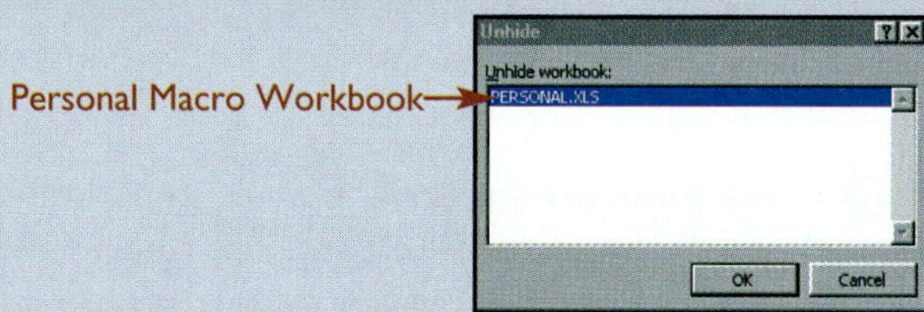

Figure 2.8
The Window, Unhide command is used to reveal the Unhide dialog box.

2 Click Personal from the Unhide workbook list and then click OK.

3 Select Tools, Macro, Macros (see Figure 2.9).

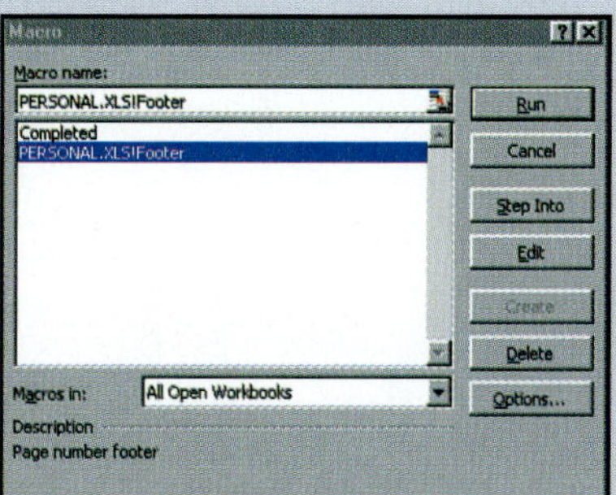

Figure 2.9
The Macro dialog box lists the names of the macros in the Project List workbook, as well as the Personal Macro Workbook.

continues ▶

To Unhide and Edit the Personal Macro Workbook (continued)

4 Click Footer from the Macro name list and then click Edit.

The Visual Basic window is displayed and reveals the Visual Basic code for the macro (see Figure 2.10). Make sure the Personal.xls window and the Code window are maximized.

You want to view the window that contains the macro code. The first line will be: `Sub Footer()`. If other windows are open (such as Project or Immediate) close them by clicking their Close buttons.

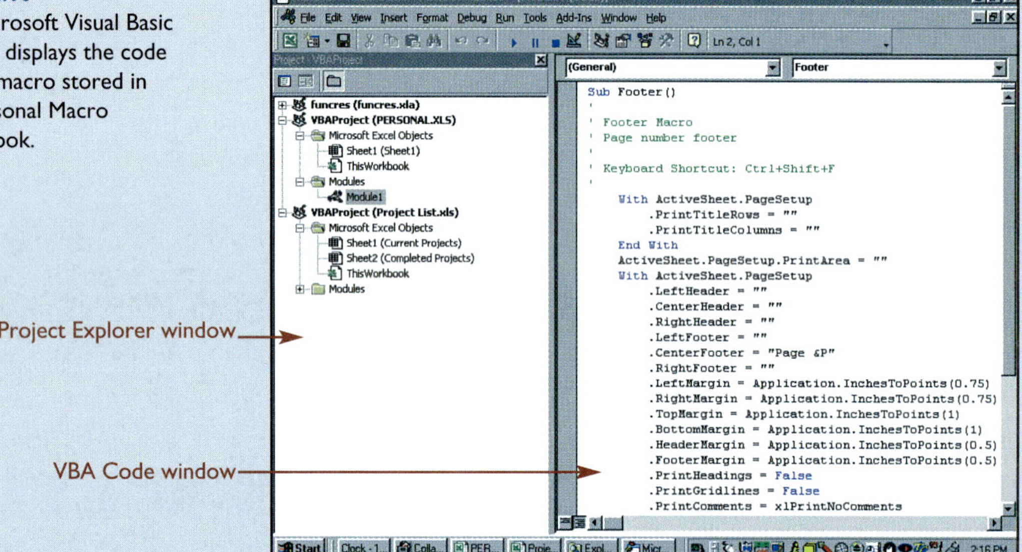

Figure 2.10
The Microsoft Visual Basic window displays the code for the macro stored in the Personal Macro Workbook.

5 Using the Office Assistant, type the query: `What is the project explorer?` Then, click Search.

Explore some of the Help topics and try other Help queries relevant to the Visual Basic Editor. Then close the Help window.

6 In the Module1 sheet window on the right side of the screen, scroll through the procedure code and find the line `.LeftFooter =""`.

You are going to edit this line to add your name to the footer.

7 Click between the " " (double quotation marks) symbols, type `Prepared by`, and then type a colon and a space (:) followed by your initials (see Figure 2.11).

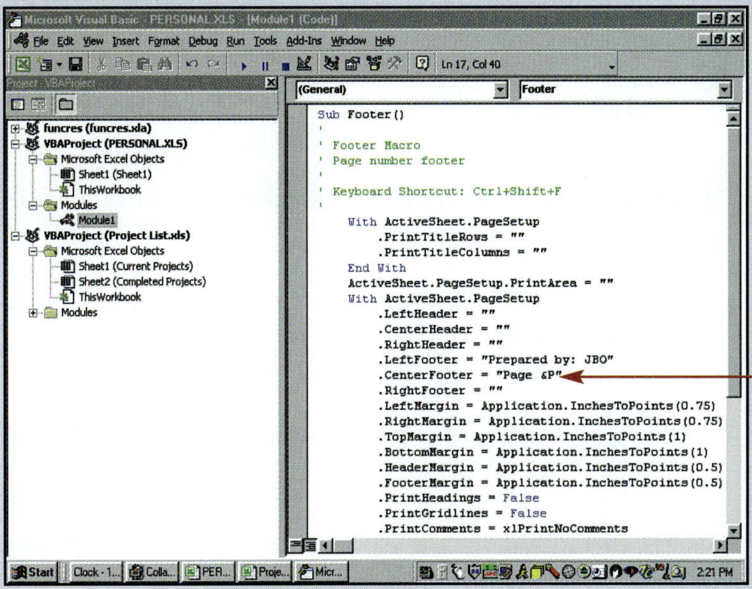

```
Sub Footer()
'
' Footer Macro
' Page number footer
'
' Keyboard Shortcut: Ctrl+Shift+F
'
    With ActiveSheet.PageSetup
        .PrintTitleRows = ""
        .PrintTitleColumns = ""
    End With
    ActiveSheet.PageSetup.PrintArea = ""
    With ActiveSheet.PageSetup
        .LeftHeader = ""
        .CenterHeader = ""
        .RightHeader = ""
        .LeftFooter = "Prepared by: JBO"
        .CenterFooter = "Page &P"
        .RightFooter = ""
        .LeftMargin = Application.InchesToPoints(0.75)
        .RightMargin = Application.InchesToPoints(0.75)
        .TopMargin = Application.InchesToPoints(1)
        .BottomMargin = Application.InchesToPoints(1)
        .HeaderMargin = Application.InchesToPoints(0.5)
        .FooterMargin = Application.InchesToPoints(0.5)
        .PrintHeadings = False
        .PrintGridlines = False
        .PrintComments = xlPrintNoComments
```

Edited instruction

Figure 2.11
The new macro after modifying the code for the left footer.

8 Select File, Save PERSONAL.XLS.
You have now edited and saved the macro. Now you will close the Visual Basic Editor.

9 Select File, Close and Return to Microsoft Excel.

10 Select Window, PERSONAL.XLS; then select Window, Hide.
You have not closed the Personal Macro Workbook; you have just hidden it.

11 Press Ctrl+Shift+F.
This plays your macro in the current worksheet.

12 Click the Print Preview button to view the edited footer.

13 Click the Close button.
Save the changes you have made, keep the Project List workbook open, and go on to Lesson 7.

If You Close a Personal Macro Workbook
If you should happen to close the Personal Macro Workbook, you will be unable to access it without reloading Excel. Excel automatically opens the Personal Macro Workbook every time you start the application.

Lesson 7: Creating a Macro Button in a Workbook

Because the entire idea behind macros is to save the user time, Excel has three quick use options for your macros. The first is shortcut keys, which we have already discussed. This lesson demonstrates the second method, which is placing a macro button in a workbook. A ***macro button*** is simply an alternative to a shortcut key. It appears on the worksheet as a button similar to any toolbar button. The third timesaver, adding a macro button to a toolbar, is covered in Lesson 8.

To Create a Macro Button in a Workbook

1. **Display the Current Projects worksheet in the Project List workbook, and click cell G2.**
   This is where you are going to place the macro button.

2. **Select View, Toolbars and click Forms to display the Forms toolbar.**

3. **Click the Button icon on the Forms toolbar.**

4. **Click on cell G2 and drag the mouse to draw a box the full size of the cell. Release the mouse button.**
   The Assign Macro dialog box should now be displayed, as shown in Figure 2.12.

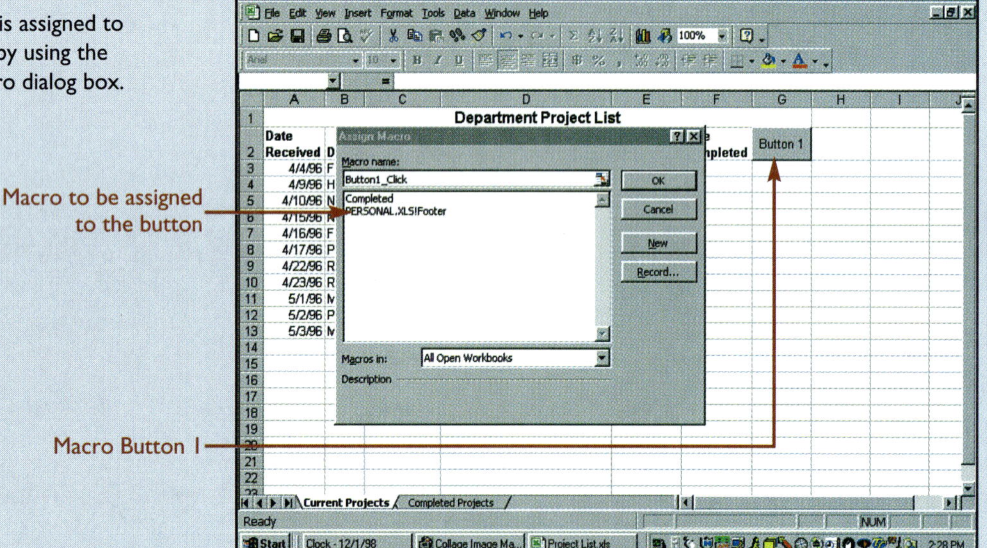

Figure 2.12
The macro is assigned to the button by using the Assign Macro dialog box.

5. **Click on the `Completed` macro name from the Macro name list, and then click OK.**
   That macro has now been assigned to the button.

6. **Click inside the button in cell G2, and delete the words `Button 1`. Type the word `Completed`.**
   If the button is too small to contain the word, you can resize the button by using the handles. If the handles are not apparent, press Ctrl while clicking the button with the left mouse button. This activates the handles.

7. **Close the Forms toolbar.**

8. **Click cell F7. Type `4/13/98` and press Enter. Click the row 7 heading.**
   The project in row 7 is now completed. Now you can test your macro button.

9. **Click the Completed button.**
   The project from row 7 should have been moved to the Completed Projects worksheet and removed from the Current Projects worksheet.

If your macro did not work, it may be that you did not click on the row heading in step 8 above. The macro button in this example only works if the row heading is activated.

Save the changes you have made to the Project List workbook, keep the workbook open, and go on to Lesson 8.

Altering a Macro Button

You can change characteristics of the macro button, such as the font, by right-clicking the button and selecting Format Control from the shortcut menu. You may remove the button from the screen by selecting Cut from the same shortcut menu. The macro button can be located anywhere on the worksheet. Just press Ctrl while left-clicking on the button border and then drag the button to the new location.

Lesson 8: Adding a Macro Button to a Toolbar

The third quick access for a macro is to place a macro button on a toolbar. In this lesson, you create a toolbar macro button for the footer macro you created in Lesson 4. The button icon will be a Smiley Face.

To Add a Macro Button to a Toolbar

1. **Click the New button on the Standard toolbar.**
2. **Select View, Toolbars, Customize.**
3. **Click the Commands tab in the Customize dialog box; then scroll down the Categories list and select Macros (see Figure 2.13).**

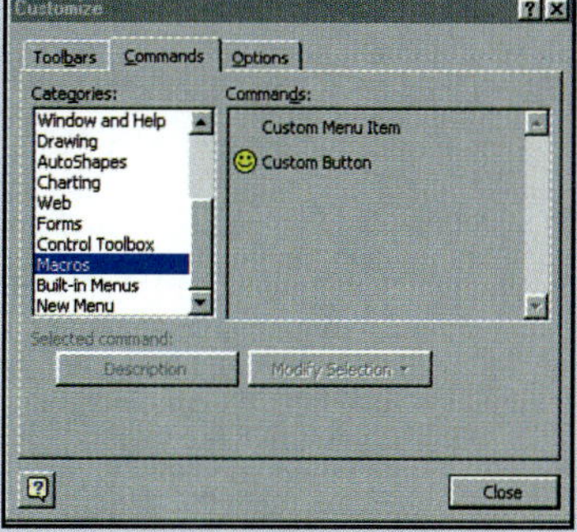

Figure 2.13
The Customize dialog box lists all toolbars, commands, and options available in Excel.

Note that the Categories are listed on the left side of the tab, with all of the available Commands listed on the right.

4. **Click the Smiley Face icon and drag it into position just to the left of the Bold button on the Formatting toolbar at the top of your screen.**

continues ▶

To Add a Macro Button to a Toolbar (continued)

5 With the Customize dialog box still displayed on-screen, right-click the Smiley Face button on the Formatting toolbar. Choose Assign Macro from the shortcut menu (see Figure 2.14).

From the Assign Macro dialog box that appears, you can assign a macro name.

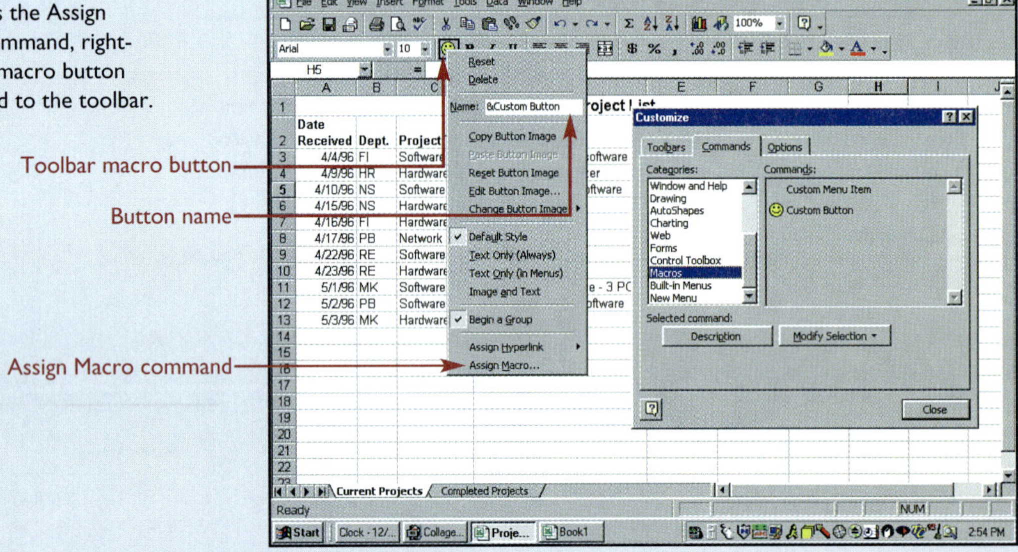

Figure 2.14
To access the Assign Macro command, right-click the macro button you added to the toolbar.

6 Click `PERSONAL.XLS!Footer` from the Macro name list in the Assign Macro dialog box, and then click OK.

7 Close the Customize dialog box.

You can now run your macro by clicking the Smiley Face button on the toolbar.

8 Save the changes to the Personal List workbook, and then close the workbook.

9 Exit Excel, and then choose Yes when prompted to save the changes to the Personal Macro Workbook.

Removing Macro Buttons from the Toolbar

You can easily remove a macro button that you added to a toolbar. Choose View, Toolbars, Customize to display the Customize dialog box. Select the toolbar button you want to delete, drag it off of the toolbar, and then close the dialog box.

Customizing a Macro Button

You can choose any one of the 42 built-in button images in Excel. Open the Customize dialog box and right-click the button you want to change. Choose Change Button Image from the shortcut menu, and select the button image you want. You can change the buttons even further and create your own button images by choosing Edit Button Image from the shortcut menu.

Summary 

Macros are a way of automating complex or repetitive tasks. In this project, you have learned to record and play macros and to store them in both a worksheet and your Personal Macro Workbook. You have also learned the three ways to have quick access to your macros—shortcut keys, macro buttons in a workbook, or macro buttons on a toolbar.

You have also been introduced, although very briefly, to the programming language of Excel, Visual Basic for Applications (VBA). With regard to macros, VBA is the means of editing; you can view this VBA code as described in Lesson 3.

You can get a lot of help on Visual Basic by using the Help menu while you are using the Visual Basic Editor. However, if you really want to develop skills in VBA programming, you are probably going to need a book. Books that discuss Excel 97 VBA programming would be useful for Excel 2000 as well.

Checking Concepts and Terms 

True/False

For each of the following, check *T* or *F* to indicate whether the statement is true or false.

__T __F **1.** If a macro is stored in a Personal Macro Workbook, the macro can be opened from any workbook. [L4]

__T __F **2.** The Personal Macro Workbook is opened every time Excel starts. [L6]

__T __F **3.** A macro with an absolute reference can be applied anywhere on a designated worksheet. [L1]

__T __F **4.** You must know Visual Basic programming to record a macro. [L1]

__T __F **5.** You can assign a macro to a toolbar button or a shortcut key. [L1,7]

__T __F **6.** If you have a macro that is specific to a particular workbook, you would store it in the Personal Macro Workbook. [L5]

__T __F **7.** A macro is like a fast typist. [Why Would I Do This?]

__T __F **8.** You need to be a skilled programmer in order to use the Visual Basic Editor. [L6]

__T __F **9.** The fastest way to run a macro is with the Tools menu. [L7]

__T __F **10.** If you put a macro button on a toolbar, it will still be there the next time you run Excel. [L8]

Multiple Choice

Circle the letter of the correct answer for each of the following.

1. When you are recording a macro, the __________ toolbar should be on the screen. [L1]

a. Stop Recording

b. Macros

c. Recording

d. Edit

2. If you want to play a macro in multiple workbooks, you need to store it in ______________. [L4]

a. the workbook in which it was created

b. a new workbook

c. the Personal Macro Workbook

d. either a or c

3. To create a macro button in the current workbook, use the ______________ toolbar. [L7]

a. Visual Basic

b. Forms

c. Drawing

d. Formatting

4. The default cell reference for a macro is _______________. [L1]
   a. a relative cell reference
   b. an absolute cell reference
   c. the previous reference selection
   d. none of the above
5. If you no longer need a macro, you _______________. [L6]
   a. cannot delete it
   b. can delete it only from the Visual Basic window
   c. can delete it from the Macro dialog box
   d. can delete it by unhiding the window and selecting Delete from the Edit menu
6. An Excel *macro* can be defined as _______________. [Why Would I Do This?]
   a. instructions
   b. a complex function
   c. recorded keystrokes
   d. stored operations
7. If you do not like any of the available custom toolbar icons, you _______________. [L8]
   a. can import one from another application
   b. are limited to existing icons
   c. can create a new icon
   d. can modify one of the existing icons
8. A macro may be stored in _______________. [L2,4]
   a. a workbook
   b. the Personal Macro Workbook
   c. the Templates workbook
   d. both a and b
9. If you close the Personal Macro Workbook, _______________. [L6]
   a. you can reopen it
   b. you must restart Microsoft Excel to reopen it
   c. you must reboot your computer to reopen it
   d. your current macro will not play
10. A macro may be assigned to _______________ [L1,7,8]
   a. a shortcut key
   b. a workbook button
   c. a toolbar button
   d. all of the above

Discussion Questions

1. Under what circumstances is it better to write a macro than to perform Excel operations manually?
2. Should all spreadsheet users learn to use Visual Basic for Applications, and if not, who should?
3. When should you store a macro in PERSONAL.XLS, and why would you choose not to?
4. When would it be useful to assign a shortcut key to a macro? When would a toolbar button be more appropriate?
5. What are the differences between object-oriented macros and recorded keystroke macros?

Skill Drill

Skill Drill exercises reinforce project skills. Each skill reinforced is the same, or nearly the same, as a skill presented in the project. Detailed instructions are provided in a step-by-step format.

Several exercises in this project direct you to access a new blank workbook. Starting Excel displays a new blank workbook. If you have been working on another file, you can display a new workbook by clicking the New button at the left end of the Standard toolbar.

1. Recording a Macro to Enter an Address

One of the common tasks that can be done with a macro is to enter a frequently used address.

1. Open a new workbook file in Excel.

   Your macro will be recorded in this workbook.
2. Select Tools, Macro, Record New Macro.
3. Name the macro **COMPANY**. The macro is to be stored in This Workbook only. Click OK.
4. Click the Relative Reference button to deselect it.
5. Select cell A1.
6. Type the following address in cells A1:A3.

```
Memex Corporation
5151 Smith Road
Columbus, OH 42221
```

7. Select cells A1:A3 and click the Bold button on the Formatting toolbar.
8. Click cell A4.
9. Click the Stop Recording button.

The macro is recorded and assigned the name COMPANY. Keep the workbook open and continue with the next exercise.

2. Playing the Address Macro

Once an address macro has been recorded, it can then be run to enter the address wherever it would normally be typed.

1. Select cell A10.
2. Choose Tools, Macro, Macros.
3. Select COMPANY and click Run.
4. Save the workbook with the filename Macro1 test.
5. Close the workbook.

3. Recording a Macro to Enter the Current Date

You are going to create a macro for the TODAY function and save it in the Personal Macro Workbook.

1. Open a new workbook and save it as Macro2 test.
2. Select Tools, Macro, Record New Macro.
3. Name the macro **TODAY**.
4. Assign the macro a shortcut key (Ctrl+Shift+T) and store the macro in the Personal Macro Workbook; then click OK.
5. Click the Relative Reference button to deselect it.
6. Type **=TODAY()** in cell A1 and press Enter. Click the Stop Recording button.
7. Save the changes and leave the workbook open.

4. Testing the Current Date Macro

Any time you create a new macro, you should test it.

1. In the Macro2 test workbook, select cell A4.
2. Press Ctrl+Shift+T. Excel enters today's date in cell A4.
3. Save the Macro2 test workbook and then close it.

5. Modifying a Macro

You are now going to modify the address in the Macro1 test workbook.

1. Open the Macro1 test workbook and display Sheet 1.
2. Select Tools, Macro, Macros.
3. Select the COMPANY macro and click Edit.
4. Change the zip code from **42221** to **43245**.
5. Click the Save button in the toolbar.
6. Click File, Close and Return to Microsoft Excel.

   You are now going to create a button on the worksheet to play the COMPANY macro.

6. Creating a Macro Button

When a macro is going to be used frequently or by someone else, it may be more convenient to place a macro button on the worksheet.

1. Display Sheet1 of the Macro1 test workbook.
2. Display the Forms toolbar.
3. Create a button in cell range B15:B16.
4. Assign the COMPANY macro to the button.
5. Delete the `Button 1` text and replace it with `Company`.
6. Close the Forms toolbar.
7. Activate cell F6; then click the Company macro button.
8. Right-click the macro button.
9. Select Format Control, and then click the Properties tab.
10. Make sure a check mark appears in the Print object check box and click OK.
11. Save the changes and close the workbook.

7. Creating a Toolbar Button

You are now going to create a button for the TODAY macro and place it on the Formatting toolbar.

1. Open a new workbook.
2. Choose View, Toolbars, Customize.
3. Select the Commands tab.
4. Select the Macros category.
5. Drag the Smiley Face (or another button) to the Formatting toolbar.
6. Right-click the Smiley Face button in the toolbar.
7. Assign the `PERSONAL.XLS!Today` macro to it; then close the dialog box.
8. Test the macro by clicking the Smiley Face button.
9. Remove the Smiley Face button from the toolbar by using the Customize dialog box.
10. Close the workbook without saving it.

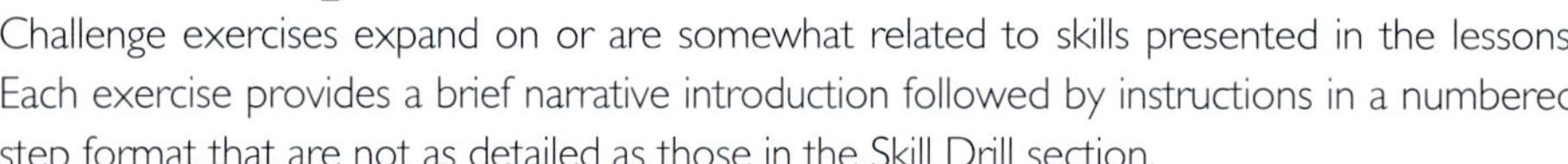

Challenge

Challenge exercises expand on or are somewhat related to skills presented in the lessons. Each exercise provides a brief narrative introduction followed by instructions in a numbered step format that are not as detailed as those in the Skill Drill section.

Each exercise is independent of the others, so that you may complete the exercises in any order. Be sure to save the workbook after completing each exercise. If you need a paper copy of the completed exercise, enter your name centered in a header before printing.

1. Editing the Module Sheet

If you want to make changes in a macro, you can modify it with the Visual Basic Editor, which is often faster and easier than re-recording the macro.

1. Open the Macro1 test workbook, save it as Macro1b test, and select Tools, Macro, Macros.
2. Click COMPANY from the Macro name list and then click Edit to open the Visual Basic Editor.
3. Scroll until you find the text `5151 Smith Road`. Replace this text with `10 North Sunset Lane`.
4. Make sure the quotation marks still surround the street address.

5. Make the address italic as well as bold (hint: insert a new line similar to the one that makes the address bold).
6. Save the changes and exit the Visual Basic window.
7. Click the Sheet2 tab and then activate cell F1.
8. Play the macro.
9. Save the changes to the workbook and then close it.

2. Customizing a Macro Toolbar Button

Once a macro is assigned to a toolbar button, the properties of that button can be changed.

1. Open a new workbook.
2. Select View, Toolbars, Customize.
3. Select the Commands tab.
4. Select the Macros category.
5. Drag the Smiley Face to the Formatting toolbar.
6. Right-click the Smiley Face button in the toolbar.
7. Assign the `PERSONAL.XLS!Footer` macro to the button.
8. With the Customize dialog box open, right-click on the Smiley Face button on the toolbar.
9. Select Edit Button Image from the shortcut menu.
10. Modify the smile to make it look different, for example, no smile and a different color.
11. Close the Button Editor, and then close the Customize dialog box.

3. Testing a Macro Toolbar Button

Your Footer macro is now assigned to the toolbar button. Use the following steps to test your button.

1. Open a new workbook.
2. Select View, Toolbars, Customize.
3. Click the Modify Selection button, and then type `&Footer` in the Name box. This name will appear as the ScreenTip when you point to the toolbar button. Close the Customize dialog box.
4. Type your first name in cell A1 of the new worksheet and press ↵Enter.

   You cannot preview a document unless there is something in a cell.
5. Select File, Print Preview.

   The worksheet should appear without the footer.
6. Click the Close button.
7. Click the Smiley Face button on the Formatting toolbar.
8. Select File, Print Preview.

   The worksheet should now appear with the footer in place.
9. Click the Close button to exit the Preview, and then close the workbook without saving changes.

4. Removing a Macro Button from a Toolbar

If you want to remove the button from the toolbar, follow these steps:

1. Open a new workbook.
2. Select View, Toolbars, Customize.
3. Drag the button off the toolbar.

   Next, you want to delete the macro itself.
4. Select Window, Unhide; then choose Personal and click OK.

   Your Personal Macro Workbook should be displayed.
5. Select Tools, Macro, Macros.

   This should display the Macro dialog box that lists all your macros.
6. Use the Delete button to remove the macro you no longer want, which in this case is the Footer macro.
7. Select Window, Hide.
8. Select File, Exit. Click Yes to save your changes to the Personal Macro Workbook.

Discovery Zone

Discovery Zone exercises require advanced knowledge of topics presented in *Essentials* lessons, application of skills from multiple lessons, or self-directed learning of new skills. Each exercise is independent of the others, so that you may complete the exercises in any order.

1. Recording Multiple Macros

Experiment with recording several macros. Just about any Excel menu item or operation can be recorded. Then choose Tools, Macro, Macros; select a macro and click the Edit button to look at the macro and perhaps edit it. Use the same procedure to view other macros you've recorded. Looking at recorded macros can provide a lot of insight about how Excel works.

2. Writing a Subroutine with VBA

If you have a little programming experience from another course, try writing a subroutine from scratch using the Visual Basic Editor. Visual Basic is a full programming language and the editor has extensive help for concepts and syntax. The subroutine you write will appear in the macros list and can be used like any other macro.

Working with Advanced Functions

Objectives

In this project, you learn how to

- **Use the Formula Palette**
- **Use the Future Value Function**
- **Use the Present Value and ROUND Functions**
- **Examine a User-Defined Function**
- **Use Concatenation to String Text Together**
- **Insert Symbols and Characters**
- **Extract Text with the MID Function**
- **Use the TEXT Function**

Key terms introduced in this project include

- ANSI codes
- ASCII codes
- concatenation
- Formula palette
- future value
- present value
- substring
- user-defined function

Why Would I Do This?

Microsoft Excel has more than 500 built-in functions. In earlier projects you have learned how to use some basic functions. This project examines a few of the many advanced functions. If you need help with almost any function, check the Formula palette or Microsoft Excel Help.

Visual Summary

Figure 3.1 shows the Formula palette and the Paste Function dialog box, which lists all of Microsoft Excel's built-in functions. Figure 3.2 is an example of the Visual Basic Editor showing a user-defined function. Later in this project, you'll learn how to use these elements to help you work with Excel's functions.

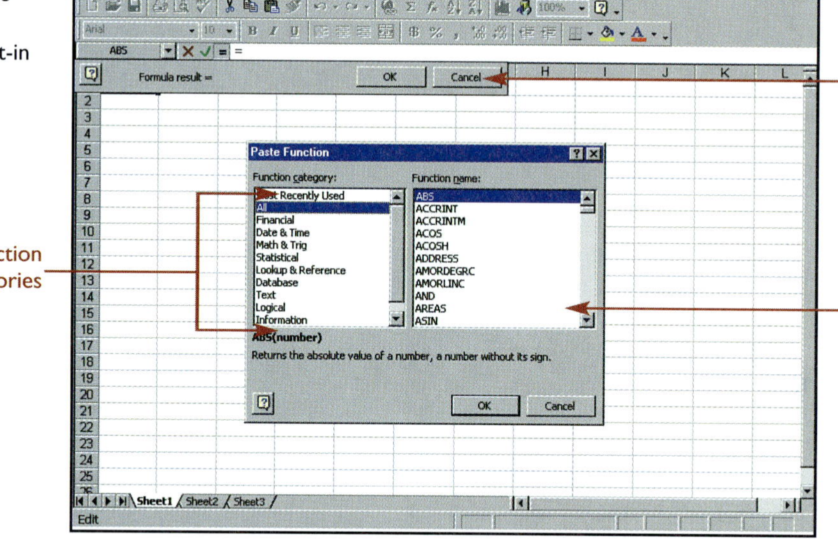

Figure 3.1
The Formula palette provides access to more than 500 built-in functions.

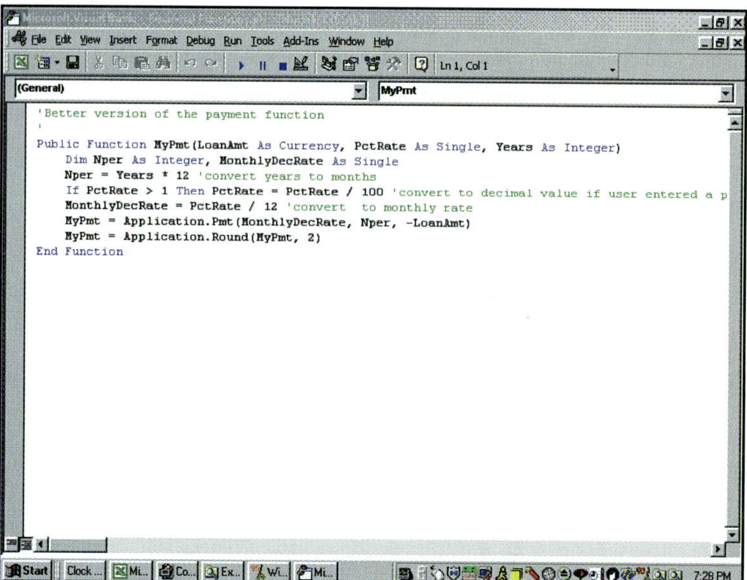

Figure 3.2
The VBA editor shows the VBA code for the MyPmt function.

Lesson 1: Using the Formula Palette

If you know the name of the function you want and you know what inputs it needs, you can type it into any cell and begin the function with an '=' sign. However, for infrequently used functions, it is easier to use the ***Formula palette***, which lists all of Microsoft Excel's functions and assists you in specifying the proper input values. This lesson explores the Formula palette while looking for the future value (FV) function that is used in the next lesson.

To Use the Formula Palette

1. **Open the file XL3-0301 and save it as `Financial Functions`.**

2. **Click on the = in the formula bar.**

   The Formula palette appears, just below the formula bar.

3. **Click the drop-down arrow to the left of the = (equal sign) in the formula bar and you see a list of the 10 most recently used functions (see Figure 3.3).**

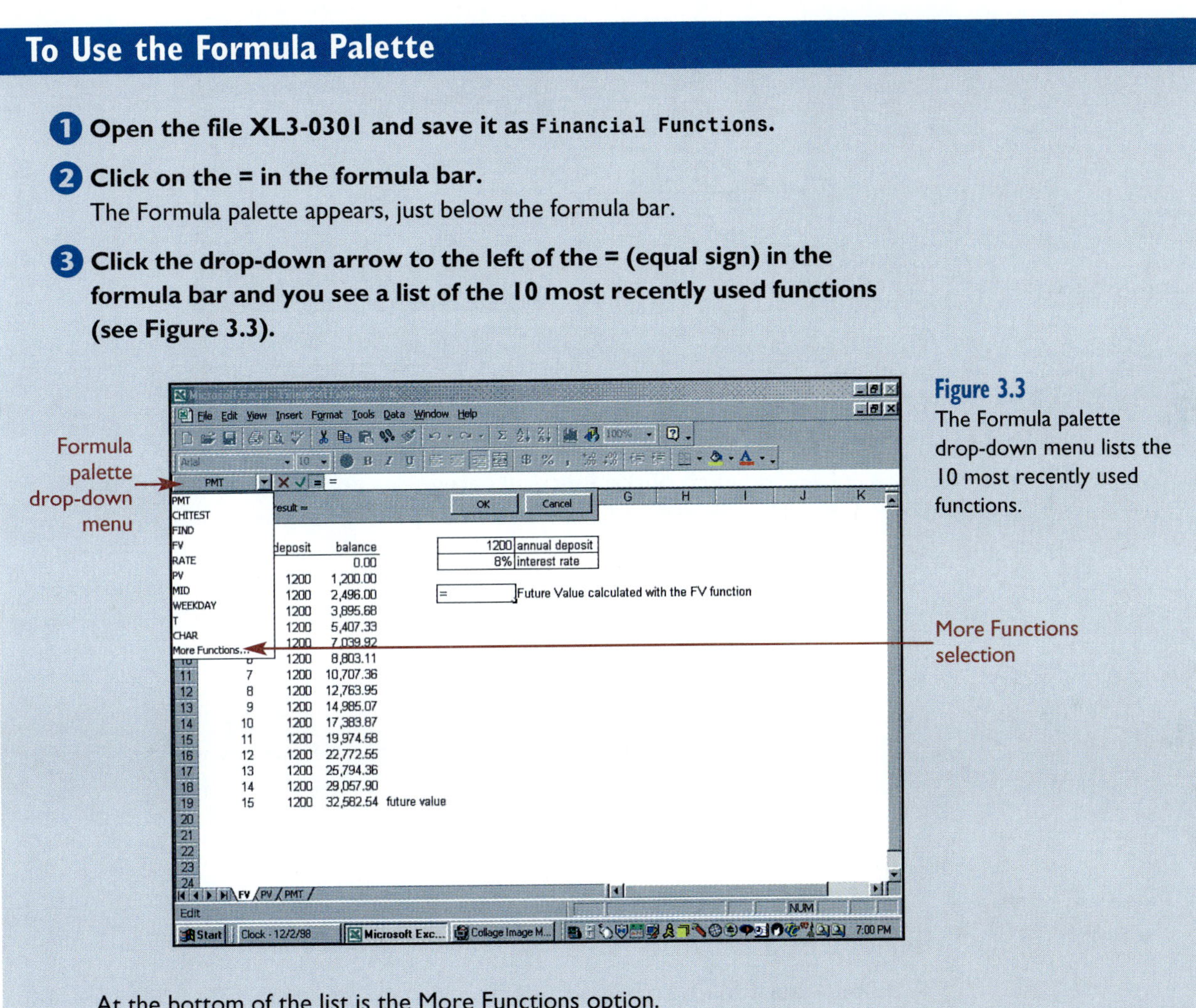

Figure 3.3
The Formula palette drop-down menu lists the 10 most recently used functions.

At the bottom of the list is the More Functions option.

4. **Click on More Functions.**

   The Paste Function dialog box appears, as shown in Figure 3.4.

continues ▶

To Use the Formula Palette (continued)

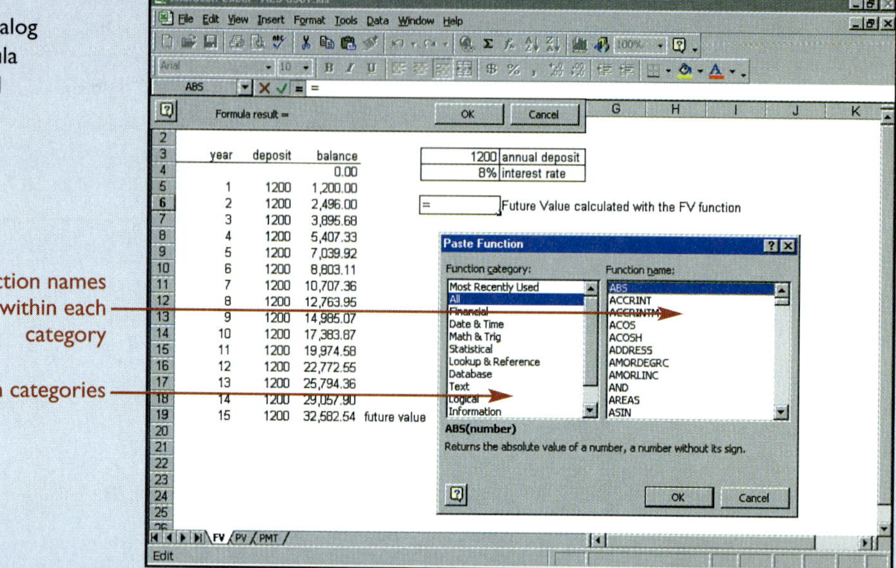

Figure 3.4
The Paste Function dialog box shows the Formula palette categories and names.

5 Take a few minutes to browse through the functions.

6 Click on each of the function categories and then scroll through the function names and click on a few to see what they do.

A brief description of the selected function appears at the bottom of the dialog box (refer to Figure 3.4). You can click the Office Assistant button in the lower-left corner of the dialog box to obtain more information on the selected function.

7 Click Cancel.

8 Click the red X on the formula bar.

The Formula palette closes. Leave the Financial Functions workbook open, and go on to Lesson 2.

Lesson 2: Using the Future Value Function

This lesson explores a typical financial function. Assume you put $1,200 in the bank at the end of each year for 15 years at 8% interest. How much money would you have at the end of the 15 years? You can use the ***future value (FV)*** function in Excel to determine the answer.

To Use the Future Value Function

1 In the Financial Functions workbook, take a moment to examine the FV worksheet.

In cells A3:C19 we see the year numbers, deposit amounts, and account balance at the end of each of the 15 years. The formulas in column C increase the balance by the stated percent and add the new deposit for each year.

Look at the cell formulas to see how they work. Notice that the worksheet is set up so that we can change the deposit and/or interest rate in cells E3 and E4 and the worksheet would show the new result. This is good worksheet practice. Never enter a number into a formula unless you are certain that you will never want to change the number.

The value in cell C19 is called the future value. While it is educational and interesting to see what it means and how it is calculated, if we are just interested in the bottom line, we can calculate the future value more easily with the FV function.

2 Click on cell E6.

3 Use the Formula palette as described in Lesson 1 to activate the FV function in the Financial functions category.
The FV Formula palette appears (see Figure 3.5).

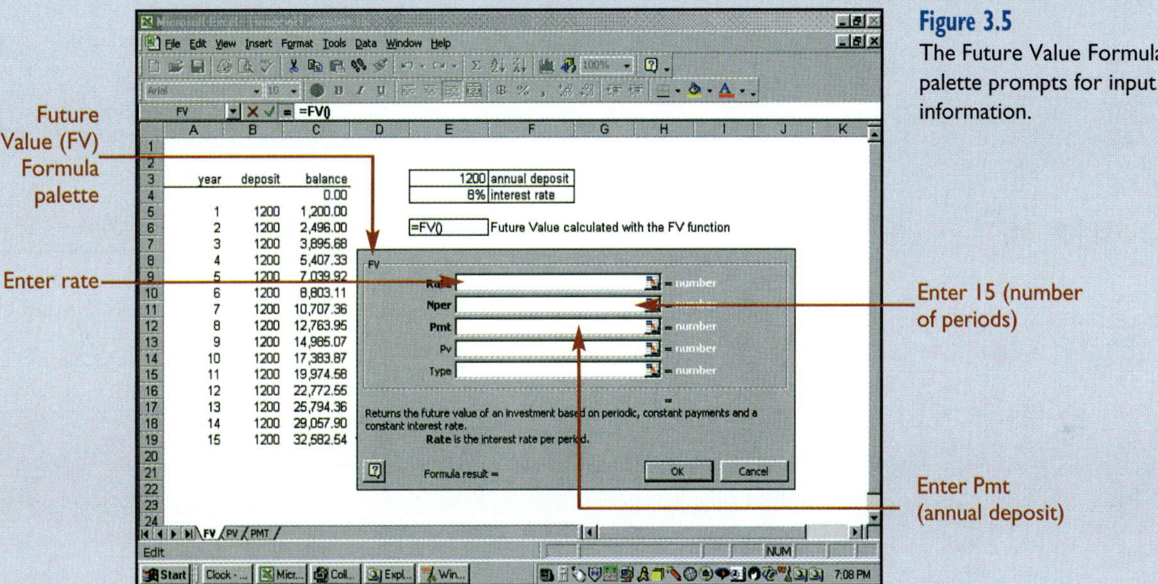

Figure 3.5
The Future Value Formula palette prompts for input information.

4 Click the Formula palette and drag it so you can see the underlying worksheet cells.

5 The cursor should be blinking in the Rate input box. Click on cell E4 to select the rate.

6 Press Tab to go to the Nper input box and type 15.
The FV function will work for any number of periods, but this example is set up only for 15.

7 Press Tab to go to the Pmt input box. Type a minus sign (–), and then click on cell E3 for the annual payment.

continues ▶

To Use the Future Value Function (continued)

If you don't type the minus sign, the resulting future value would be negative. All of the financial functions work this way to reflect that one party's cash out-flow is the other party's cash in-flow. For example, if you are paying off a loan, the payment is a negative cash flow to you, but it would be a positive cash flow from the bank's point of view.

The Formula palette now displays the formula result that should correspond to the value in cell C19. If it doesn't, try to figure out what you did wrong.

Leave the other two input boxes (PV and Type) blank. They are for advanced calculations and are not often used.

8. **Click OK to complete the function.**

9. **Try entering some different payment and interest rates in cells E3 and E4.**
   It is not necessary to open the Formula palette again; just change the values in the cells and the result automatically updates.

   Save the changes in the Financial Functions workbook, keep the workbook open, and go on to Lesson 3.

Entering Percentages
When you enter the percent as `8%`, the entry is treated numerically the same as if you had typed `.08`.

Viewing Cell Formulas
You can see all of the cell formulas on a worksheet without clicking them individually; just press Ctrl+~. Press this key combination again to return the display to values (it acts as a toggle).

Lesson 3: Using the Present Value and ROUND Functions

Assume you want to be able to *withdraw* $1,200 at the end of each year for 15 years. How much money would you have to put into an account at the start of the first year for it to earn exactly enough interest to generate the payments (withdrawals) and have the account equal zero after the last payment? This amount is known as the ***present value***. Banking transactions are usually computed to the nearest penny, whereas computer functions calculate the answer to many decimal places. If you want the computer to reflect rounding to the nearest penny, you must use the ROUND function.

To Use the Present Value and ROUND Functions

1. **Click on the PV sheet tab in the Financial Functions workbook and take a moment to examine the worksheet.**
   In cells A3:C19, we see the year number, withdrawal amount, and the account balance at the end of each of the 15 years. The formulas in column C increase the balance by the stated percent and subtract the withdrawal for each year. Look at the cell formulas to see how they work. You have probably noticed that the value in cell C19 is not zero, as it is supposed to be. That is because we have not yet made our deposit in cell C4 with the PV function.
2. **Click on cell C4.**
3. **Use the Formula palette to select the PV function in the Financial functions category. Click OK.**
4. **Click anywhere on the PV Formula palette and drag it so you can see the underlying cells.**
5. **The cursor should be blinking in the Rate input box. Click on cell E8 to specify the rate.**
6. **Press Tab to go to the Nper input box and type `15`.**
   The PV function will work for any number of periods, but this example is set up only for 15.
7. **Press Tab to go to the Pmt input box. Type a minus sign (–), and then click on cell E7 for the annual payment.**
   The Formula palette now displays the formula result. If it doesn't, try to figure out what you did wrong.

   Leave the other two input boxes (FV and Type) blank. They are for advanced calculations and are not often used.
8. **Click OK; cell C19 shows zero.**
   The present value is `10,271.37`. However, if you increase the number of decimal places, you see it is actually `10,271.3744255116`. While this number is mathematically correct and makes the balance go to exactly zero after 15 years, it does not reflect reality, because dollar amounts are typically rounded to the nearest penny. The way to handle this with Microsoft Excel is with the ROUND function.
9. **Double-click on cell C4.**
10. **Place the cursor between the `=` and the `P` and type `ROUND(`.**
11. **Now place the cursor at the end of the formula, and type `,2)`.**
    The resulting formula should look like this:

    ```
    =ROUND(PV(E8,15,-E7),2)
    ```

    The final argument of `2` specifies the number of decimal places to round to. If you want to round to an integer value, you would use `0`. If you want to round to the nearest thousand, you would use `-3`.

continues ▶

To Use the Present Value and ROUND Functions (continued)

12 Press 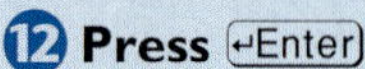**.**

Figure 3.6 shows the screen as it should appear after you have completed the ROUND function.

Figure 3.6
This screen shows the effect of the ROUND function on the final balance.

Microsoft Excel - Financial Functions.xls

C4 = =ROUND(PV(E8,15,-E7),2)

	year	withdrawal	balance		
4			10,271.37	Present Value	
5	1	1200	9,893.08		
6	2	1200	9,484.53		
7	3	1200	9,043.29	1200	annual deposit
8	4	1200	8,566.75	8%	interest rate
9	5	1200	8,052.09		
10	6	1200	7,496.26		
11	7	1200	6,895.96		
12	8	1200	6,247.64		
13	9	1200	5,547.45		
14	10	1200	4,791.24		
15	11	1200	3,974.54		
16	12	1200	3,092.51		
17	13	1200	2,139.91		
18	14	1200	1,111.10		
19	15	1200	-0.01		

Present value

Final balance

If you increase the number of decimal places, you see that the number is now `10,271.3700000000`. Since the rounded number is slightly less than the original number, the balance at the end of year 15 turns out to be slightly negative. If you always want to round *up*, there is, as you probably guessed, a ROUNDUP function.

Save the Financial Functions workbook, and leave it open for the next lesson.

Function Names Are Not Case Sensitive

The ROUND function in this lesson was typed in capital letters; however, that is not necessary. You may use lowercase or a mixture. When you press Enter, the function name is automatically converted to uppercase.

Lesson 4: Examining a User-Defined Function

The objective of this lesson is to show that you do not have to be a skilled programmer to create your own simple functions, which are called ***user-defined functions***. User-defined functions are listed in the Formula palette and can be used just like the standard Excel functions. If there are some computations that you often use, you will find it worth the effort to create user-defined functions for them. It will save a lot of typing and probably reduce errors.

This lesson simply looks at an example that has already been written; however, by examining it you can see how it works. Later we will modify it to make another function.

In the Excel 2000 Essentials Basic, Project 5, Lesson 3, you saw how to calculate a monthly loan payment using the PMT function. However, you had to know a couple of tricks to make the function work correctly. You had to divide the annual percentage by 12 to make it a monthly rate, and you had to start the PV field with a minus sign.

When asked to enter the rate, you needed to know whether to enter `8`, `.08`, or `8%`. Also, the form displayed a couple of fields that are rarely used, and the calculated value was not rounded to the nearest penny. Our "new and improved" payment function will fix all of those problems. First use the function and then examine it.

To Examine a User-Defined Function

1. **Click on the PMT sheet tab of the Financial Functions workbook.**

2. **Click cell B7, open the Formula palette, and go to More Functions.**

3. **Scroll down to the User-Defined category, click on MyPmt, and then click OK.**

4. **Drag the MyPmt Formula palette so you see the cells underneath (see Figure 3.7).**

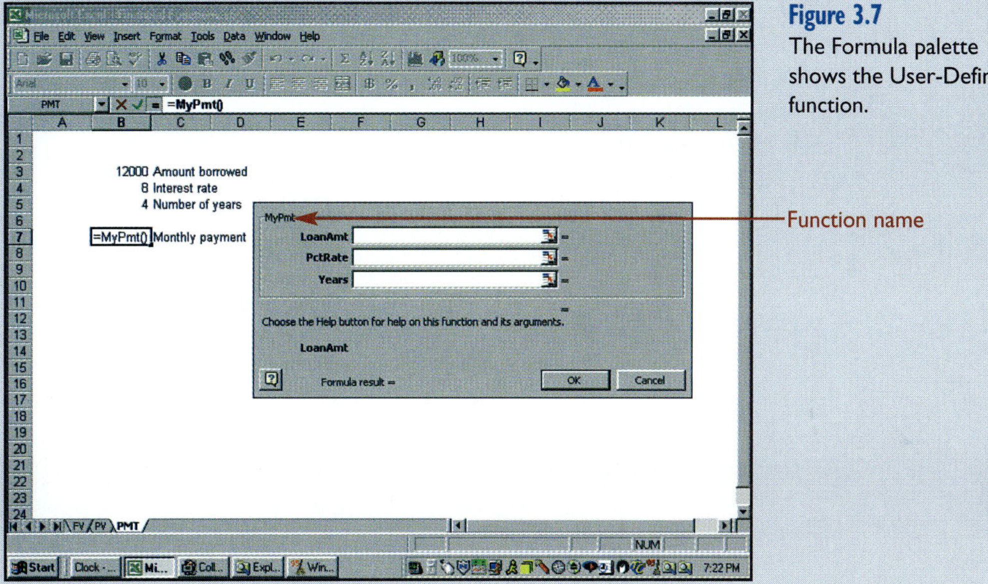

Figure 3.7
The Formula palette shows the User-Defined function.

5. **Enter the appropriate values in the cells.**
   The $12,000 amount borrowed at 8% interest for 4 years should result in a monthly payment of `$292.96`. Increase the decimal places to see that this amount has been rounded to the nearest penny.

6. **Click OK.**
   Now let's take a look at the function.

7. **Select Tools, Macro, Visual Basic Editor.**
   The MyPmt function appears in the Module 1 (Code) window (refer to Figure 3.2). If you do not see it, click on View, Project Explorer, and then double-click Module 1 under `Financial Functions.xls`.

   Remember that a user-defined function is not a standard Excel function, and is only available in the workbook in which it was created (unless you store it in `Personal.xls`).

continues ▶

To Examine a User-Defined Function (continued)

8 Examine the function code.

It is beyond the scope of this book to get into the details of Visual Basic programming; however, if you carefully look at each line you can see how the function works. Note that the variable names are used as input box labels in the Formula palette, so if you write a function, use descriptive names for the function name and its arguments.

If you change MyPmt to something else, or change any of the variable names, you will see that those changes are reflected in the Formula palette. (To jump back to Microsoft Excel to test it, you can click the Microsoft Excel icon at the left end of the toolbar.) If you change the name of the function from MyPmt to something else, you must also change MyPmt to the same thing wherever MyPmt appears in the function.

9 Click File, Close and Return to Microsoft Excel.

Save and then close the Financial Functions workbook.

As you probably noticed, there are many more financial functions available in Excel; however, our purpose here is to give you a sample of them and show how they could be used.

Lesson 5: Using Concatenation to String Text Together

This lesson deals with a different category of functions: text functions, sometimes known as string functions. Microsoft Excel is used primarily for working with numbers; however, cells can also contain text. Labels and descriptive cells are comprised of text, but supporting data can also be text. For example, gender could be entered as M and F. Text functions allow you to manipulate text cells. While these functions would rarely be the main focus of a worksheet, they are frequently useful utility functions.

One common operation with text is putting text cells together to make longer strings of text. This process is called ***concatenation***. There is a function called CONCATENATE; however, concatenation is usually done with the concatenation operator, &.

Assume one column of your worksheet has first names and another column has last names. You want to put them together to read last name, comma, space, first name.

To Use Concatenation to String Text Together

1 Open XL3-0302 and click on the Data I tab. Save the file as `String Functions`.

2 In cell C3, type `=B3&", "&A3`

The `&` in the preceding formula is the concatenation operator, and we are concatenating three things—the last name, the first name, and the comma and space between them. You could also have typed `=CONCATENATE(B3,", ",A3)`, but using the `&` operator is easier and can be used when typing text.

3 Copy the formula in cell C3 to cells C4:C9.

All names now appear in the correct format, as shown in Figure 3.8.

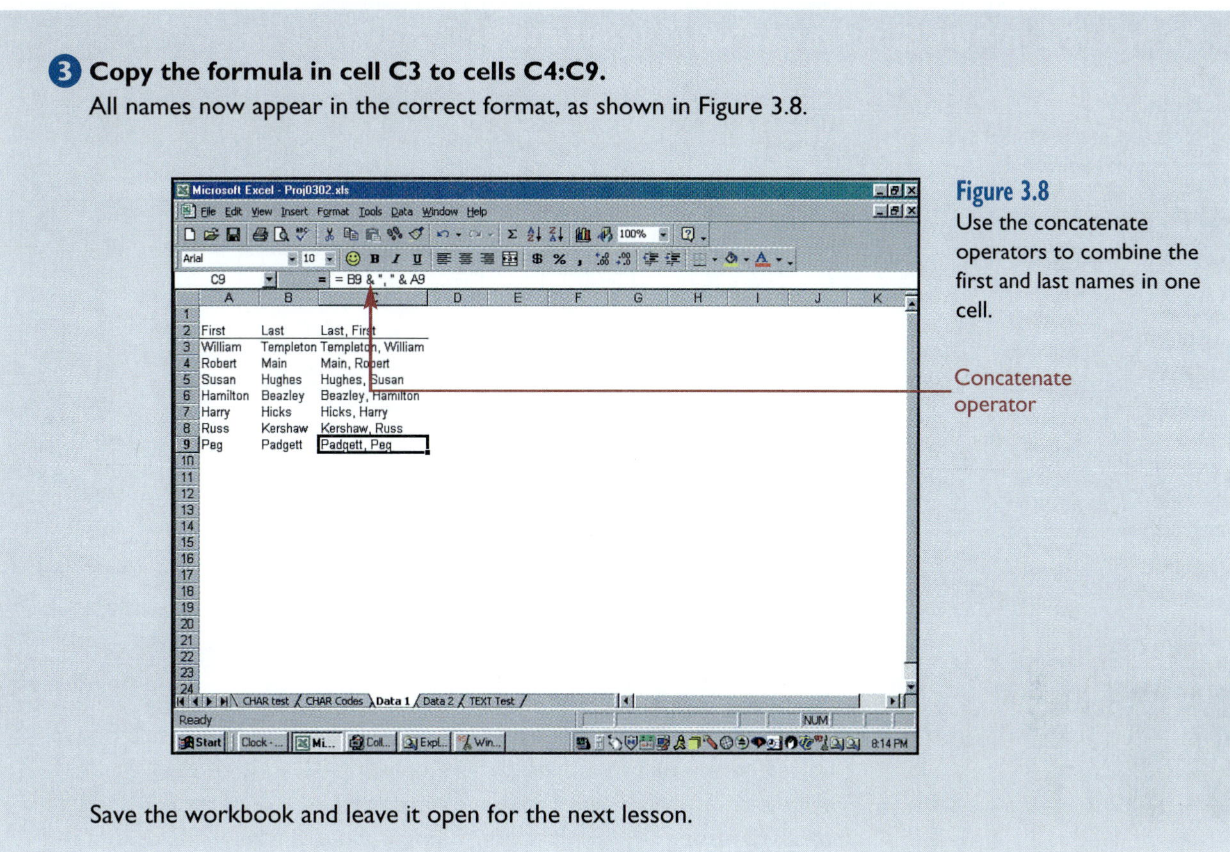

Figure 3.8
Use the concatenate operators to combine the first and last names in one cell.

Save the workbook and leave it open for the next lesson.

Lesson 6: Inserting Symbols and Characters

You can insert special characters or symbols such as the copyright symbol (©), international currency (£) or mathematical expressions (±) into worksheet text. In Microsoft Word this is done with the Insert, Symbols command, but in Microsoft Excel, you need to use the CHAR function.

To Insert Symbols and Characters

1 In the String Functions workbook, click on the CHAR test tab.

This is a blank worksheet.

2 Click in cell B4, type `=CHAR(169)`, and press Enter.

In the cell, you see the copyright symbol (©). How do you know what characters are available? Typing the `=CHAR()` formula multiple times would be a bit tedious.

3 Click the CHAR Codes tab of the workbook (see Figure 3.9).

continues ▶

To Insert Symbols and Characters (continued)

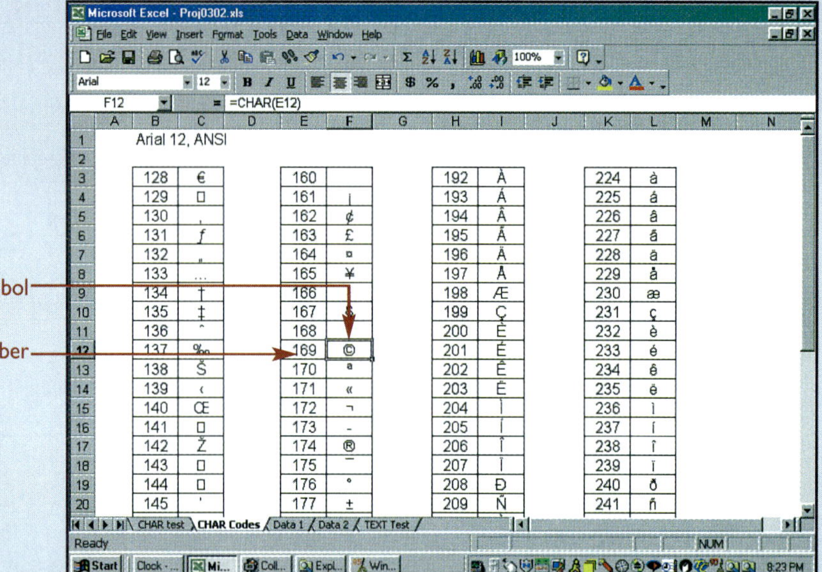

Figure 3.9
Note the active symbol's formula in the formula bar.

4 Examine formulas in the worksheet by clicking on the result box. (This is the right box of the pair in columns C, F, I, and L.)

The cells repeat the CHAR function to form a table. You can see all of the formulas by pressing Ctrl+~. Pressing Ctrl+~ again will take you back to normal worksheet view.

5 Select all the cells by pressing Ctrl+A, and then select another font from the Formatting toolbar.

How do you use the special characters along with other data in Excel? You need to use concatenation, as described in Lesson 5. For example, to enter © 1999 you would type `=CHAR(169)&" 1999"`. Fortunately, there is a more efficient method. If you hold Alt down while typing the character code, you automatically enter the ANSI symbol. Let's try it.

6 Click the CHAR test tab and click cell B5 to select the cell.

7 While holding down the Alt key, type `0169` using the numeric keypad, then release the Alt key and press Enter.

You will see the copyright symbol in the cell. You can then proceed to type other characters in the cell.

Save the workbook and keep it open for the next lesson.

You must type the leading 0 — `0169`, not `169`. Also, you must use the numeric keypad, not the numbers across the top of the keyboard, and the Num Lock key must be activated.

Standard Codes

If you have taken an introductory computer course, you know that text characters are represented by a single byte. Since the eight bits in a byte can be arranged in 256 patterns, a byte can represent 256 different characters. The first 128 (0 to 127) represent the upper- and lowercase alphabet and other commonly used characters. The upper half (128-255) can be used to represent special characters such as mathematical symbols and international alphabet characters. In the early PC days, the codes were referred to as ***ASCII codes***, and the upper codes were standardized to a set of codes defined by IBM. With the advent of Windows, the standard character set uses ***ANSI codes***.

About Code Characters

You can print the table to have a reference sheet of special characters. You might want to shade the cells of characters you will be using frequently. The special characters are the same for many fonts; however, if you select an unusual or decorative font you may find some of the characters different or missing.

Lesson 7: Extracting Text with the MID Function

In computer terminology, text is often referred to as a string; that is, a string of characters. Excel has several functions for manipulating text strings. This lesson demonstrates how to extract a section of a string (sometimes called a ***substring***) using the MID function. In other words, it can get characters from the middle of a string. You might want to use this to extract a person's last name from a name field, or to display only part of an ID field.

To Extract Text with the MID Function

1. **In the String Functions workbook, click on the Data 2 tab.**
   Assume the items in column A are ID numbers for students in a computer course. The instructor wants to post grades using the last four digits of the ID number.
2. **Counting each digit and the dashes, verify that the last four digits in the ID number would be characters 8, 9, 10, and 11.**
3. **Click on cell C3.**
4. **Open the Formula palette and go to the MID function under Text functions. Click OK and drag the MID Formula palette so you can see the underlying cells.**
5. **For the Text input box, click on cell A3, and then press Tab.**
6. **For the Start_num input box, type 8, and then press Tab.**
7. **For the Num_chars input box, type 4.**
   This means you want to start at character 8 in cell A3, and extract the next 4 characters (see Figure 3.10).

continues ▶

To Extract Text with the MID Function (continued)

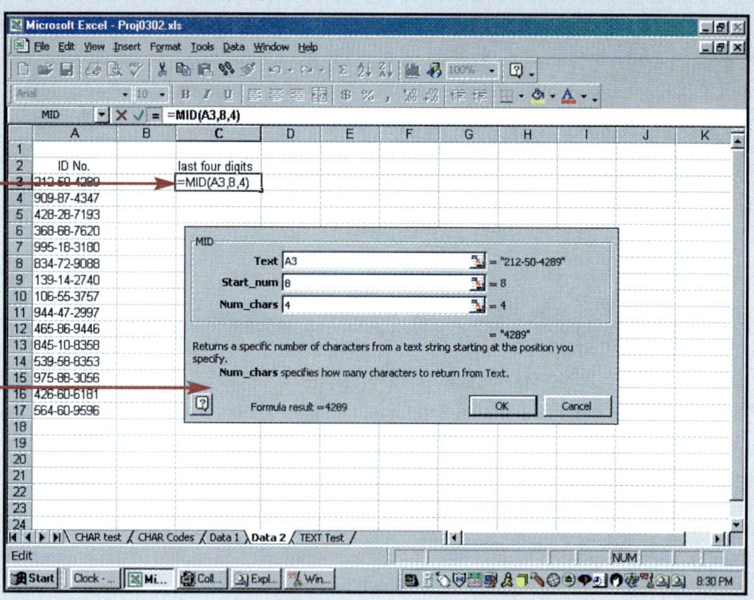

Figure 3.10
The MID Formula palette enables you to enter the MID formula parameters.

MID function formula

MID Formula palette

8 **Click OK and make sure cell C3 contains the appropriate characters (4289).**

9 **Copy the formula in cell C3 to cells C4:C17.**

If the instructor wanted to use these numbers in another worksheet he/she would want to put the results of the function in each cell, rather than the function. This would be done with the following steps.

10 **Select cells C3:C17 and then choose Edit, Copy.**

11 **With the cells still selected, select Edit, Paste Special.**

12 **In the Paste Special dialog box, select Values, and then click OK (see Figure 3.11).**

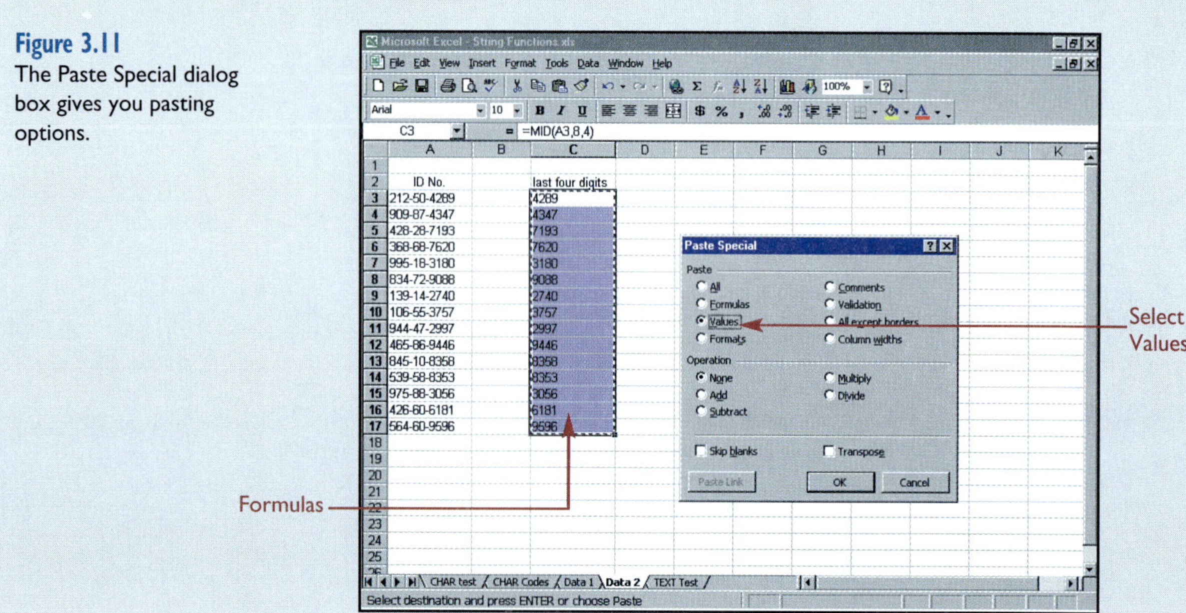

Figure 3.11
The Paste Special dialog box gives you pasting options.

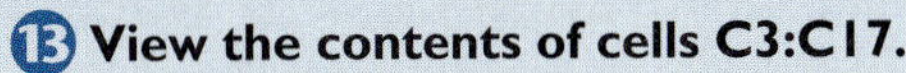

13 View the contents of cells C3:C17.

Notice that there are no longer any formulas, just the extracted strings. Indeed, you could now delete the original values in A3:A17.

Save the changes in the String Functions workbook, keep the workbook open, and go on to Lesson 8.

Lesson 8: Using the TEXT Function

Recall from your earliest introduction to spreadsheets that cells can contain two things: text or numeric values. The TEXT function converts a numeric value to text. Why would you want to do this? One reason would be if you wanted to concatenate two numbers to create a sentence or a title. For example, let's say that you want to calculate the square root of 23.45 and display the result in a sentence, such as: `The square root of 23.45 is 4.8425.` You can use Excel's TEXT function to create a sentence that includes a formula.

To Use the TEXT Function

1 In the String Functions workbook, click on the TEXT Test tab.

2 Click on cells B3 and B4 and examine the contents.

3 Click on cell B6, type the following formula, and press Enter (see Figure 3.12):

```
="The square root of "&B3&" is "&TEXT(B4,"0.0000")&"."
```

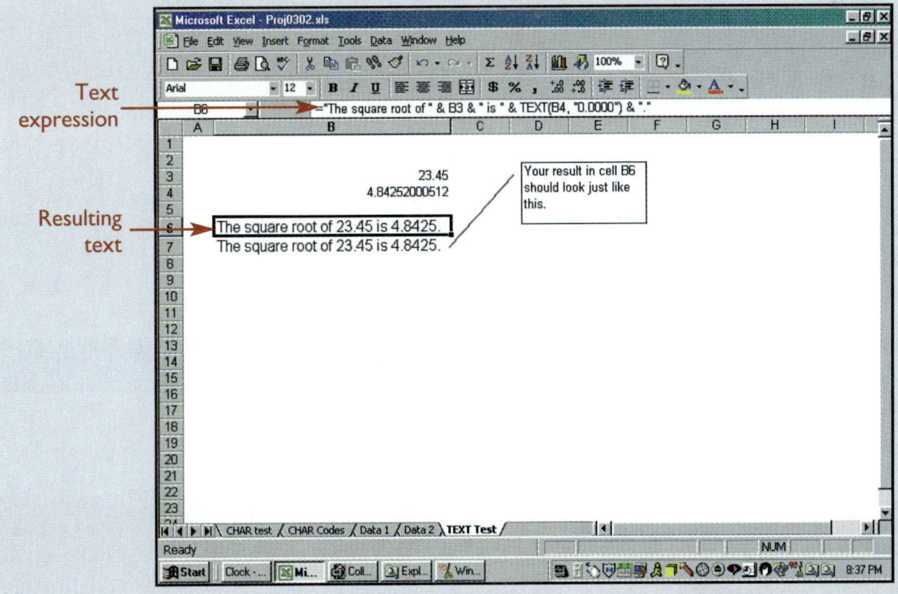

Text expression

Resulting text

Figure 3.12
This figure shows an example of the text created by a TEXT function.

continues ▶

To Use the TEXT Function (continued)

Note a couple of things about this formula. If we do not want to format a value, we do not have to use the TEXT function, we just refer to it with the `B3` in the above expression. Since `B3` follows the concatenation operator, Microsoft Excel knows to convert the contents of that cell to text. Since the result of the square root is to be displayed to 4 decimal places, the `"0.0000"` in the TEXT function specifies the numeric format, with four decimals.

Another useful feature of the TEXT function is to convert a date to a day of the week. Assume you want to know the day of the week for January 1, 2000.

4. **In the TEXT Test tab, click on cell B11, type `1/1/2000`, and press Enter.**

5. **In cell B12, type `=TEXT(B11,"dddd")`, and press Enter.**
The `"dddd"` format tells Microsoft Excel that you want to display the day of the week of the indicated date.

Save your changes to the String Functions workbook, and then close the workbook.

Summary

In this project you have looked at a sampling of advanced functions. We looked at specific examples of Financial and Text functions, but, more importantly, we examined the Formula palette in detail and saw that there are hundreds of Microsoft Excel functions that can handle just about any operation.

In working with the Financial functions we saw the concept of financial modeling, that is, we used standard worksheet formulas to look at an account balance over time and then we used the Microsoft Excel functions to verify the bottom line value. We also looked at the concept of a user-defined function and hopefully inspired some of you to pursue Visual Basic for Applications in more detail.

The Help system provides detailed information on every function. You can also use the Help menu to obtain help while you are using the Visual Basic Editor.

Checking Concepts and Terms

True/False

For each of the following, check *T* or *F* to indicate whether the statement is true or false.

__T __F **1.** Pressing Ctrl+~ will reveal all of the formulas on a worksheet. [L2,6]

__T __F **2.** The minus sign is typed into the Pmt text box to get a positive result. [L2]

__T __F **3.** When typing formulas you must use uppercase letters. [L3]

__T __F **4.** You must know VBA programming language to write a user-defined function. [L4]

__T __F **5.** Characters and symbols are inserted into Microsoft Excel worksheets from the Insert, Symbols command. [L6]

__T __F **6.** All character codes must be preceded by a zero. [L6]

__T __F **7.** FV and MID are both Financial functions. [L7]

__T __F **8.** The Formula palette lists all of Microsoft Excel's functions. [Why Would I do This]

__T __F **9.** The STRING function is used to round decimal places. [L5]

__T __F **10.** The DATE function can determine the day of the week for any future date. [L8]

Multiple Choice

Circle the letter of the correct answer for each of the following.

1. Microsoft Excel has more than ______________ built-in functions. [Why Would I do This]

a. 300

b. 50

c. 500

d. 150

2. To enter a percent into a formula, you must type it using which of the following formats? [L2]

a. 5%

b. 5

c. .05

d. 0.05

3. For a result to reflect the closest real dollar amount, you must use which function? [L3]

a. NPR

b. MID

c. ROUND

d. NPV

4. Text functions are also known as [L5]

a. concatenates

b. String functions

c. Logic functions

d. none of the above

5. The keystroke or operator for concatenate is [L5]

a. &

b. *

c. ^

d. !

6. The MID function is used for [L7]

a. rounding numbers

b. extracting text

c. concatenating text

d. creating text

7. To convert formulas to actual values in a worksheet, you select which commands? [L7]

a. Edit, Copy; Edit, Paste

b. Edit, Cut; Edit, Paste Special

c. Edit, Copy; Edit, Paste Special

d. Edit, Cut; Edit, Paste

8. The "dddd" format tells Microsoft Excel that you want to display [L8]

a. the day, month, and year

b. the day of the week

c. the number of days between two dates

d. the year only, using four digits

9. In order to make the PMT function work properly, you must [L4]

a. multiply the annual percentage by 12

b. divide the annual percentage by 12

c. use a plus sign in the Pmt text box

d. none of the above

10. To access the Formula palette, you [L1]

a. click X and the drop-down arrow

b. click = and the drop-down arrow

c. select Tools, Wizard

d. select Tools, Wizard, Look-up

Discussion Questions

1. Review the Formula palette functions and think of three situations where you could create a user-defined function.
2. Discuss at least four reasons why a spreadsheet is a preferable method of doing financial modeling.
3. Discuss the situations where rounding is appropriate and where it is not.
4. Discuss why text manipulation is important in a Microsoft Excel worksheet.

Skill Drill

Skill Drill exercises reinforce project skills. Each skill reinforced is the same, or nearly the same, as a skill presented in the project. Detailed instructions are provided in a step-by-step format.

1. Calculating Future Value

If you put $100 in the bank every month for 20 years, how much would you have at the end with a 6% annual interest rate?

1. Open a new workbook file and save it as `SkillDrill 1-3`.
2. In Sheet 1, enter `100`, `20`, and `6%` in three cells and label them as `Payment`, `Years`, and `Rate`.
3. Use the Formula palette to calculate the FV function. Make sure you do the following: put a minus sign in front of the payment cell reference; multiply the Years cell times 12 to get the number of months; and divide the Rate cell by 12 to get the monthly rate.
4. Calculate the future value using a financial model similar to that used in Lesson 2. It will have 240 rows (representing the months) and you would use the monthly interest rate in the calculations.
5. Save the workbook and leave it open for the next exercise.

If steps 3 and 4 give the same answer, you have probably done them correctly.

2. Computing Present Value

If you had an auto lease that required 36 payments of $259.37, how much would you have to put into an account at 6.2% interest in order for the account to make the payments and go to zero after the last payment?

1. Click on the Sheet2 tab of SkillDrill 1-3 that should be open from the previous lesson.
2. Enter `259.37`, `36`, and `6.2%` in three cells and label them as `Payment`, `Months`, and `Rate`.
3. Use the Formula palette to calculate the PV function. Make sure you do the following: put a minus sign in front of the payment cell reference, and divide the Rate cell by 12 to get the monthly rate.
4. Calculate the account balance using a financial model similar to that used in Lesson 3. It will have 36 rows representing the months, and you will use the monthly interest rate in the calculations.

   If the balance in step 4 goes to zero after the last payment, you have calculated the present value correctly.
5. Save the workbook and leave it open for the next exercise.

[?] 3. Using Another Financial Function: RATE

You saw in Lesson 1 that there were many other Financial functions. Let's look at one more.

Refer to the lease example in Exercise 2. What interest rate would you need in order for an initial deposit (present value) of $8,000 to generate the 36 payments of $259.37?

1. Click on the Sheet 3 tab of SkillDrill 1-3 that should be open from the previous exercise.
2. Enter `259.37`, `36`, and `8000` in three cells and label them `Payment`, `Months`, and `Present Value`.
3. Use the Formula palette to calculate the RATE function. Make sure you put a minus sign in front of the payment cell.
4. Click on the "?" Help button in the Formula palette to get information on the Rate function.

   The result is the monthly interest rate. Multiply it by 12 to get the annual rate.
5. Calculate the account balance using a financial model similar to Lesson 3. It will have 36 rows representing the months and you will use the monthly interest rate in the calculations. Use $8,000 as the present value, and the rate calculated in step 3 as the interest rate.

   If the balance in step 4 goes to zero after the last payment, you have calculated the present value correctly.
6. Save and close the workbook.

4. Creating a User-Defined Function

Create a MyFV function similar to the MyPmt function in Lesson 4.

1. Open the Financial Functions workbook, open the Visual Basic Editor and locate the MyPmt function.
2. Copy all of the lines of the MyPmt function (everything from the Public Function statement through the End Function statement) and paste the copy below the End Function statement.
3. Make the following changes:

   Change the four occurrences of `MyPmt` to `MyFV`. (You can use any name you want, but make sure all four occurrences are the same.)

   Change the two occurrences of `LoanAmount` to `MonthlyPmt`.

   Change `Application.Pmt` to `Application.FV`.

   Change the comment statement in the first line to read appropriately.
4. Go back to the worksheet and test the function by comparing its results with the Excel FV function. Remember that it assumes monthly payments.
5. Close the workbook without saving your changes.

5. Practicing with Additional Text Functions

Occasionally you want to do the opposite of concatenation, namely splitting a text string into components (the fancy word for this is 'parsing'). For example, let's say that you have cells that contain last and first names separated by a comma and you want to place the first and last names in different cells.

1. In a blank workbook, enter `Smith, Tom` into cell A4.
2. In cell C4 type `=MID(A4,1,FIND(", ",A4)-1)`
3. In cell D4 type `=MID(A4,FIND(", ",A4)+1,LEN(A4))`
4. Study the two functions until you can explain them to someone else. Note that embedded in the MID function are two new functions—FIND and LEN. Use Help or the Formula palette to see how they work.

Splitting Text

You could also use the Data, Text to Columns Wizard to split text into different columns; however, that is a one-time operation and the functions above are 'live' and can be copied to other cells.

5. Close the workbook without saving your changes.

6. Using the TEXT Function

Assume you take out a short-term loan for 90 days. Find the due date and determine what day of the week it falls on.

1. In a blank workbook, enter any date in cell A4, such as **11/28/99**.
2. In cell C4, type **=A4+90** and you see the due date.
3. In cell D4, type **=TEXT(C4,"dddd")** and you see the day of the week.
4. In cell E4, type **=TEXT(C4,"ddd")** and see what happens.
5. Close the workbook without saving your changes.

Challenge

Challenge exercises expand on or are somewhat related to skills presented in the lessons. Each exercise provides a brief narrative introduction followed by instructions in a numbered step format that are not as detailed as those in the Skill Drill section.

Each exercise is independent of the others, so that you may complete the exercises in any order. Be sure to save the workbook after completing each exercise. If you need a paper copy of the completed exercise, enter your name centered in a header before printing.

1. Writing a User-Defined Function

A common operation is strangely missing from the hundreds of Microsoft Excel functions: a RANGE function that calculates the difference between the largest and smallest numbers in a range of cells. So let's write one and put it in your PERSONAL.XLS file to use with any workbook.

1. From any workbook, open the Visual Basic Editor from the Tools, Macro menu. Use the Project Explorer to locate Module 1 of PERSONAL.XLS and type in the following three lines of code:

```
Public Function Range(X)
Range = Application.Max(X) - Application.Min(X)
End Function
```

2. Save PERSONAL.XLS and then select File, Close and Return to Microsoft Excel.
3. Type a few numbers in a worksheet, and use the User Defined functions of the Formula palette to test your RANGE function.

2. Renaming an Existing Function

If you have ever studied statistics, you know that the "average" technically should be called the "mean." This exercise will create a new function that works the same as the built-in AVERAGE function, but it will let you use the proper name, MEAN.

1. From any workbook, open the Visual Basic Editor from the Tools, Macro menu. Use the Project Explorer to locate Module 1 of PERSONAL.XLS and type in the following three lines of code:

```
Public Function Mean(X)
Mean = Application.Average(X)
End Function
```

2. Save PERSONAL.XLS and then select File, Close and Return to Microsoft Excel.

3. Type a few numbers in a worksheet, and use the user-defined functions of the Formula palette to test your MEAN function. Test it using both AVERAGE and MEAN.

3. Using the CELL Function to Obtain Cell Information

Excel has the capability to give you information about your worksheet cells. This can be handy if you are trying to debug a worksheet. For example, assume you are looking at a worksheet where the numbers in two cells do not line up like they should and you want to know what format was used for each cell.

1. Open a new workbook.
2. Type any number into cell C5 and click the Percent Style button on the Formatting toolbar.
3. In cell C6, type: `=CELL("format",C5)` and press ↵Enter. You must type the quotation marks.
4. To interpret the resulting code, use the Office Assistant or the Help Answer Wizard to search for `CELL()`.
5. While you are reading the Help information, look at some of the other types of information and try them. If you change something in a cell, you need to press the F9 function key to update and recalculate the worksheet.
6. Close the workbook without saving your changes.

4. Using the INFO Function to Obtain System Information

Using Excel functions, you can determine interesting and useful information about Excel and your computer's operating environment. For example, assume you want to put a message in a cell reminding users to press F9 to do a recalculation if the recalculation mode is not set for automatic recalculation. You would use the INFO function nested in an IF function to check the current recalculation mode and display the appropriate message.

1. Open a new workbook.
2. Type the following formula into any cell:

```
=IF(INFO("recalc")="Manual","Press F9 to
➥recalculate","Automatic recalculation is ON")
```

3. Choose Tools, Options, and click the Calculation tab.
4. Select Manual, and click the Calc Now button.
5. Now use the same procedure to set the calculation back to Automatic and note how the cell message changes.
6. Use the Office Assistant or the Help Answer Wizard to search for `INFO()`.
7. Try some of the other INFO items.
8. Close the workbook without saving your changes.

Discovery Zone

Discovery Zone exercises require advanced knowledge of topics presented in *Essentials* lessons, application of skills from multiple lessons, or self-directed learning of new skills. Each exercise is independent of the others, so that you may complete the exercises in any order.

1. Exploring Visual Basic

Open the Visual Basic Editor and explore a bit. Use the Help feature, right-click everything you see; try clicking various menu items, clicking toolbar buttons, and entering code (you can't break anything).

If you are going to be doing much work with Visual Basic, you will find the Visual Basic toolbar useful. Activate it (while in Excel, not the Visual Basic Editor) and try it.

2. Using Visual Basic in Other Applications

The Visual Basic Editor and the Visual Basic Language work the same in all Office applications. If you have created macros in Microsoft Word or any of the other applications, take a look at them. Obviously the different applications have different commands and objects, but the editing procedures and the general structure of the language is the same across applications.

Project 4

Project 4

Worksheet Simulation and Statistical Functions

Objectives

In this project, you learn how to

- **Create Random Numbers with the RAND Function**
- **Create a Recalculation Macro and Button**
- **Generate Two Random Values**
- **Simulate Expected Values**
- **Generate a Distribution of Values**
- **Examine a Business Inventory Simulation Example**
- **Perform a Chi-Square Goodness of Fit Simulation**
- **Use Descriptive Statistics in a Simulation**

Key terms introduced in this project include

- chi-square
- conditional formatting
- expected value
- normal distribution
- p-value
- RAND
- RANDBETWEEN
- RANDNORM
- random data sets
- simulation
- uniform distribution

Why Would I Do This?

One of the most powerful features of worksheet analysis is the ability to perform "what-if" analyses. One simple way of doing this is to change certain cells of a worksheet and see how the change affects other cells. This is a useful approach, and Data Tables and the Scenario Manager discussed in Project 6, "Using Goal Seek, Scenarios, Solver, and Auditing Tools" enhance this method. However, there are times when you may want to try out more situations than you could possibly type in yourself. Having Excel create many random input values and studying the effect on certain cells is called ***simulation***.

In this project you will create some simple business simulation models and use simulation to create ***random data sets*** in order to study some commonly used statistical functions.

Visual Summary

Figure 4.1 shows an example of a business simulation. The random numbers in columm B are used to simulate different levels of demand. The output from each of the worksheets is summarized in the Top sheet to determine the optimal level of inventory.

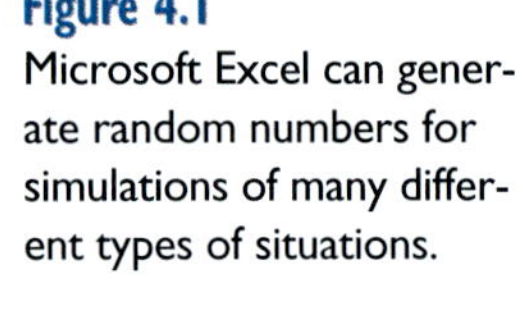

Figure 4.1
Microsoft Excel can generate random numbers for simulations of many different types of situations.

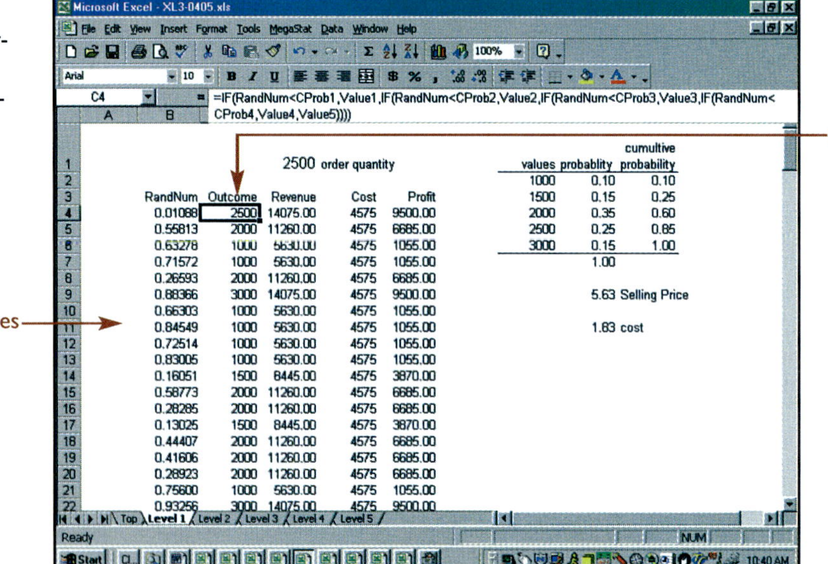

Lesson 1: Creating Random Numbers with the RAND Function

Random numbers are the building blocks of a simulation because they are recalculated over and over to represent possible real-world values. In this lesson you learn how to create and manipulate random numbers using the ***RAND*** function. RAND calculates random numbers between 0 and 1 with every value being equally likely. In later lessons you will learn how to calculate discrete random values and specific distributions of random values.

To Create Random Numbers with the RAND Function

1. **Open the XL3-0401 workbook, and save it as `RandTest`.**
2. **Click in cell A3, type `=RAND()` and press Enter.**
   This creates a random number between 0 and 1.
3. **Use the Office Assistant or Excel Help to get further information on the RAND function.**
4. **Choose Tools, Options; then select the Calculation tab, and click the Calc Now (F9) button (see Figure 4.2).**

   If the Options command appears dimmed on the Tools menu, check to be sure that you have entered the RAND formula in cell A3.

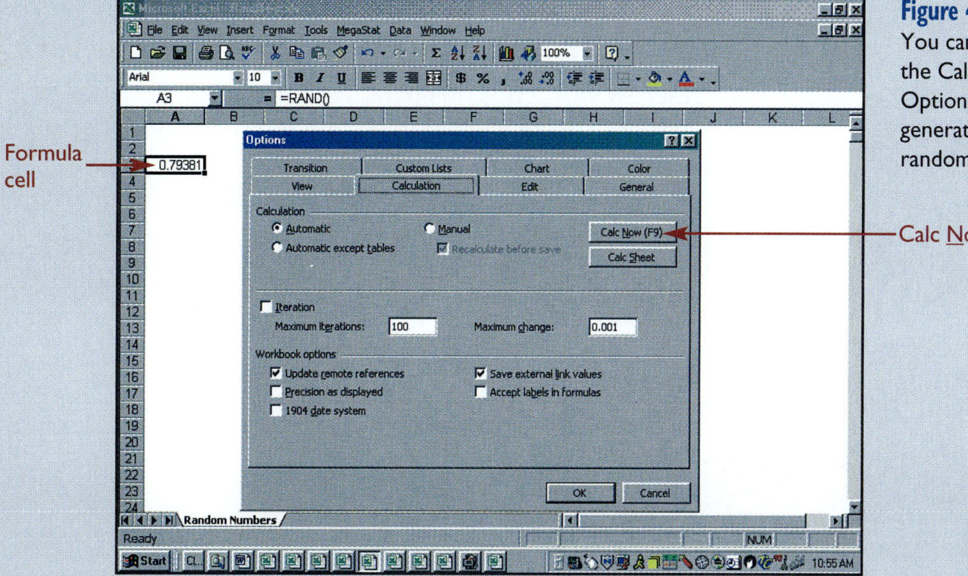

Figure 4.2
You can press F9 or use the Calculation tab in the Options dialog box to generate new sets of random numbers.

5. **Press F9 a few times and observe the number as it recalculates in cell A3.**
6. **Edit cell A3 to read: `=RAND()*100`.**
   This formula results in random numbers between 0 and 100. (To obtain random numbers for a different range, such as between 0 and 25, you would multiply the RAND function by 25.)
7. **Copy cell A3 to the range A4:A15 and press F9 a few times to observe changes in the random numbers.**
8. **Edit cell A3 to read `=ROUND(RAND()*100,2)`.**
   This formula results in random numbers between 0 and 100, rounded to two decimal places.
9. **Copy the revised formula in cell A3 to the range A4:A15, and then press F9 a few times to observe changes in the random numbers.**
   Save the RandTest workbook and leave it open for the next lesson.

Recalculating Worksheets with the F9 Function Key
When creating simulations with random data, you frequently need to recalculate the worksheet to get a new set of random numbers. A faster way to do this is to press the F9 function key. You also can add a recalculation button to the worksheet.

Lesson 2: Creating a Recalculation Macro and Button

Others who use a workbook with random numbers might not be familiar with the F9 recalculation key (or they may have difficulty remembering which function key to use). In this case, you can create a recalculation macro and assign it to a button in the worksheet. Then, they could simply click the button to recalculate the worksheet.

To Create a Recalculation Macro and Button

1. **In the RandTest workbook, prepare to record a macro by selecting Tools, Macro, Record New Macro. Name the macro `Recalc` and store it in your Personal Macro Workbook.**
   By placing this macro in your Personal Macro Workbook, it will be available in any workbook, and you can quickly draw a recalc button or add a recalc button to a toolbar.

2. **Click OK to close the Record Macro dialog box and begin recording the macro.**

   If you need a refresher on creating and recording macros, refer to Lessons 1 and 2 in Project 2, Automating Tasks with Macros."

3. **Press F9 when you have begun recording the macro.**

4. **Click the Stop Recording button.**
   This is a very short macro. All it does is record the recalculation operation.

5. **Display the Forms toolbar and draw a button in cell E3.**
   Review Project 1, "Designing Onscreen Forms," if you do not remember how to draw form controls. After you finish drawing the button, the Assign Macro dialog box appears.

6. **Assign the Recalc macro to the button by selecting Assign Macro from the list in the dialog box.**
   Project 2, Lessons 6 and 7 give more details on assigning macro buttons.

7. **Name the button `Recalc`.**

8. **Click the button a few times to test it.**
   Each click should generate a new set of random numbers (see Figure 4.3).

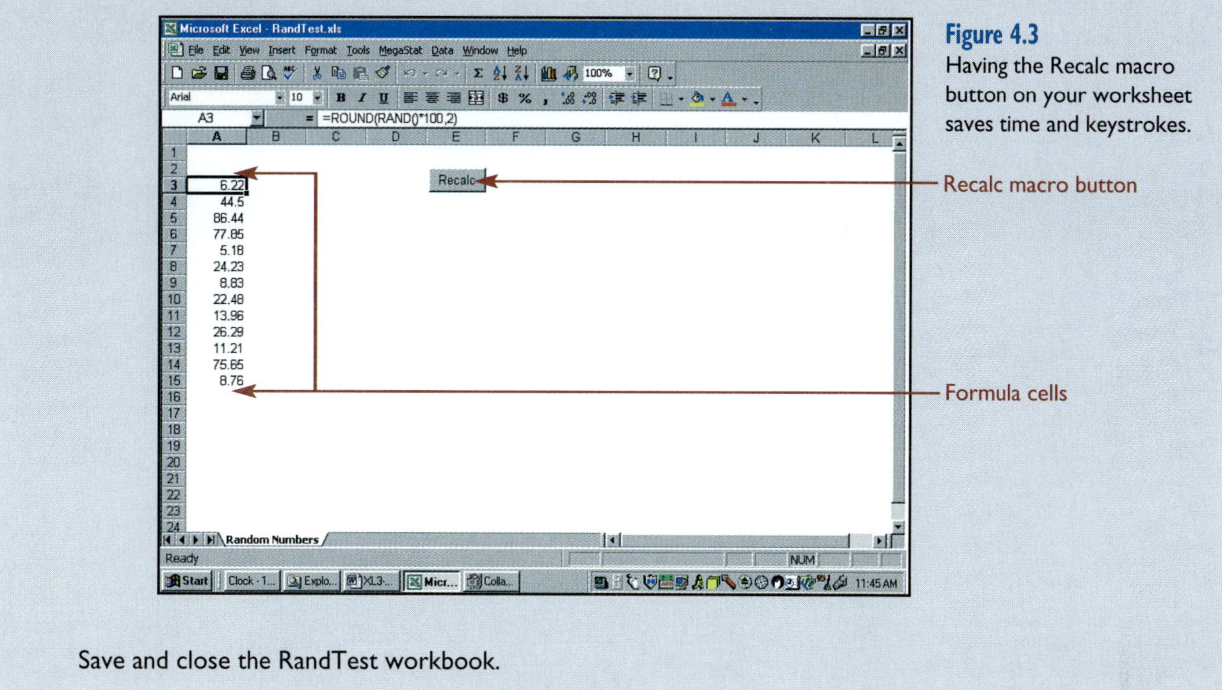

Figure 4.3
Having the Recalc macro button on your worksheet saves time and keystrokes.

Save and close the RandTest workbook.

Lesson 3: Generating Two Random Values

It is easy to generate random numbers with the RAND function, but what if we only want to simulate two values? For example, we may want to simulate a situation where you win a game 6 percent of the time, and lose 94 percent of the time. The trick is to use a RAND function inside an IF function. If the random number is less than .06, it is considered a win; otherwise, it is a loss.

To Generate Two Random Values

1. **Open the XL3-0402 workbook and save it as `WinLose`.**
2. **Examine the workbook, taking note of the named ranges.**
3. **In cell A3, type `=IF(RAND()<Prob_win,"Win","Lose")` and copy cell A3 to the range A4:A202.**
   The IF function has three arguments: the logical condition, the return value if logical condition is true, and the return value if logical condition is false. Thus, if the random value is less than .06 (the Prob_win value entered in cell D2), the IF function returns `Win`; otherwise, it returns `Lose`.
4. **Press F9 a few times to generate new random outcomes.**
   It is better to use the named cell 'Prob_win' rather than .06, because you may then change the value in cell D2, without needing to change the formula cells.

   This example enters the text string `Win` or `Lose` in the cells, but you also could set up the worksheet to enter numbers—for example, the amount of money won or lost. Indeed, that would be more common in a simulation worksheet.

continues ▶

To Generate Two Random Values (continued)

5 Click on any cell in the data range A3:A202.

6 Choose Format, Conditional Formatting.

As shown in Figure 4.4, note how the cells have been formatted to highlight the wins. This feature is called ***conditional formatting***.

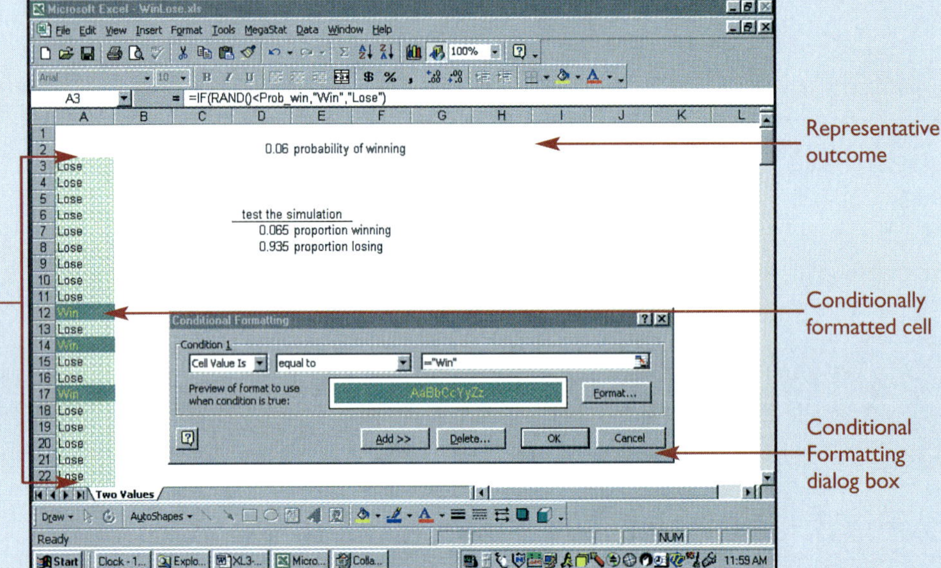

Figure 4.4
Conditional formatting can be used to highlight specific outcomes within a simulation.

7 Use the Office Assistant or Excel Help to get information about Conditional Formatting.

8 Close the Conditional Formatting dialog box, and then examine the formulas in cells D7 and D8.

Cells D7 and D8 use the COUNTIF function to determine the actual proportion of wins and losses. If you are creating a simulation model, it is a good idea to test the simulation. It will rarely be perfect but it should be reasonably close.

9 Press F9 several times to see how the simulation works.

10 Change cell D2 to .5 to simulate tossing a coin.

You could even change "Win" and "Lose" in cells A3:A202 to "Heads" and "Tails" respectively.

Save and close the WinLose workbook.

Lesson 4: Simulating Expected Values

This lesson utilizes the simulation procedure introduced in Lesson 3. The statistical concept of ***expected value*** calculates the expected outcome given a probability distribution. For example, let's assume that an insurance company sells a $10,000 one-year term policy for $250. If the person is alive at the end of the year, all bets are off and the insurance company keeps the $250. If the person dies during the year, the insurance company loses $9,750 (it pays out the $10,000 but keeps the $250 premium). Assuming there is a 2 percent chance that the policyholder will die during the year, we calculate the average amount the insurance company is expected to make per policy sold (that is, the expected value) and then simulate the outcome for 1,000 policies.

To Simulate Expected Values

1. **Open the XL3-0403 workbook, click the Expected Value tab, and save the workbook as `Expected Value`.**

2. **Examine the worksheet. Make note of the named ranges.**

3. **Click cell B13.**
   The expected value is found by summing the products of value times probability. In other words, you could type `=C8*D8+C9*D9`. However, let's use the SUMPRODUCT function instead.

4. **Type `=SUMPRODUCT(value,probability)` in cell B13, and press Enter.**
   Note that `value` and `probability` are named ranges in the Expected Value worksheet. In this situation, either formula would be satisfactory, but if you wanted to sum the products of two large ranges, the SUMPRODUCT method is much more efficient.

   In this example, the expected value is 50—meaning that the insurance company should expect to make an average of $50 per policy sold.

5. **Activate the Simulation worksheet.**
   Cells A3:E202 show the outcomes of 1,000 policies.

6. **Click in one of the cells in the range A3:E202, and examine the formula `=IF(RAND()<0.02,AmtDie,AmtLive)`.**
   The `AmtDie` and `AmtLive` variables are the named cells containing the gains to the insurance company. We want to place `AmtDie` in a cell if a person dies. This should be 2 percent of the time, so if the random number is less than .02, we assume the person dies; otherwise, the person lives.

7. **Type `=AVERAGE(policies)` in cell G3 to calculate the average of all 1,000 policies. If the expected value computation is valid, this number should be near the expected value of 50; however, for any given recalculation it could be quite different. See Figure 4.5.**

continues ▶

To Simulate Expected Values (continued)

Figure 4.5
An expected value simulation can provide both the average result and the expected result per iteration.

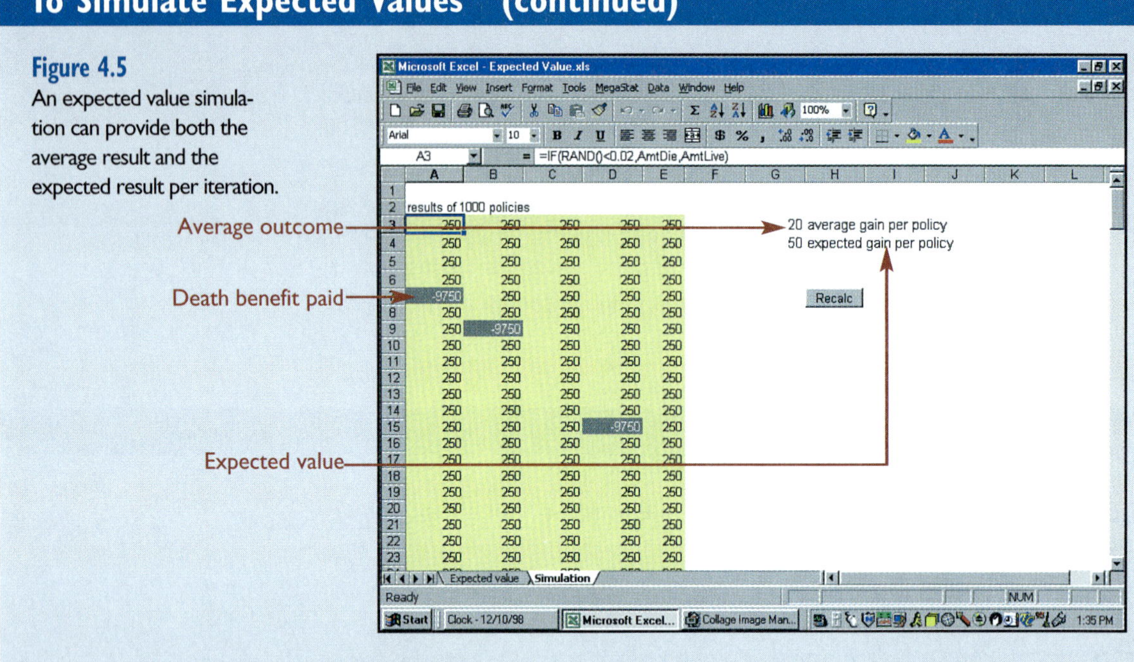

8 Click the Recalc button in the worksheet until you get an average gain per policy of exactly 50.
Why isn't the average outcome always 50? Because the world is random. Even if the mortality rate is .02, that doesn't mean for any given batch of 1,000 policies you will get exactly 20 deaths.

Save and close the Expected Value workbook.

Lesson 5: Generating a Distribution of Values

In the previous two lessons we have seen how to simulate two values. In this lesson we will extend the concept to more than two values. This technique provides a building block for many business simulations.

Assume we want to simulate a situation where there are five levels of sales (for example, 1000, 1500, 2000, 2500, and 3000), each of which has a corresponding probability of occurrence (for example, .10, .15, .35, .25, and .15).

To Generate a Distribution of Values

1 Open the XL3-0404 workbook and save it as `SimTest`.
Our steps in working with this workbook will involve examining how it works, since the building blocks of the workbook involve the use of statements and procedures that have been discussed previously.

2 Click on the Name box, and then click on each of the named ranges in order to see what range is represented by each name.

Two hundred random outcomes were calculated in order to give reasonably stable results without using an undue amount of space or computing time. With a large or fast computer, you would use more values.

3 Examine cells E5:F9.

Cells E5:F9 contain five possible outcomes and their corresponding probabilities of occurrence. The probabilities would be determined by past history or managerial judgment. In a simulation context they could be arbitrary values that you want to explore.

Note that the cumulative probability is simply each probability being added to the previous one, and that the last value is 1.00.

4 Examine cells F16:F20.

Note that the COUNTIF statement is used to determine the observed proportions, to verify that the simulation is working properly. Press F9 a few times to see that the observed outcomes are reasonably close to the input probabilities.

5 Click on cell B6.

The formulas in cells B6:B205 are the heart of this worksheet (see Figure 4.6). One of the formulas is shown below.

```
=IF(RandNum<CProb1,Value1,IF(RandNum<CProb2,Value2,IF(RandNum
➥<CProb3,Value3,IF(RandNum<CProb4,Value4,Value5))))
```

This is a nested IF statement. It takes a random number, determines where it falls in the range of cumulative probabilities, and assigns the corresponding value to the cell. It is similar in concept to the previous lesson, except that several values are involved.

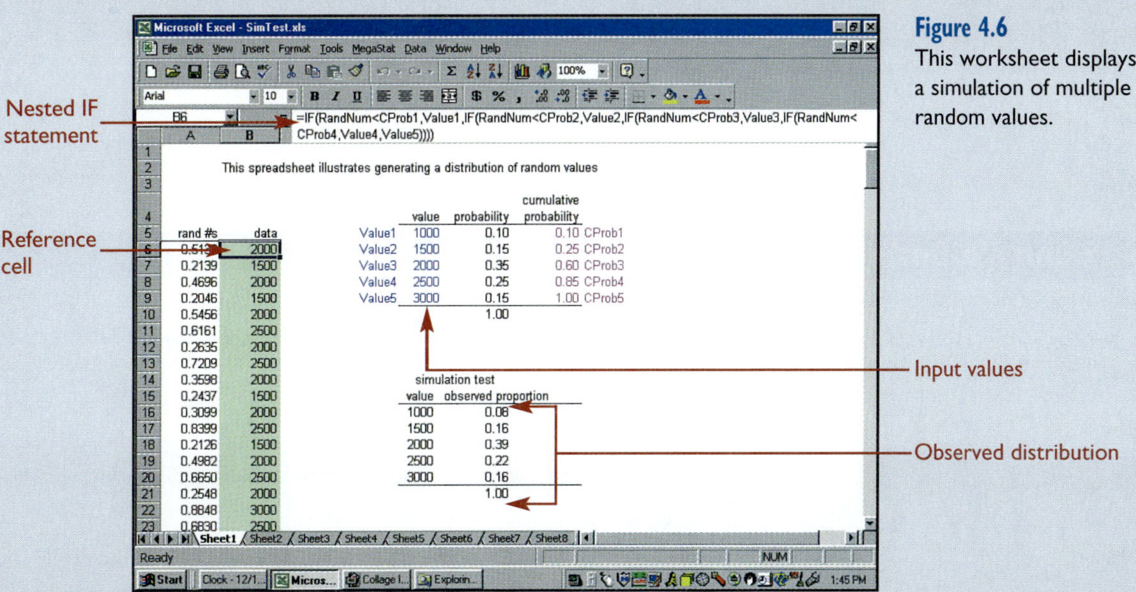

Figure 4.6
This worksheet displays a simulation of multiple random values.

Save and close the SimTest workbook.

Examining the IF Statement

The IF statement used in this lesson illustrates several issues regarding worksheet formula techniques:

- While it is certainly a complicated formula, it would be even more difficult to read if cell addresses were used instead of the named ranges.
- The random number must be calculated outside the formula. If the RAND function were used instead of using a random number from the named range RandNum, it would calculate a different value each place it appeared in the formula, and would defeat the purpose of the statement, namely converting a given random number in a specific value.
- 'RandNum' is a range name referring to all 200 random numbers. When it appears in the IF statement, the value in the same row as the statement is used.
- Why does the statement use '<' rather than '<='? Actually it doesn't make any difference. The random numbers are calculated to 16 digits, so the probability of getting an exact match approaches zero.

Lesson 6: Examining a Business Inventory Simulation Example

This worksheet will take the concepts learned in Lesson 5 and expand them into a business simulation.

The purpose of this simulation is to determine which of five different ordering quantities would maximize profit for a company that purchases items wholesale and sells them retail. We are assuming unsold items have no salvage value, such as a perishable item. It is a simple model; however, it can be expanded to model more complex situations.

The workbook looks at five possible sales levels, each with a specified probability of happening. It also looks at five ordering quantities. The ordering quantities correspond to the sales levels, although that would not have to be the case. The best outcome would be when the amount of inventory purchased turns out to be the same as the demand. If you purchase too little inventory, your revenue is not as high as it could have been. If you purchase too much inventory, the cost of the unsold inventory reduces profit and in some cases can actually cause a loss.

To Examine a Business Inventory Simulation Example

1. **Open the XL3-0405 workbook and display the worksheet labeled 'Top'.**

   Note that there are six worksheets in the workbook. The first sheet, 'Top', contains input and summary values. Worksheets named Level 1 through Level 5 show the simulation outcomes for five different ordering quantities.

2. **Examine cells B3:B7.**

   These cells contain values for five possible ordering quantities. These cells also represent five possible sales outcomes, each associated with a probability. In practice, these ordering quantities and sales level values would not have to be the same values, but it makes the worksheet simpler.

3 **Examine each of the worksheets.**
Each worksheet provides a simulation for a given ordering quantity. Figure 4.1 in the Visual Summary shows the sheet for Level 1. Also notice that the random numbers are generated in Level 1 and are used in the other sheets.

Note in the Level 5 worksheet there are some negative profits (for example, a loss) when demand is low and there is a lot of unsold inventory.

4 **Click on the 'Top' worksheet and examine the formulas in cells F3:F7. These cells give the average profit from each simulation (see Figure 4.7).**

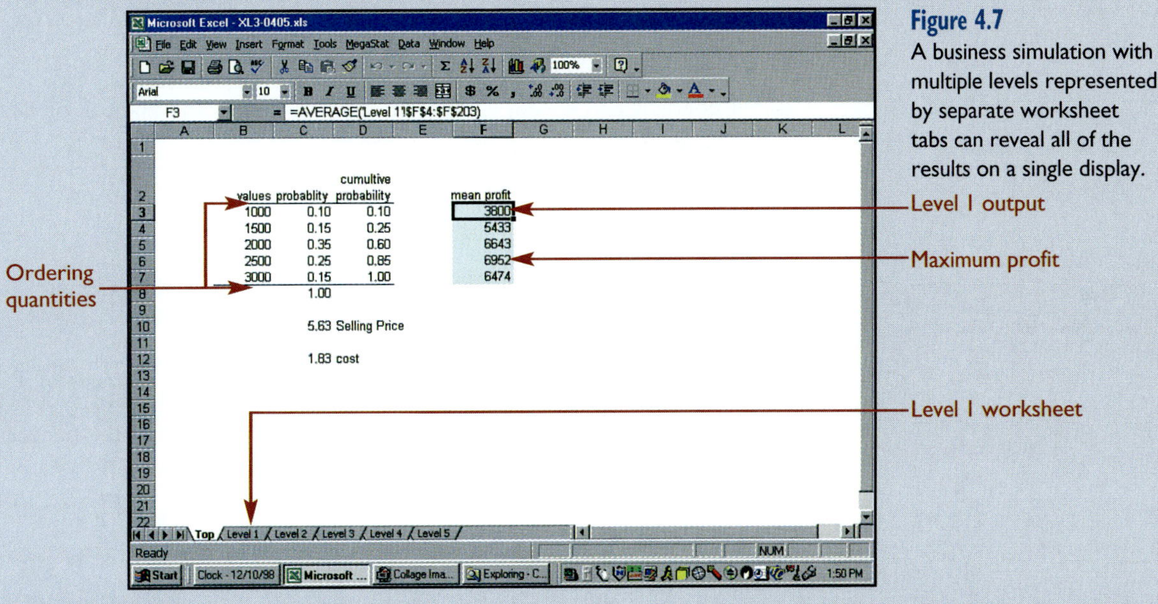

Figure 4.7
A business simulation with multiple levels represented by separate worksheet tabs can reveal all of the results on a single display.

5 **Press F9 a few times.**
What ordering quantity would maximize the profit?

Close the workbook without saving it.

Lesson 7: Performing a Chi-Square Goodness of Fit Simulation

A commonly used statistical procedure is the ***chi-square*** goodness of fit test. In this lesson we will simulate dice tossing and use the goodness of fit test to test the accuracy of the simulation.

To Perform a Chi-Square Goodness of Fit Simulation

1 **Open the XL3-0406 workbook, and save the workbook as GOF.**

2 **Examine the contents and layout of the worksheet.**
Cells A3:F102 (named 'dice') use the ***RANDBETWEEN*** function to generate random integers between 1 and 6 to simulate tossing a die 600 times.

continues ▶

To Perform a Chi-Square Goodness of Fit Simulation (continued)

If you get a `#NAME` error in cells A3:F102, it probably means that the Analysis ToolPak Add-in is not activated or not installed. RANDBETWEEN is an Analysis ToolPak function. Choose Tools, Add-Ins; if Analysis ToolPak is not selected, check it, and then click OK and press F9 to recalculate the worksheet. If Analysis ToolPak is not listed in the Add-Ins Available list, you need to re-run the Excel setup and install the Analysis ToolPak.

If you cannot install the Analysis ToolPak, the statement `=INT(RAND()*6)+1` will provide the same results as `=RANDBETWEEN(1,6)`.

3 Enter `=COUNTIF(dice,H4)` in cell I4.

Cell H4 contains a 1, so the COUNTIF function counts the number of 1's in the dice range.

4 Copy cell I4 and then paste it into cells I5:I9.

Cell I10 sums the six counts and should display `600`.

5 Enter `=CHITEST(observed,expected)` in cell I13.

Note that the variables `observed` and `expected` are named ranges.

The CHITEST function gives the p-value for the goodness of fit test. The ***p-value*** gives the probability of getting the observed deviation from the expected value by chance alone. Small p-values indicate that the deviations from the expected values are greater, and traditionally if the p-value is under .05, we would say that the deviations are large enough to say that the dice are unfair.

Since Excel has a good random number generator, as you click the Recalc button you will typically see p-values larger than .05.

6 Click the Recalc button (or press F9) until you get a p-value under .05 (see Figure 4.8).

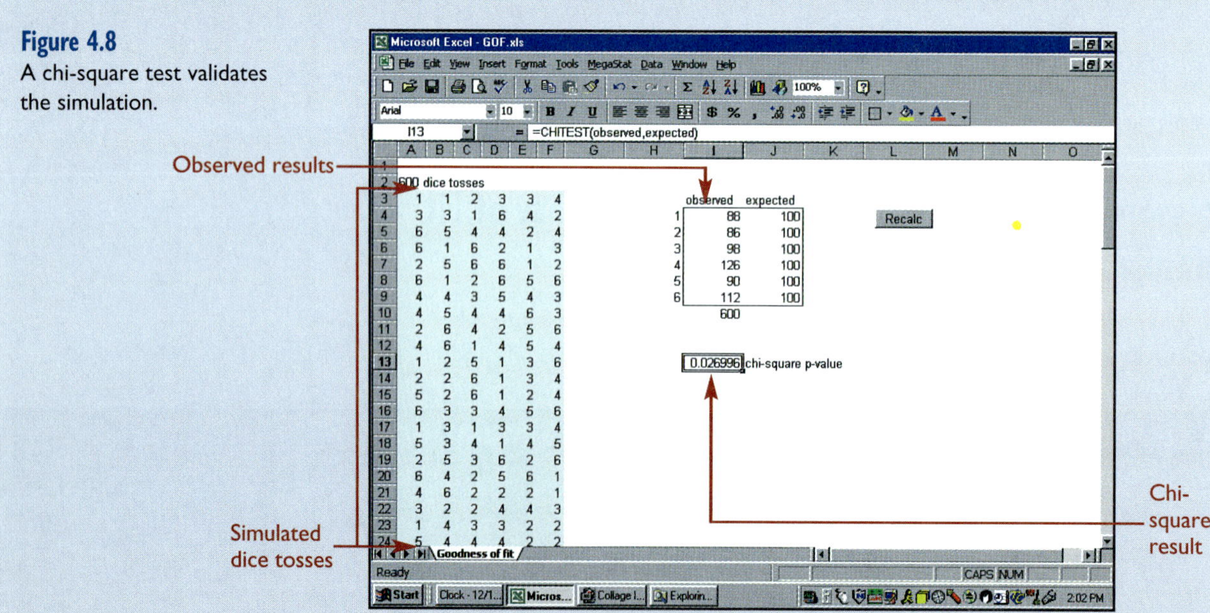

Figure 4.8
A chi-square test validates the simulation.

Notice that the deviation between the observed and expected is fairly large. If this were the only result you looked at, you would say that the Excel random number generator was unfair; however, you would be making what statisticians call a Type I Error—a conclusion based on a chance outcome, not by any failure of our electronic die.

Save and then close the GOF workbook.

Lesson 8: Using Descriptive Statistics in a Simulation

This lesson uses the ***RANDNORM*** distribution to generate random numbers with a mean of 100 and a standard deviation of 15. RAND and RANDBETWEEN create a ***uniform distribution*** of random numbers; for example, any value in the range is as likely to occur as any other value. Sometimes you want numbers to exhibit a ***normal distribution***; for example, a bell-shaped curve with most of the values near the center of the distribution. This lesson uses the RANDNORM user-defined function.

RANDNORM Is a User-Defined Function

RANDNORM is not a standard Excel function. It is a user-defined function that is a part of the XL3-0407 workbook. If you want to have it available to any workbook, copy and paste it into your PERSONAL.XLS Personal Macro Workbook. (See Project 3, "Working with Advanced Functions," Lesson 4 for more information on user-defined functions.)

To Use Descriptive Statistics in a Simulation

1. **Open the XL3-0407 workbook, and save it as `Descriptive Statistics`.**

2. **Examine the contents of the worksheet.**
   Note that cells A3:A202 contain 200 normally distributed random numbers created with RANDNORM, and that the range is named 'data'.

3. **In cell D5, enter `=AVERAGE(data)`.**
   Note that entering the range name `data` is much easier than selecting a range containing 200 cells.

4. **In cell D6, enter `=STDEV(data)`.**

5. **Press F9 several times and notice how close the mean and standard deviation values are to the target value (see Figure 4.9).**
   Notice that cells C9:D9, which indicate the number of decimal places, tend to clutter the output and would not be used very often. There are various ways to hide cells. Here is one quick way:

continues ▶

To Use Descriptive Statistics in a Simulation (continued)

Figure 4.9
A simulation can be done with normally distributed numbers by using the user-defined RAND-NORM function.

Normally distributed random numbers

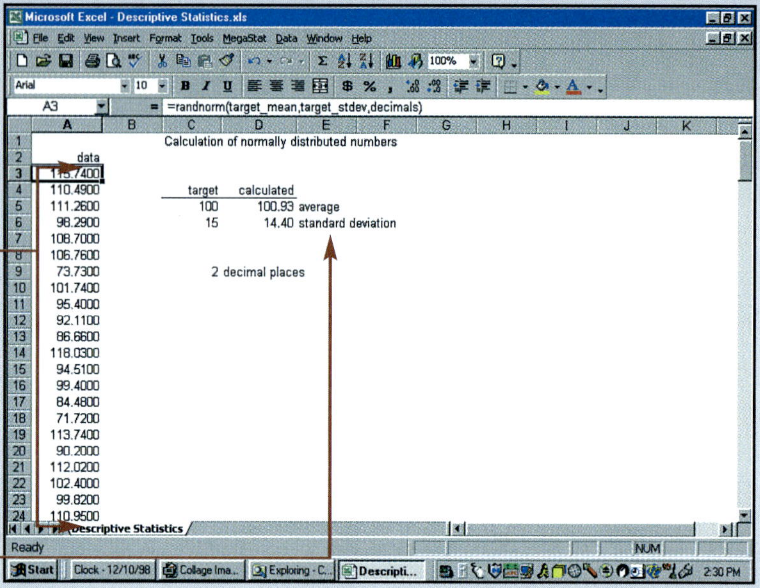

Observed results

6. **Select cells C9:D9.**
7. **Click the drop-down menu on the Font Color button on the Formatting toolbar.**
8. **Select white as the font color.**
9. **To unhide the cells, select the cells and select a different color.** Save the Descriptive Statistics workbook and close it.

Use Named Cells Instead of Constants
In keeping with good spreadsheet practice, the target mean, target standard deviation, and the number of decimal places should be in named cells and not used as constants in the formulas. This allows you to change the values without editing all of the cells.

Summary

In this project, you generated random numbers and used them in simulation. Random numbers are generated by the Excel functions RAND and RANDBETWEEN. You also used a user-defined function, RANDNORM, that created normally distributed random numbers that more accurately reflect real-life distributions than the uniformly distributed random numbers of RAND and RANDBETWEEN.

The dice-toss simulation demonstrated how to create random integers and also how to test the accuracy of the results using the goodness of fit test. This test could be used for any simulation. The expected value simulation showed how to use uniform random numbers to simulate events that do not occur with equal frequency.

The methods illustrated in this project are not the only ways simulations can be used. However, simulation is a straightforward technique, and with a little imagination, it can be used in many situations to bring your worksheets to life.

Checking Concepts and Terms 

True/False

For each of the following, check *T* or *F* to indicate whether the statement is true or false.

__T __F **1.** The RAND function generates random numbers. [L1]

__T __F **2.** The RAND function cannot be used inside of any other function. [L3]

__T __F **3.** Uniformly distributed numbers form a bell-shaped curve. [L8]

__T __F **4.** Conditional formatting is used to highlight particular results. [L3]

__T __F **5.** Simulations are a form of what-if analysis. [Why Would I Do This]

__T __F **6.** A cell can be hidden by changing the font color to white. [L8]

__T __F **7.** A chi-square test is used to determine the accuracy of a simulation. [L7]

__T __F **8.** RANDBETWEEN generates random numbers in a normal distribution. [L7]

__T __F **9.** The COUNTIF function counts cells meeting a given criteria. [L7]

__T __F **10.** The Calc Now button is on the Standard toolbar. [L2]

Multiple Choice

Circle the letter of the correct answer for each of the following.

1. Simulation is useful when [Why Would I Do This]

a. you want to base your results on random data

b. your data is specific but too large to type in

c. you want to generate a sensitivity report

d. none of the above

2. Which of the following can be used to generate a new set of random numbers? [L1]

a. Calc Now

b. Regenerate

c. the F9 function key

d. both a and c

3. The RAND function is found in the [L7]

a. Formula palette, Statistics category

b. Formula palette, Data category

c. Analysis ToolPak

d. Formula palette, Math & Trig category

4. RANDNORM is a [L8]

a. built-in statistical function

b. user-defined function

c. Analysis ToolPak function

d. data function

5. The result of a chi-square test is [L7]

a. a p-value

b. an r-factor

c. a standard deviation

d. none of the above

6. =RAND()*200 generates [L1]

a. random numbers between 0 and 200

b. random numbers 0 and 200

c. any 200 random numbers

d. 200 random numbers between 0 and 100

7. Expected value validation is based on [L7]

a. a normal distribution

b. a probability distribution

c. a goodness of fit test

d. a p-value

8. RANDBETWEEN is found in the [L7]

a. Formula palette, Data category

b. Analysis ToolPak

c. Formula palette, Math & Trig category

d. Formula palette, Statistical category

Discussion Questions

1. What are three business situations where a simulation would be appropriate?
2. What type of simulation would be important for the data to be a normal distribution?
3. What could be changed in the business inventory simulation of Lesson 6 to make it more realistic?
4. Under what circumstance might you want to use conditional formatting, including hiding cells?
5. Think of a situation (other than the insurance example) when an expected value simulation would be useful.

Skill Drill

Skill Drill exercises reinforce project skills. Each skill reinforced is the same, or nearly the same, as a skill presented in the project. Detailed instructions are provided in a step-by-step format.

1. Creating Random Numbers

In this exercise, you will create 100 integers between 1 and 10.

1. Open the XL3-0408 workbook and save it as `XL3-skill`. Activate the Exercises 1-3 sheet.
2. Examine the formulas in the worksheet.
3. In cell A1, type `=RANDBETWEEN(1,10)`.
4. Copy the formula in cell A1 to cells A2:A100.

   You should see the sum of the observed values become 100.
5. Save your changes and keep the workbook open for the next exercise.

2. Adding a Recalc Button

You want to have your supervisor try the simulation you have created. Because he has little experience with simulations, you are going to add a Recalc button to your worksheet.

1. In the XL3-skill workbook, activate the Exercises 1-3 sheet.
2. Open the Forms toolbar.
3. Draw a button and label it `Recalc`.

   Assign the Recalc macro that should be in your Personal Macro Workbook (PERSONAL.XLS) from Lesson 2.
4. Click the Recalc button a few times to make sure it works.
5. Save your changes and keep the workbook open for the next exercise.

3. Performing a Goodness of Fit Test

Your simulation is going to be presented at a meeting with several vice presidents. To ensure the accuracy of your workbook, you perform a chi-square test.

1. In the XL3-skill workbook, activate the Exercises 1-3 sheet.
2. Name cells D5:D14 `observed`.
3. Name cells E5:E14 `expected`.
4. In cell G9, type `=CHITEST(observed,expected)`.
5. Click your Recalc button until you get a test value greater than .95. Note the observed frequencies.
6. Click your Recalc button until you get a test value less than .05. Note the observed frequencies.
7. Save your changes and keep the workbook open for the next exercise.

4. Calculating Normally Distributed Random Numbers

Assume you want to simulate the amount customers purchase in a store. You have reason to believe the average amount is $120 with a standard deviation of 20.

1. In the XL3-skill workbook, activate the Exercises 4-5 sheet.
2. Name cells C3, C4, C5 as **mean**, **sd**, and **dec** respectively.
3. In cell A1, enter `=RANDNORM(mean,sd,dec)`.
4. Copy the formula in cell A1 to cells A2:A100.
5. Press F9 several times, and note if the observed outcomes are close to the target values specified in cells C3:C4.
6. Save your changes and keep the workbook open for the next exercise.

5. Calculating the Mean and Standard Deviation

Now test the numbers created in Exercise 4, and see if they really have a mean of 120 and a standard deviation of 20.

1. In the XL3-skill workbook, activate the Exercises 4-5 sheet.
2. In cell C8, use the AVERAGE function to calculate the average of the 100 numbers you created in Exercise 4.
3. In cell C9, use the STDEV function to calculate the average of the 100 numbers you created in Exercise 4.
4. Press F9 a few times to see how close the mean and standard deviation are to the target values.
5. Save your changes and keep the workbook open for the next exercise.

You can also right-click the Recalc button from the Exercises 1-3 worksheet, and then copy and paste it into the Exercises 4-5 worksheet.

6. Simulating an Expected Value

Given four possible outcomes each with a corresponding probability, what is the expected outcome? Simulate the values and see if the average outcome is close to the expected value.

1. In the XL3-skill workbook, activate the Exercise 6 sheet.
2. Create random numbers in cells B3:B202 using `=RAND()`.
3. Use a nested IF statement to generate simulated random values in cells A3:A202. Use the probability distribution in cells D3:D6.
4. Use a COUNTIF function to count the simulated outcomes in cells G3:G6.
5. Calculate the expected value in cell C13.
6. Calculate the average outcome in cell C15.
7. Save the changes and close the workbook.

Challenge 

Challenge exercises expand on or are somewhat related to skills presented in the lessons. Each exercise provides a brief narrative introduction followed by instructions in a numbered step format that are not as detailed as those in the Skill Drill section.

Each exercise is independent of the others, so that you may complete the exercises in any order. Be sure to save the workbook after completing each exercise. If you need a paper copy of the completed exercise, enter your name centered in a header before printing.

1. Setting Up a Frequency Distribution

In this exercise, you will use the FREQUENCY function to count the normally distributed random numbers.

1. Open the XL3-0409 workbook and save it as `XL3-challenge`. Click the Descriptive Statistics tab.
2. Set up a frequency distribution (using the FREQUENCY function that you learned about in `Level II`; or you could look it up in Excel Help) that will summarize the distribution of random values.

   Hint: Use interval boundaries of 55, 65, … 155.
3. Save the workbook and keep it open for the next exercise.

2. Inserting a Column Chart

In this exercise, you will create a chart to see whether the normally distributed random numbers really do have a bell-shaped distribution.

1. In the XL3-challenge workbook, use the output of the frequency distribution from Challenge Exercise 1 to insert a column chart in the worksheet.
2. Press F9.

   The chart will change, but it should be more or less bell-shaped.
3. Save your changes to the workbook, and keep it open for the next exercise.

3. Copying and Testing a RANDNORM Function

Since a normal random number generator function is not a part of Excel, you may want to place it in your PERSONAL.XLS file so you can use it in any workbook.

1. In the XL3-challenge workbook, open the Visual Basic Editor by choosing Tools, Macro, Visual Basic Editor.
2. Find the RANDNORM function in Module1.
3. Select and copy the RANDNORM function.
4. In the Visual Basic Editor Project Explorer, find the PERSONAL.XLS workbook and paste the RANDNORM function into Module1.
5. Close the Visual Basic Editor.
6. In a new workbook, use the Formula palette to find RANDNORM under user-defined functions. Create some normal random numbers.
7. Save your changes to the workbook, and keep it open for the next exercise.

4. Using a LOOKUP Table to Generate Discrete Random Values

In Lesson 5, you created a distribution of discrete random values. In this exercise you will use an alternative method.

1. In the XL3-challenge workbook, click the Challenge 4 tab.
2. Use the Office Assistant or Excel Help to review the LOOKUP function.

3. In cell B4, type the following formula:

```
=LOOKUP(RAND(),$E$7:$E$10,$F$7:$F$10)
```

   Make sure you could explain to someone else how this LOOKUP function works.

4. Copy cell B4 to cells B5:B253.
5. Save and then close the workbook.

Discovery Zone 

Discovery Zone exercises require advanced knowledge of topics presented in *Essentials* lessons, application of skills from multiple lessons, or self-directed learning of new skills. Each exercise is independent of the others, so that you may complete the exercises in any order.

1. Using a LOOKUP Statement as an Alternative to a Nested IF Statement

Open the SimTest workbook from Lesson 5 and convert it to use a LOOKUP table instead of a nested IF statement. (See Challenge Exercise 4.)

2. Creating a Time Series Simulation Model

Create a worksheet that simulates possible growth scenarios for a company starting at year 2000 through year 2020. Make the starting value 1000, and increase the growth 10% ±1% random fluctuation per year, with a ±100 units random fluctuation around the trend value.

Project 5

Analyzing Data Using the Analysis ToolPak

Objectives

In this project, you learn how to

- **Use the Data Analysis ToolPak to Generate Random Numbers**
- **Select a Random Sample**
- **Smooth Time Series Data with a Moving Average**
- **Perform a t-Test Analysis for Two Independent Groups**
- **Perform a t-Test Analysis for Two Paired Groups**
- **Compare Multiple Groups with Anova**
- **Perform a Regression Analysis**
- **Plot a Regression Line and Make a Prediction**

Key terms introduced in this project include

- Analysis ToolPak
- Anova
- moving average
- random sample
- regression analysis
- regression line
- t-Test analysis

Why Would I Do This?

Excel has the capability to perform most commonly used statistical analyses. These procedures allow us to summarize data, test group differences, study relationships, and make predictions. Excel also provides utilities for sampling and generating random numbers.

Some statistical operations can be done with Excel functions; however, Excel also has an add-in known as the ***Analysis ToolPak*** (which is usually referred to as the Data Analysis Tools because that is the way the menu item appears). This add-in allows you to perform many statistical procedures with the output organized and labeled.

This project focuses on using the Analysis ToolPak. The Analysis ToolPak add-in should already be installed since you used it in Project 4. The lessons in this project give some guidance regarding the tests, but deciding which procedure to use, what data is appropriate, and interpreting the results, are statistical issues, not Excel issues.

Visual Summary

Figure 5.1 shows the Data Analysis dialog box that enables you to select various statistical procedures, several of which are explored in this project. Figure 5.2 shows an example of the Data Analysis Tools—a moving average is calculated to smooth time series data. The regression analysis output shown in Figure 5.3 shows another typical Data Analysis output.

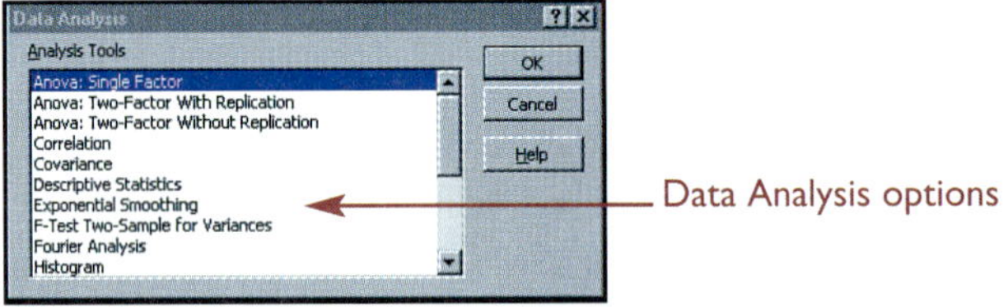

Figure 5.1
The Data Analysis dialog box shows the Analysis ToolPak options.

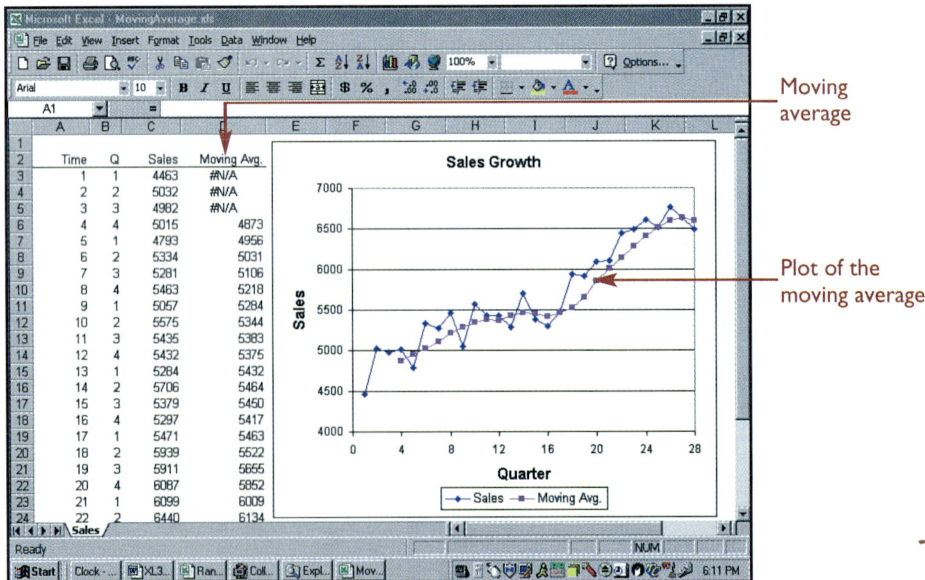

Figure 5.2
The chart shows the smoothing effect of a moving average.

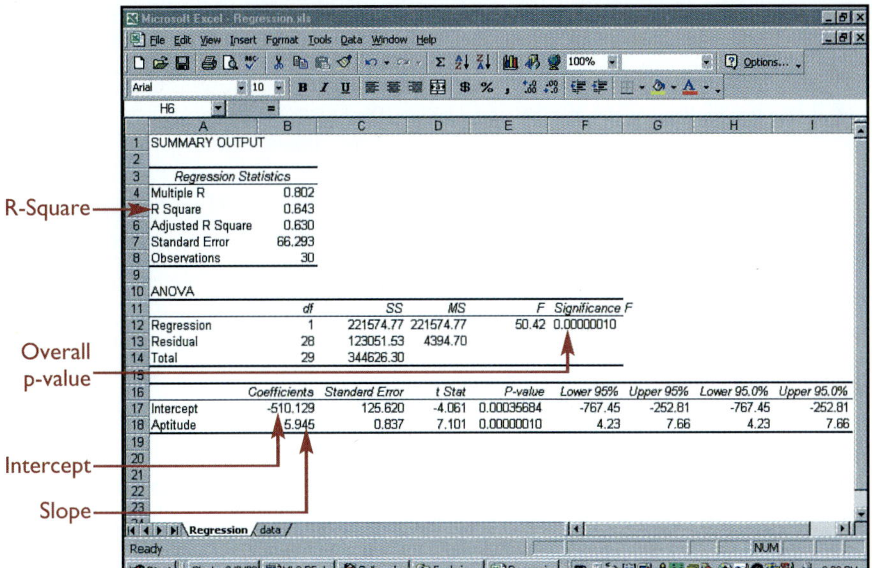

Figure 5.3
The R-Square in cell B5 indicates a moderate degree of relationship; the p-value in cell F12 is well under the .05 alpha level, indicating a statistically significant degree of relationship.

Lesson 1: Using the Analysis ToolPak to Generate Random Numbers

In Project 4, "Worksheet Simulation and Statistical Functions," you saw how to create random numbers using Excel functions. In this lesson you will create random numbers using the Analysis ToolPak. The Analysis ToolPak is easy to use and offers many options. In the process of generating random numbers, we will see some of the procedures of the Analysis ToolPak that are common to all of the options.

To Use the Analysis ToolPak to Generate Random Numbers

1. **Open a new, blank workbook and save it as `RandomNumbers`.**

2. **Choose Tools, Data Analysis.**
   Scroll through the options in the Data Analysis dialog box (refer to Figure 5.1 in the Visual Summary).

   The Analysis ToolPak is not an intrinsic part of Microsoft Excel—it is an add-in. If your Tools menu does not list the Data Analysis command, you will need to install the Analysis ToolPak. To do so, choose Tools, Add-Ins. Then, scroll down until you find Analysis ToolPak, select it, and click OK. When Excel asks if you want to install, click Yes. You will probably need your Microsoft Office CD.

3. **Click the Help button in the dialog box.**
   This will give general help regarding the Data Analysis ToolPak.

4. **In the Analysis Tools list box, select Random Number Generation and click OK.**
   The Random Number Generation dialog box is displayed.

continues ▶

To Use the Analysis ToolPak to Generate Random Numbers (continued)

5. **In the Number of Variables text box, type `1`.**
   This is the number of columns of random numbers.

6. **In the Number of Random Numbers text box, type `1000`.**
   This is the number of random numbers in each column.

7. **Click the Distribution drop-down arrow and click Normal.**
   Make note of the other options for Parameters, Random Seed, and Output options. Some of them will be explored later.

8. **In the Parameters area, enter `200` for the Mean, and `20` for the Standard Deviation.**

9. **In the Output options area, click the Output Range option button, and then click in the text box and type `A1` (see Figure 5.4).**
   The Output Range is the upper left-hand corner of the output that will be created. Make sure the cell or range you select is below any existing data in the worksheet. You may also want to place the output in a new worksheet or new workbook.

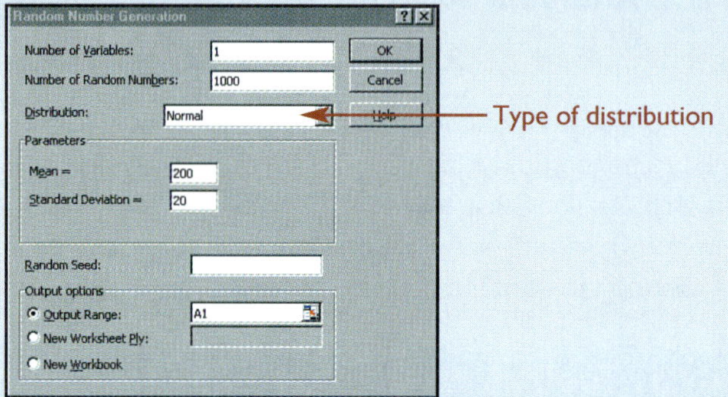

Figure 5.4
Random numbers can be generated by using the Random Number Generation dialog box, accessed through the Data Analysis Tools.

10. **Click OK to generate the numbers.**
    The random numbers are created and placed in cells A1:A1000.

11. **With the output range (A1:A1000) selected, click in the Name box and name the random numbers: `data`.**

12. **In cells C3 and C4 type `=AVERAGE(data)` and `=STDEV(data)`, respectively.**
    These cells should verify that the mean and standard deviation are approximately 200 and 20. Since these are random numbers, your results will not be identical to the ones shown in Figure 5.5.

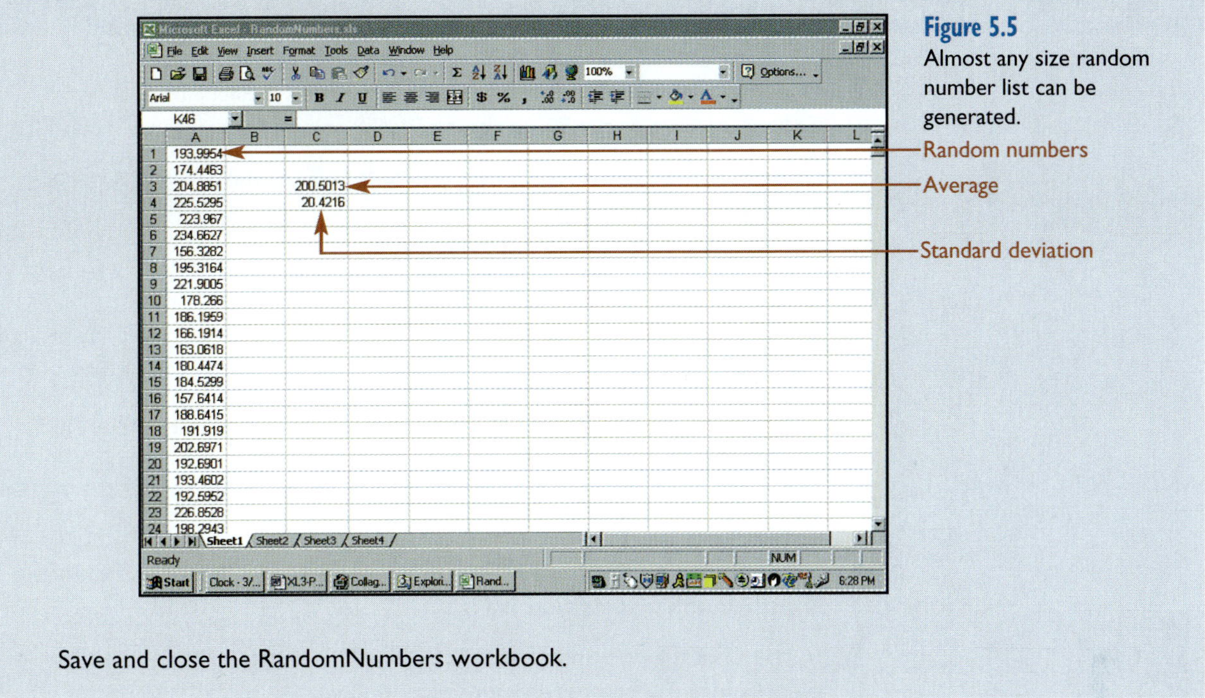

Figure 5.5
Almost any size random number list can be generated.

Save and close the RandomNumbers workbook.

Which Method of Generating Random Numbers Is Best?
Which is better for calculating random numbers—the Excel functions or the Data Analysis Tools? The Data Analysis Tools provide more flexibility and are easy to use; however, the Excel functions have an advantage for simulation because they are "live" and can be recalculated (whereas the Data Analysis Tools generate one fixed sample).

Repeating a Series Of Random Numbers with a Seed Value
A "seed" value for random numbers is a value that starts a particular sequence of random numbers. The Random Seed text box in the Random Number Generation dialog box is typically left blank, which means you get a different sequence of random numbers every time. If you enter a number, you can use that same number later to re-create the exact same set of random numbers.

Lesson 2: Selecting a Random Sample

Often you are faced with taking a ***random sample*** from a population. For a sample to be truly random, every item must have the same likelihood of being sampled and there must be no bias.

Assume we have several hundred employees, and we want to select a random sample of 20 employees to test a pilot copy of a questionnaire we are developing.

To Select a Random Sample

1. **Open the XL3-0501 workbook and save it as `RandomSample`.**
   Column A contains the ID numbers of 1,128 employees in a range named ID.

2. **Choose Tools, Data Analysis; then select Sampling in the Analysis Tools list box and click OK.**
   The Sampling dialog box is displayed.

3. **Click the Help button in the dialog box.**
   Clicking the Help button in the dialog box for a specific option will give information regarding the purpose of the various elements of the dialog box.

4. **In the Input Range box of the Sampling dialog box, type `ID`. Leave the Labels box unchecked.**
   You could have selected cells A2:A1129, but it is easier to use the named range, ID.

5. **In the Sampling Method area, click Random and then type `20` in the Number of Samples text box.**

6. **In the Output options area, click New Worksheet Ply, and then type `Sample` in the corresponding text box.**
   This creates a new worksheet named Sample. The completed dialog box is shown in Figure 5.6.

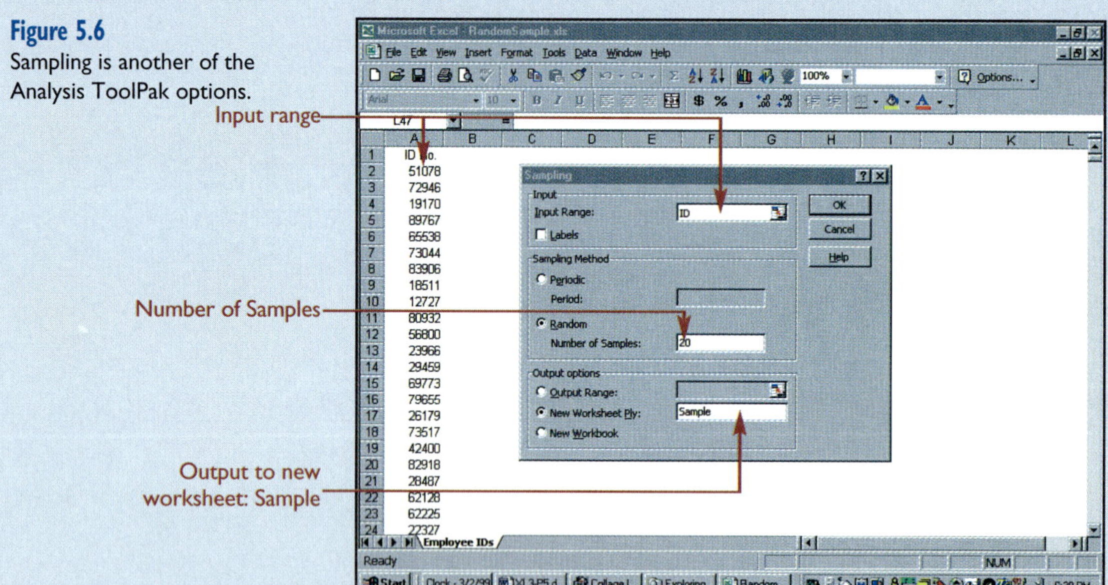

Figure 5.6
Sampling is another of the Analysis ToolPak options.

7. **Click OK and examine the sample.**
   You see 20 randomly selected ID numbers in cells A1:A20 of the Sample worksheet. You might try using Edit, Find to locate some of the sample values in the original data.

Save and close the RandomSample workbook.

Lesson 3: Smoothing Time Series Data with a Moving Average

If you have data measured over time, it is useful to smooth the data by averaging a few periods of data. By doing this, random fluctuations above and below the trend line will be averaged and the resulting line will be smoother and will better reflect the long-term trend. This can be done with a ***moving average***. In this example we have seven years of quarterly data, and we will smooth it by averaging four quarters.

To Smooth Time Series Data with a Moving Average

1 Open the XL3-0502 workbook and save it as `MovingAverage`.

The worksheet contains 28 quarters of data; a plot of the data is shown in Figure 5.7.

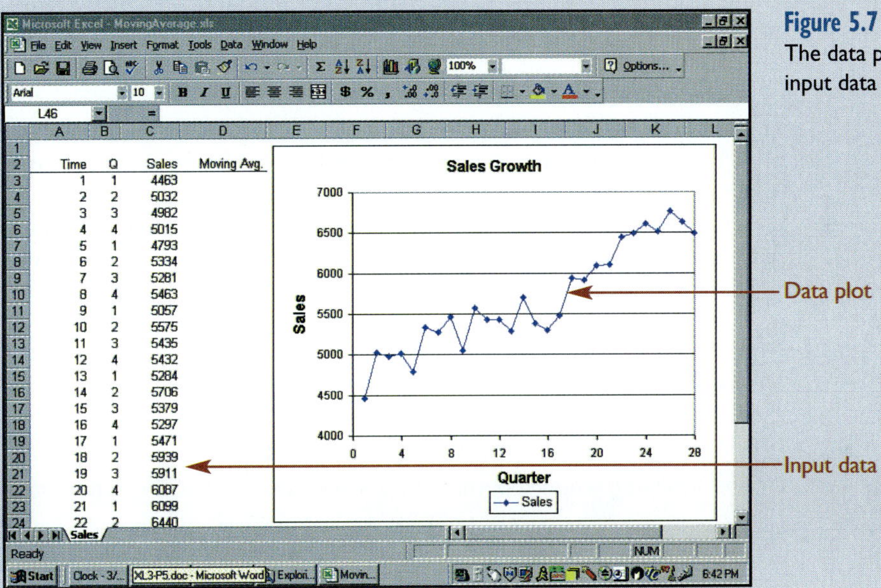

Figure 5.7
The data plot shows the input data in chart form.

2 Choose Tools, Data Analysis; then select Moving Average and click OK.

3 Select cells C3:C30 in the Input Range box. Leave the Labels in First Row box unchecked.

4 Type `4` in the Interval text box.

5 Type `D3` in the Output Range box. Leave the Chart Output and Standard Errors boxes unchecked. The completed dialog box is shown in Figure 5.8.

continues ▶

To Smooth Time Series Data with a Moving Average (continued)

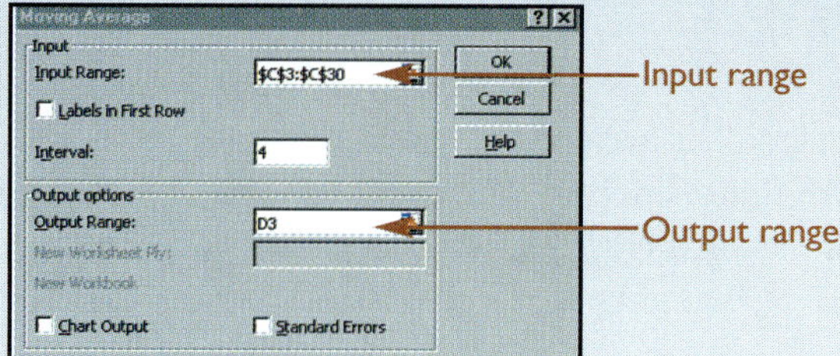

Figure 5.8
The Moving Average option is used to smooth the data plot.

6. **Click OK to calculate the moving average.**
   Note that the first three cells contain `#N/A`, since the first three cells are averaged into the first moving average value. These cells can be cleared.

7. **Select cells D2:D30. Drag the selected cells over the chart and drop them.**
   The moving average will now be plotted in addition to the original data. The completed worksheet is shown in Figure 5.2 in the Visual Summary. Note that the moving average is much smoother than the actual data.

If you have difficulty dragging the selected range over the chart, you may have disabled drag-and-drop. To enable this feature, choose Tools, Options. Then click the Edit tab, check the Allow cell drag and drop option, and click OK. You could also add the series by copying the cells and pasting them into the chart.

8. **Click any one of the Moving Average cells in the range D6:D30.**

9. **Note the contents of the cell, and then choose Tools, Auditing, Trace Precedents.**
   Most Data Analysis output consists only of numbers and text; however, the Moving Average output actually puts an AVERAGE function in the cells.

   Save and close the MovingAverage workbook.

Lesson 4: Performing a t-Test Analysis for Two Independent Groups

A *t-Test Analysis* tests whether the means of two groups are the same. A t-Test is useful whenever you need to compare the means of two groups. For example, assume you are a manager for Indy Motor Works car rental agency. You want to know if the rental cost is different for business versus personal use because you want to know whether to focus on business or personal advertising.

To Perform a t-Test Analysis for Two Independent Groups

1. **Open the XL3-0503 workbook and save it as `t-Test`.**

2. **Click in cell B14 and then click the Sort Ascending button on the Standard toolbar.**
   This sorts the business and personal records into separate groups, as shown in Figure 5.9.

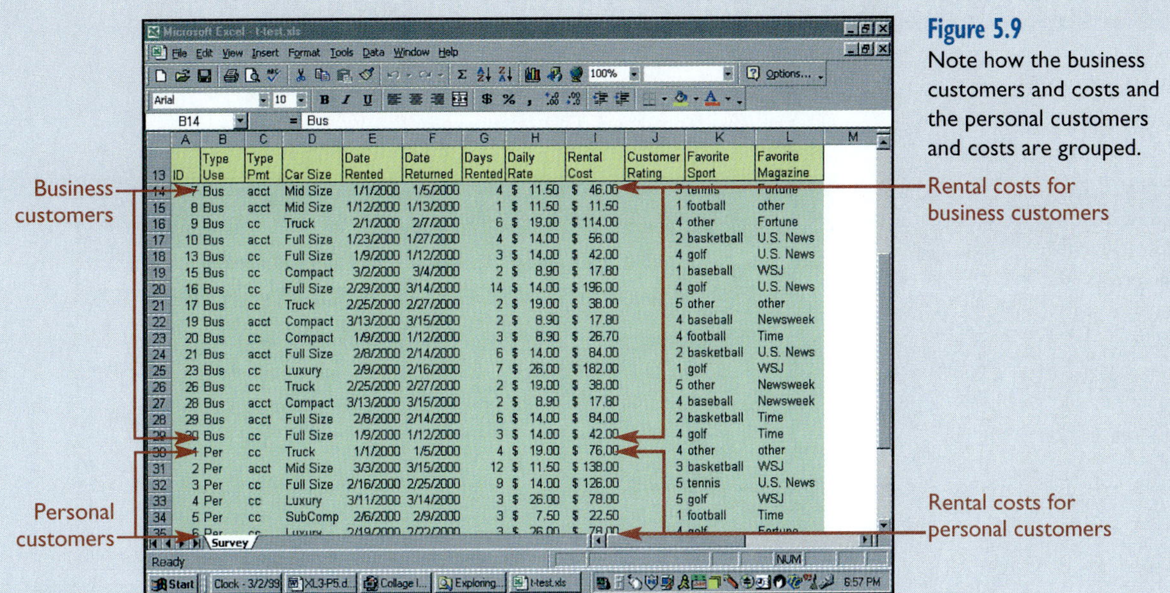

Figure 5.9
Note how the business customers and costs and the personal customers and costs are grouped.

3. **Choose Tools, Data Analysis; then select t-Test: Two-Sample Assuming Equal Variances and click OK.**
   The t-Test: Two-Sample Assuming Equal Variances dialog box is displayed.

4. **Select cells I14:I29 for the Variable 1 Range.**
   These cells contain the rental costs for the business customers.

5. **Select cells I30:I43 for the Variable 2 Range**
   These cells contain the rental costs for the personal customers.

6. **In the Hypothesized Mean Difference text box, type `0`; then type `.05` in the Alpha text box; leave the Labels box unchecked.**
   The "0" mean difference indicates we are testing that the groups have the same mean. Alpha (also called the significance level) is the probability of observing the result by chance alone. If the calculated p-value is less than alpha, we will conclude that the groups are significantly different from each other. The value that is normally used for Alpha is .05. The Labels box is checked if the first cell in the data ranges contains a label for the ranges.

7. **Select the New Worksheet Ply option button, and type the name `t-test` in the corresponding text box. The completed dialog box is shown in Figure 5.10.**

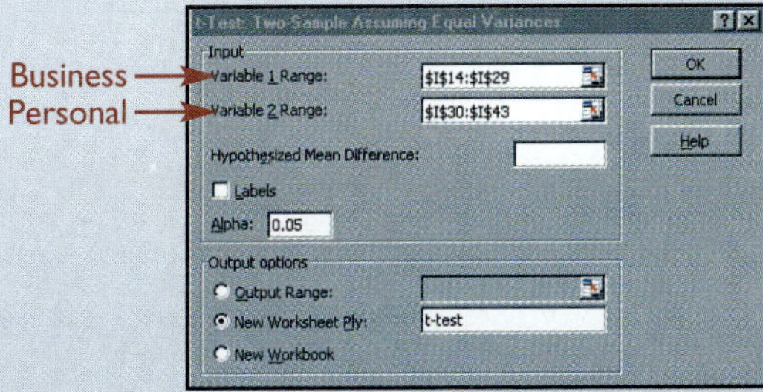

Figure 5.10
Variable ranges are specified in the t-Test: Two-Sample Assuming Equal Variances dialog box.

continues ▶

To Perform a t-Test Analysis for Two Independent Groups (continued)

8 Click OK to perform the test for output options.

The output from the t-Test is shown in Figure 5.11.

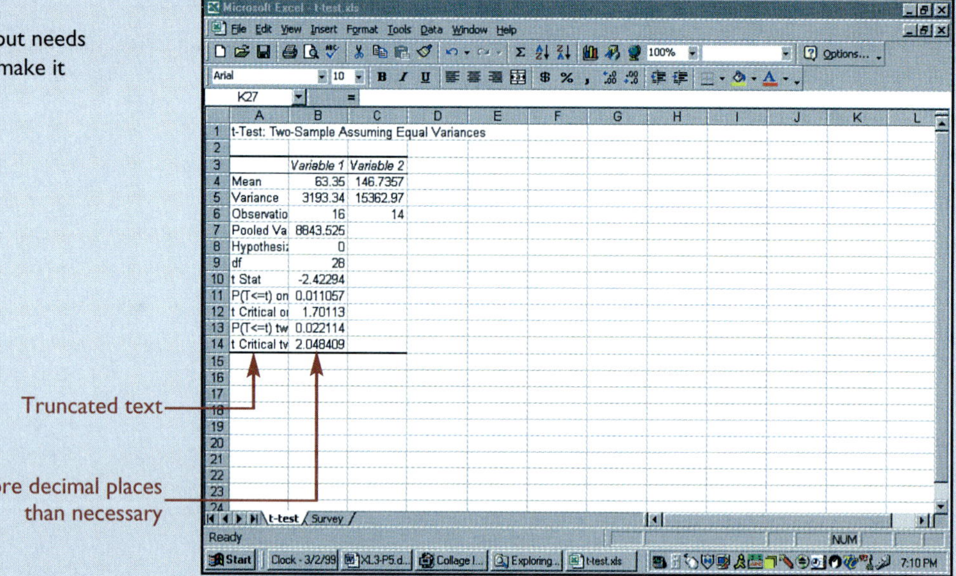

Figure 5.11
The t-Test output needs some work to make it easy to read.

The t-Test output is readable but needs a little touch-up.

9 Make the column widths the correct size, right-align the labels in the first table column, adjust the number of decimal places, and turn off the worksheet grid lines. Your output should look similar to Figure 5.12.

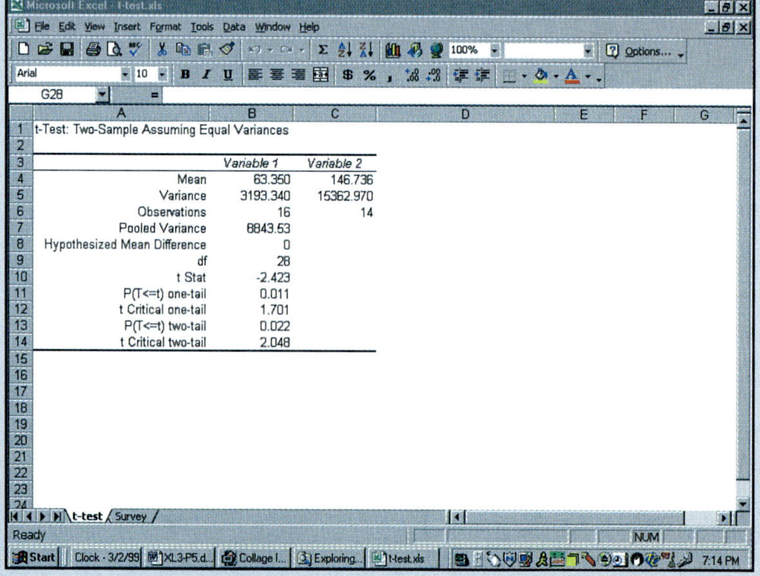

Figure 5.12
Notice how much easier it is to read the t-Test output after some adjustments are made.

The value in cell B13 is less than the specified alpha value of .05, which indicates the group means are probably different. (See discussion of alpha in step 6.) In other words, because the observed difference is unlikely by chance alone, we conclude that it is more than a chance difference, *that is,* the group means really are different.

Save and close the t-Test workbook.

Lesson 5: Performing a t-Test Analysis for Two Paired Groups

Another common situation is to have a sample of paired observations. This can happen when you have Before and After measurements, or any data where you have pairs of numbers and you want to know if the pairs have the same means.

Assume a company has produced a tutorial course that is supposed to improve college entrance exam scores. A sample of students take the entrance exam, take the tutorial course, and then re-take the entrance exam. Each student then has a pair of Before and After scores, and we want to know if there is an improvement.

To Perform a t-Test Analysis for Two Paired Groups

1. **Open XL3-0504 and save it as `PairedGroups`.**
2. **Choose Tools, Data Analysis; then select t-Test: Paired Two Sample for Means in the Analysis Tools list box and click OK.**
   The t-Test: Paired Two Sample for Means dialog box is displayed.
3. **Select cells B3:B18 for the Variable 1 Range.**
   These cells contain the post-tutorial exam scores.
4. **Select cells A3:A18 for the Variable 2 Range.**
   These cells contain the pre-tutorial exam scores.
5. **In the Hypothesized Mean Difference text box, type `0`; then type `.05` in the Alpha text box, and check the Labels box.**
6. **In the Output options area, select New Worksheet Ply, and type the name `paired t-test` in the corresponding text box. Click OK to perform the test.**
7. **Make the column widths the correct size, right-align the labels in the first table column, adjust the number of decimal places, and turn off the worksheet grid lines. Your output should look similar to Figure 5.13.**

continues ▶

To Perform a t-Test Analysis for Two Paired Groups (continued)

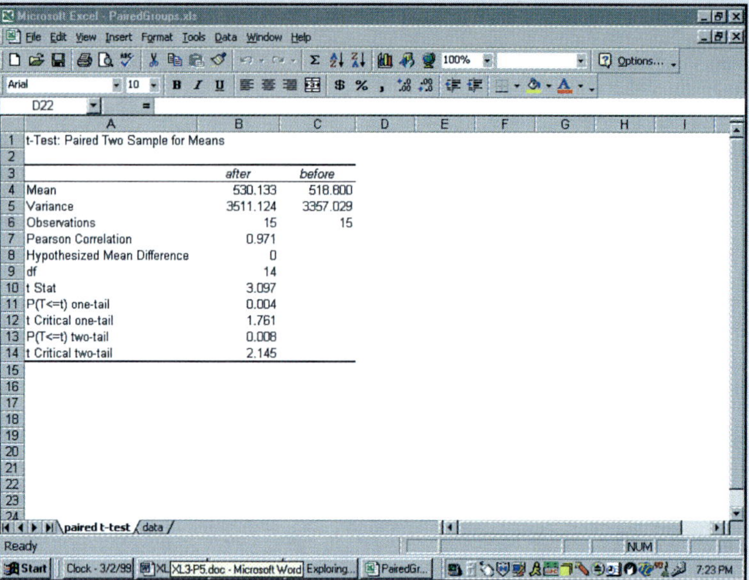

	A	B	C
1	t-Test: Paired Two Sample for Means		
2			
3		after	before
4	Mean	530.133	518.800
5	Variance	3511.124	3357.029
6	Observations	15	15
7	Pearson Correlation	0.971	
8	Hypothesized Mean Difference	0	
9	df	14	
10	t Stat	3.097	
11	P(T<=t) one-tail	0.004	
12	t Critical one-tail	1.761	
13	P(T<=t) two-tail	0.008	
14	t Critical two-tail	2.145	

Figure 5.13
This figure shows the formatted output of the test.

The value in cell B11 is less than .05, which indicates that the mean difference is greater than zero.

Save and close the PairedGroups workbook.

Lesson 6: Comparing Multiple Groups with Anova

Sometimes we need to compare more than two groups of data. The statistical tool for this procedure is Analysis of Variance (*Anova*) or, more precisely, Single Factor Anova. This is also sometimes known as One-Way Anova.

A purchasing manager wants to determine which of four brands of tires has the longest mileage. She chooses several automobiles to use one of the tire brands until it is worn out. If she only wanted to compare two brands, she would use the t-Test for independent groups (Lesson 4), but with more than two groups she would use the Anova test.

To Compare Multiple Groups with Anova

1. **Open the XL3-0505 workbook and save it as Anova.**

2. **Choose Tools, Data Analysis; then select Anova: Single Factor and click OK.**
   The Anova: Single Factor dialog box is displayed. The Single Factor Anova was selected because there were multiple independent groups, similar to the t-Test in Lesson 4, but with more than two groups.

3. **Select cells B4:E14 for the Input Range.**
   Each column in the range represents one of the groups. It is OK that some of the selected cells are empty. The groups do not all have to be the same size.

4. **Select Grouped By Columns, type `.05` in the Alpha text box, and select the Labels check box.**

5. **In the Output options area, select New Worksheet Ply, type `Anova` in the corresponding text box, and click OK.**

6. **Clean up the output by adjusting column widths, aligning the labels, setting decimal places, and turning off the gridlines. Your worksheet should resemble Figure 5.14.**
   Figure 5.14 shows the formatted Anova output. The p-value in cell F13 is less than .05 (the Alpha value), which means the groups are statistically significantly different, that is, the groups' differences are unlikely to be due to chance alone.

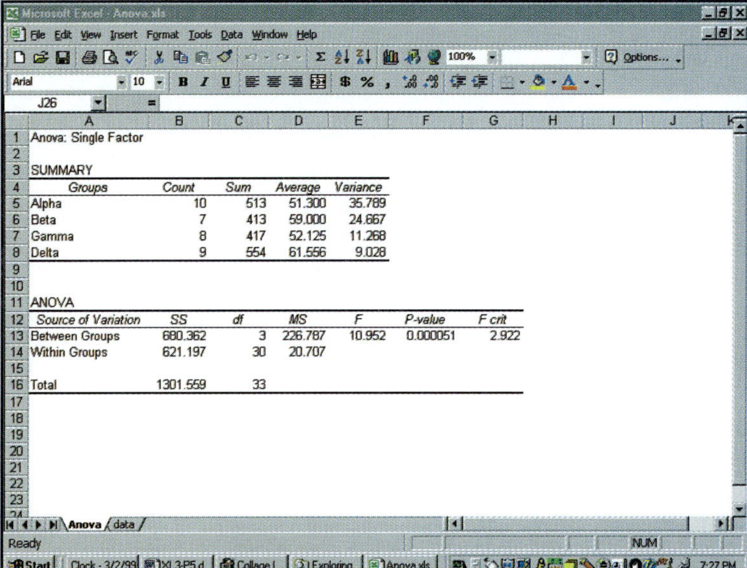

Anova: Single Factor

SUMMARY

Groups	Count	Sum	Average	Variance
Alpha	10	513	51.300	35.789
Beta	7	413	59.000	24.667
Gamma	8	417	52.125	11.268
Delta	9	554	61.556	9.028

ANOVA

Source of Variation	SS	df	MS	F	P-value	F crit
Between Groups	680.362	3	226.787	10.952	0.000051	2.922
Within Groups	621.197	30	20.707			
Total	1301.559	33				

Figure 5.14
This figure shows output from a Single Factor Anova.

Save and close the Anova workbook.

Lesson 7: Performing a Regression Analysis

One of the most commonly used statistical analyses is ***regression analysis***, which looks at the relationship between variables, with the goal of predicting one of the variables.

Regression analysis is the statistical analysis relevant to an XY scatter chart. It gives the slope and intercept of the straight line that best fits the scatter chart (trendline). The trendline can be used to predict the Y variable given a value for the X variable.

The regression analysis also gives a measure (R-Square) of the goodness of fit. If R-Square is 1.00, the points fall right on the line; if R-Square is 0.00, the points are randomly scattered. Regression analysis will also test if the degree of relationship is statistically significant, that is, better than chance.

Regression analysis (and an XY scatter chart) can be used to examine the relationship of any pairs of variables. For example, you could look at the relationship between SAT scores and college GPA. If the X variable represents time, you have a special type of regression analysis known as time series analysis.

In the example used for this lesson, a human resources manager wants to predict sales from a sales aptitude test. He collects data from 30 salespeople.

To Perform a Regression Analysis

1 Open the XL3-0506 workbook and save it as `Regression`.
Figure 5.15 shows the data and an XY scatter chart created with Excel. If we are going to be able to predict sales using the aptitude test, then sales should increase as the aptitude score increases. The scatter chart shows a moderate degree of relationship—the data points are not right on the line, but there is some upward trend with higher aptitude scores being associated with higher sales. The regression analysis will tell us if it is statistically significant.

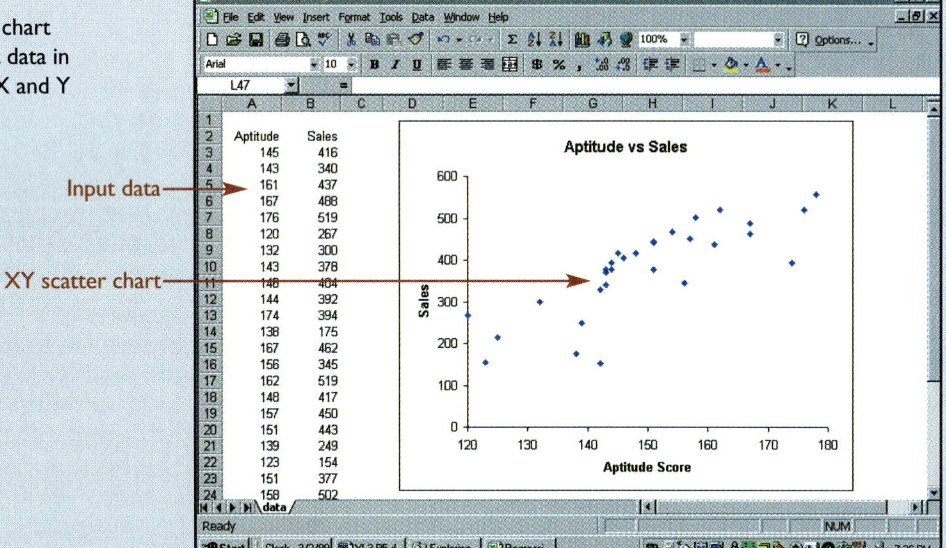

Figure 5.15
The XY scatter chart shows the input data in relation to the X and Y axes.

2 Choose Tools, Data Analysis; then select Regression and click OK.
The Regression dialog box is displayed.

3 Select cells B2:B32 for the Input Y range.
These are the Sales numbers that represent the Y (vertical) axis.

4 Select cells A2:A32 for the Input X range.
These are the Aptitude scores that represent the X (horizontal) axis.

5 Check the Labels box and leave the other input boxes unchecked.

6 In the Output options area, select New Worksheet Ply, type `Regression` in the text box, and click OK.

7 Clean up the output by adjusting column widths, aligning text, setting decimal places, and turning off the worksheet gridlines. Your worksheet should resemble Figure 5.3 in the Visual Summary.
There are a lot of numbers on the regression output, but for a quick interpretation there are two you should always check. First, examine the R-Square (cell B5). This value will always be between 0 and 1, the closer to 1 the better the regression. A "good" R-Square depends on the context, but in this case, .643 would probably be considered pretty good, especially because we are predicting human behavior.

The other value to check is the p-value in cell F12. If this value is under the specified alpha level (.05 in this example) it means that the degree of relationship is more than could be expected by chance alone; that is, the regression analysis is "statistically significant at the .05 level."

Save the Regression workbook, and leave it open for the next lesson.

Lesson 8: Plotting a Regression Line and Making a Prediction

The regression analysis calculates the slope and intercept of the best fitting straight line, the ***regression line***. Once we have the best fitting straight line, we can use it for making predictions.

To Plot a Regression Line and Make a Prediction

1 Open the Regression workbook if it is not still open from the previous lesson, and save it as `Regression2`. Click the data worksheet tab.

2 Right-click any one of the data points in the XY scatter chart to display the shortcut menu as shown in Figure 5.16.

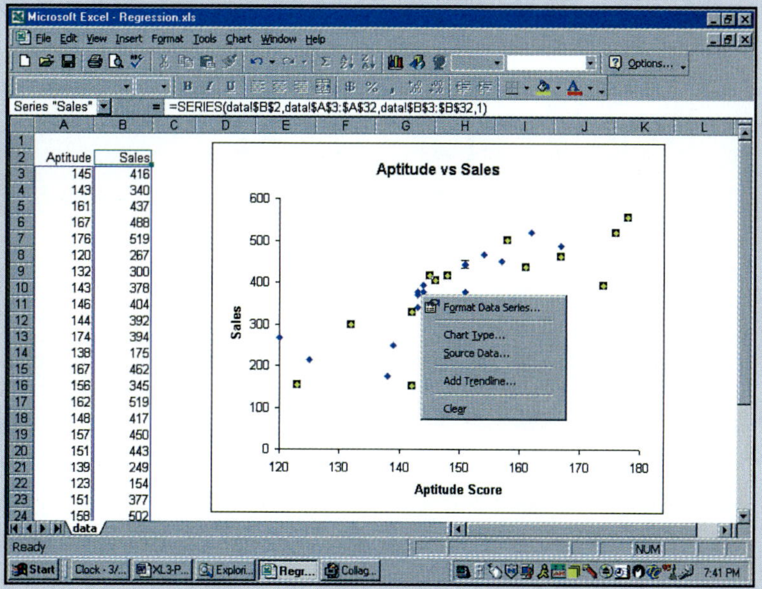

Figure 5.16
Right-clicking a data point in the scatter chart reveals this shortcut menu.

3 Select Add Trendline to display the Add Trendline dialog box as shown in Figure 5.17.

continues ▶

To Plot a Regression Line and Make a Prediction (continued)

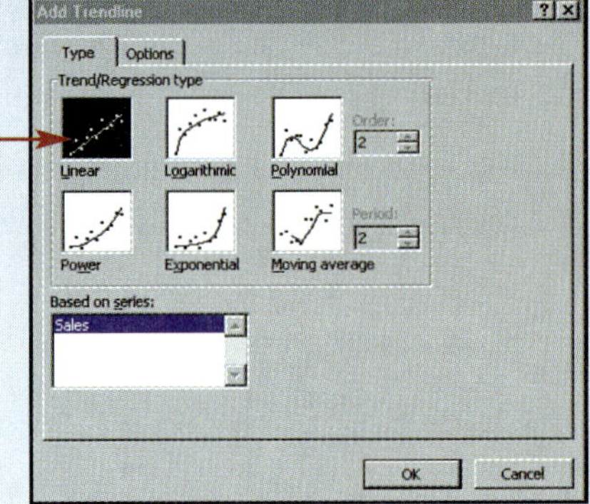

Figure 5.17
The Add Trendline dialog box offers six line type options.

4. **In the Add Trendline dialog box, click the Linear box.**

5. **Click the Options tab and check Display equation on chart and Display R-squared value on chart, and then click OK.**
   The linear trendline appears within the scatter chart as shown in Figure 5.18. Now calculate a predicted value.

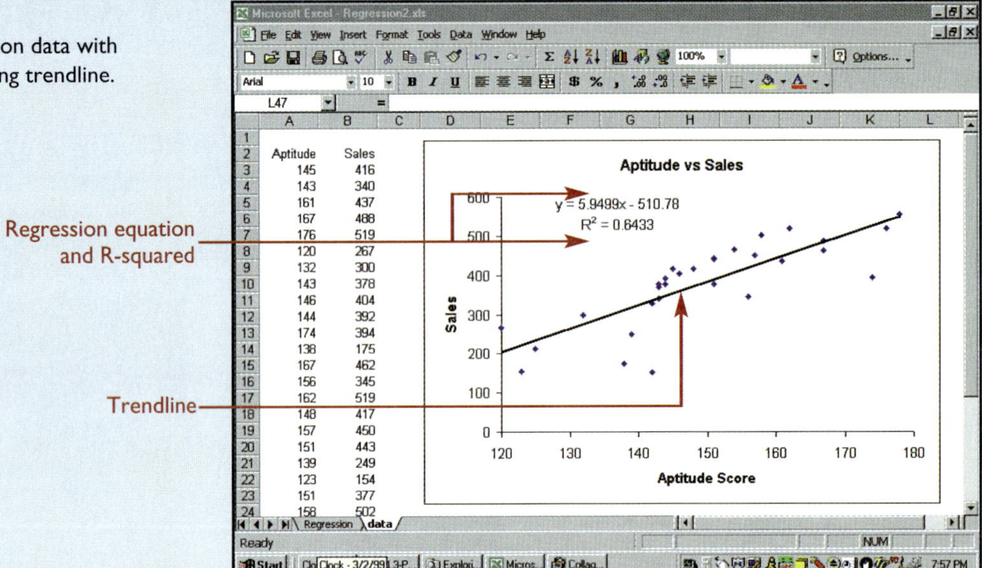

Figure 5.18
The regression data with the best fitting trendline.

6. **Click on the Regression tab of the workbook.**
   Because the manager has a statistically significant regression analysis, he wants to use it to make a prediction. If a new employee has an aptitude score of 165, what would we predict for her sales? Excel does not have a direct way of calculating predicted values, so you need to enter a formula to calculate the regression line.

   Using the slope and intercept values in cells B18 and B17, respectively, the resulting regression equation is: Y = 5.945x - 510.129. If you substitute 165 for X you will have calculated the predicted sales for someone with an aptitude score of 165. This calculation will be done in the next two steps.

7 **Enter 165 in cell A21.**

You could have entered this directly in the formula in the next step, but it is better to place it in a cell so you can change it to make predictions with other values.

8 **Enter =B18*A21+B17 in cell A22.**

This formula multiplies the input value (A21) times the slope (B18) and adds the intercept (B17). In other words, it calculates the height of the regression line at 165, which is the predicted value.

Save and close the Regression2 workbook.

When Is a Trendline Not a Trendline?

The trendline should actually be called a regression line in this example, since this is not time-related data. Excel calls all regression lines trendlines, but they are only properly called trendlines if the X variable represents time.

Summary

In this project, we have examined the Analysis ToolPak and some of its many uses. We calculated random numbers, sampled from a population, smoothed data, compared group means, and calculated predicted values using a regression line. There are other procedures that we did not examine; however, they all work similarly to the ones that we did examine.

If you want to expand your knowledge in this area, you probably need to expand your knowledge of statistics. As we have seen, using the Data Analysis ToolPak is easy; the trick is knowing what procedure to use and interpreting the results. Taking one or more courses (or reading books) on statistics would be the best approach.

Checking Concepts and Terms

True/False

For each of the following, check *T* or *F* to indicate whether the statement is true or false.

__T __F **1.** The Analysis ToolPak is an intrinsic part of Microsoft Excel. [L1]

__T __F **2.** In a truly random sample, every item must have the same chance of being sampled. [L2]

__T __F **3.** To do a Moving Average, you would choose Tools, Data Analysis. [L3]

__T __F **4.** A t-Test can only be applied to a single data group. [L4]

__T __F **5.** Anova is used to compare multiple groups. [L6]

__T __F **6.** Regression analysis looks at the relationship between constants. [L7]

__T __F **7.** Random numbers can only be generated with the Analysis ToolPak. [L1]

__T __F **8.** Regression analysis generates a scatter chart. [L7]

__T __F **9.** Regression analysis can be used to make predictions. [L7]

__T __F **10.** Frequency is not part of the Analysis ToolPak. [L1]

Multiple Choice

Circle the letter of the correct answer for each of the following.

1. Which of the following tools can be selected from the Data Analysis dialog box? [L1,6,7]
   a. Regression
   b. Anova
   c. Sampling
   d. all of the above
2. Generating random numbers for simulation is better accomplished with the Microsoft Excel functions than the Data Analysis Tools, because [L1]
   a. the function method is less time-consuming
   b. the random numbers can be recalculated
   c. the random numbers are fixed
   d. none of the above
3. The Random Seed option is used to [L3]
   a. identify the first number in the set
   b. generate the same set of random numbers again
   c. identify the mean of the sample set
   d. identify the size of the set
4. A moving average is [L3]
   a. a method of keeping the output current
   b. like an automatic macro for the average function
   c. a method of smoothing data
   d. all of the above
5. A t-Test analysis is used to [L4]
   a. test group differences
   b. test for truly random distribution
   c. test variable differences in a single group
   d. test small samples
6. Anova stands for [L6]
   a. A Normal Variance
   b. Analysis: Normal/Variant
   c. Analysis of Variance
   d. Analysis of Normal Output Variations
7. Which of the following is *not* a tool in the Data Analysis dialog box? [VS]
   a. Anova: Single
   b. Anova: Multiple
   c. Anova: Two-Factor With Replication
   d. Anova: Two-Factor Without Replication
8. The goal of regression analysis is to [L7]
   a. analyze past data
   b. make predictions based on a variable
   c. analyze a problem by working backward from a known solution
   d. make predictions based on multiple variables
9. In a regression analysis, data is displayed as a [L7]
   a. line graph
   b. formula
   c. scatter chart
   d. table
10. A regression line is [L8]
    a. the best fitting straight line
    b. constructed for time-related data
    c. based on a formula
    d. both a and c

Discussion Questions

1. The company you work for manufactures low-fat snack foods. The marketing department has been doing taste tests with three different groups—adult females, adult males, and teenagers. What type of analysis might you do on the results of their testing, and how would it impact the marketing strategy?
2. A landscaping service needs to purchase new mowers and wants the most reliable brand. They are considering five different brands. Discuss how you could set up an analysis to help make the decision.
3. Discuss which Microsoft Excel functions can also be executed using the Data Analysis Tools, and in what situations it would be appropriate to use the function or the analysis tool.
4. A business school has five years of data on student GMAT scores and student grade point averages. How might this information be useful, and how would you use Microsoft Excel to analyze the data?

Skill Drill

Skill Drill exercises reinforce project skills. Each skill reinforced is the same, or nearly the same, as a skill presented in the project. Detailed instructions are provided in a step-by-step format.

1. Generating a Sample of Yes/No Responses

In this exercise, we will generate 500 random numbers that will simulate a Yes/No questionnaire response with a 60% Yes rate.

1. Start a new workbook and save it as `Exercise1`.
2. Choose Tools, Data Analysis; then select Random Number Generation and click OK.
3. Type `1` as the number of variables, and `500` as the number of random numbers.
4. Select Bernoulli from the Distribution list, and type `.6` for the p-value.

   A Bernoulli distribution is simply a distribution with two possible outcomes: 0 and 1.
5. Select Output Range and type `A2` in the text box. Click OK.
6. Type `=IF(A2=1,"Yes","No")` in cell B2 and copy it to cells B3:B501.

   This converts `0` and `1` (in column A) to `No` and `Yes` (in column B).
7. Select cells B2:B501, and then use Copy and Paste Special Values to convert the formulas to values. Note that the copy and paste ranges are the same.
8. Use a COUNTIF function to count the number of `Yes` responses.

   The number of responses should be approximately 60% (that is, 300/500); however, your actual count will probably not be exactly that, since these are random numbers.
9. Save the Exercise1 workbook and keep it open for the next exercise.

2. Selecting a Random Sample

Assume you are creating a simulation of a questionnaire and one of the items requires a Yes/No answer. You want to simulate the response of 20 people by selecting 20 of the 500 values you just created.

1. In the Exercise1 workbook from the previous exercise, choose Tools, Data Analysis; then select Sampling and click OK.
2. Type `A2:A501` for the Input Range.

   Note that you must select the 0/1 numbers in column A, not the No/Yes values in column B.
3. Type `20` for number of samples.
4. Select Output Range, and type `C4` in the text box. Click OK.
5. Count the number of 1's in the sample.

   It should be approximately 60% (that is, 12/20).
6. Save the workbook as Exercise2 and close it.

3. Calculating a Moving Average

Assume someone invests in stock and monitors its value over 24 years. Since the value varies over the long term, you want to smooth the series.

1. Open XL3-0507 and save it as `Exercise3`.
2. Choose Tools, Data Analysis; then select Moving Average and click OK.
3. Type `B2:B26` for the Input Range. Leave the Labels in First Row box unchecked.
4. Type `3` in the Interval box.

   What should the interval be? For quarterly data, the logical number would be 4. For annual data any value could be used. Values of 3 to 5 are typically used.
5. Type `C2` in the Output Range box, and click OK.
6. Select cells `C2:C26` and drag them to the chart.
7. Re-run the moving average using other values for the Interval box.
8. Save and close the Exercise3 workbook.

4. Comparing Two Groups of Data

A sales manager wants to know whether his sales staff is different in the East and West regions.

1. Open XL3-0508 and save it as `Exercise4`.
2. Choose Tools, Data Analysis; then select t-Test: Two-Sample Assuming Equal Variances and click OK.
3. Select cells `B4:B18` for the Variable 1 Range.

   These cells contain the sales for the East region.
4. Select cells `C4:C13` for the Variable 2 Range.

   These cells contain the sales for the West region.
5. In the Hypothesized Mean Difference text box, type `0`, type `.05` in the Alpha text box, and leave the Labels box unchecked.
6. In the Output options area, select New Worksheet Ply, and type the name `t-test` in the text box. Click OK to perform the test.
7. Format the output, as desired.

   Is there a difference between the groups; that is, is the p-value in cell B13 less than .05?
8. Save the changes and close the workbook.

5. Testing for Two Paired Groups of Data

A general manager wants to know whether the number of accidents has decreased after a safety campaign. He collects the number of annual accidents from 15 departments before and after the campaign.

1. Open XL3-0509 and save it as `Exercise5`.
2. Choose Tools, Data Analysis; then select t-Test: Paired Two Sample for Means and click OK.
3. Select cells `B4:B19` for the Variable 1 Range.

   These cells contain the number of accidents before the safety campaign.
4. Select cells `C4:C19` for the Variable 2 Range.

   These cells contain the number of accidents after the safety campaign.
5. In the Hypothesized Mean Difference text box, type `0`, type `.05` in the Alpha text box, and check the Labels box.
6. In the Output options area, select New Worksheet Ply, and type the name `t-test` in the text box. Click OK to perform the test.
7. Format the output, as desired.

   Is there a difference between the groups; that is, is the p-value in cell B13 less than .05?
8. Save and close the workbook.

6. Comparing Production Rates with Anova

A production manager wants to know whether the production rates are different for four different machines.

1. Open XL3-0510 and save the workbook as `Exercise6`.
2. Choose Tools, Data Analysis; then select Anova: Single Factor and click OK.
3. Select cells `B4:E15` for the Input Range.

   Each column in the range represents one of the groups.
4. Select Grouped by Columns, and type `.05` in the Alpha text box. Select the Labels in First Row check box.
5. In the Output options area, select New Worksheet Ply, type the name `ANOVA`, and click OK.
6. Format the output, as desired.

   The p-value in cell F13 is larger than .05 (the Alpha value), which means that the groups are not quite statistically significantly different at the 5% level.
7. Save the changes and close the workbook.

7. Performing a Regression Analysis

A statistics instructor wants to use regression analysis to determine the relationship between absences and grades.

1. Open XL3-0511 and save the workbook as `Exercise7`.
2. Use the Insert, Chart command to create an XY scatter chart, with Absences as the horizontal axis (X) and Grade as the vertical axis (Y).
3. Choose Tools, Data Analysis; then select Regression and click OK.
4. Select cells **B1:B89** for the Input Y range.
5. Select cells **A1:A89** for the Input X range.
6. Check the Labels box and leave the other input boxes unchecked.
7. In the Output options area, select New Worksheet Ply, type the name **Regression**, and click OK.
8. Format the output, as desired.

   The p-value in cell F12 is well under the .05 Alpha level, indicating that there is a statistically significant negative relationship between absences and grades.
9. Save the changes and keep the workbook open for the next exercise.

8. Adding a Trendline to a Chart and Calculating a Predicted Value

The statistics instructor is presenting the results in a committee meeting and wants them in a visual format.

1. Click on the Data worksheet tab of the Exercise7 workbook from the preceding exercise and save the workbook as `Exercise8`.
2. Right-click one of the data points in the scatter chart to display the shortcut menu.
3. Select Add Trendline.
4. In the Add Trendline dialog box, click the Linear box and then click OK.
5. Click on the Regression tab in the workbook.

   Since the instructor has a statistically significant regression analysis, he wants to use it to make a prediction. Assume a student has 5 absences.
6. Type **5** in cell B21.
7. Type **=B18*B21+B17** in cell B22.

   This formula multiplies the input value (B21) times the slope (B18) and adds the intercept (B17). In other words, it calculates the height of the regression line at 5 absences.
8. Enter **2** in cell B21. Cell B22 will show the predicted grade.
9. Save the changes and close the workbook.

Challenge 

Challenge exercises expand on or are somewhat related to skills presented in the lessons. Each exercise provides a brief narrative introduction followed by instructions in a numbered step format that are not as detailed as those in the Skill Drill section.

Each exercise is independent of the others, so that you may complete the exercises in any order. Be sure to save the workbook after completing each exercise. If you need a paper copy of the completed exercise, enter your name centered in a header before printing.

1. Replicating Random Numbers

Occasionally you may want to repeat a particular sequence of random numbers. For example, you may be creating worksheet simulations and you want to be able to replicate particularly interesting outcomes.

1. Start a new workbook and save it as `Challenge1`.
2. Using the Data Analysis Random Number Generation, specify that you want 20 random numbers in cells A1:A20. Select whatever distribution you wish.
3. Enter some integer value in the Random Seed box and click OK.
4. Repeat the operation, but change the output to B1:B20.

   You should find that the numbers in columns A and B are the same.
5. Save and close the workbook.

2. Generating a Distribution of Discrete Random Numbers

The Data Analysis ToolPak allows you to create discrete random numbers that follow a specified distribution. A discrete random number is one where only certain specific values can occur.

1. Start a new workbook and save it as `Challenge2`.

   Assume you want to generate 200 random numbers that would correspond to 40% Chicago, 35% Denver, 25% Phoenix.
2. Enter the following table in cells C2:D4 of your worksheet:

1	40%
2	35%
3	25%

   Assume 1, 2, and 3 represent the three cities. You must enter integer values; you cannot enter the city names.
3. Using the Data Analysis Random Number Generation, specify that you want one variable of 200 random numbers in cells A1:A200.
4. Select Discrete from the Distribution drop-down list and specify `C2:D4` for the Value and Probability Input Range. Click OK.
5. Use a nested IF function or a LOOKUP function to convert the integers to the corresponding city names.
6. Use COUNTIF functions to see how close the distribution is to what you wanted. Repeat the random number generation a few times.
7. Save and close the workbook.

3. Centering a Moving Average

When you create a moving average, the average is aligned with the last value that is averaged; however, the moving average will often fit the original data if it is aligned with the center value.

1. Open the XL3-0512 workbook and save it as `Challenge3`.

   This workbook should have the three-term moving average calculated and plotted on the chart.
2. Select cells C4:C26 and drag them up one row to C3:C25.

   On the chart, note how the moving average line fits the data better because the moving average value is now on the same row as the middle of the three values that are averaged. Check it by choosing Tools, Auditing, Trace Precedents. This is why an odd number of terms is often used in a moving average—so that the moving average can be placed on the center row.

3. Experiment with different moving average terms, such as 4, 5, and 7.
4. Save and close the workbook.

4. Preparing Data for Anova

Often the data for groups you want to compare is in a single column. Because the Anova program requires that the groups be side by side, you need to sort the data into groups and then move the groups so they are side by side.

1. Open the XL3-0513 workbook, and save it as **`Challenge4`**.

   The worksheet contains sales data for three states, and we want to know if the mean sales for the states are different. In order to perform the Analysis of Variance, the data for the three states needs to be placed side-by-side.
2. Click in cell A2 and click the Sort Ascending button.
3. Copy cells B2:B8 to D2:D8; copy B9:B16 to E2:E9; copy B17:B26 to F2:F11.
4. Place the labels **`California`**, **`Florida`**, and **`Indiana`** in cells D1:F1.
5. Run the Anova: Single Factor Data Analysis.

   You should find an F value of 5.69 with a p-value of .0102.
6. Save the workbook and keep it open for the next exercise.

5. Comparing the Anova Test and the t-Test

This exercise shows that when comparing two groups, the single factor Anova and the independent groups t-Test give the same results.

1. Open the Challenge4 workbook from the preceding exercise, and click on the Data tab. Save the workbook as **`Challenge5`**.

   This worksheet should show the completed version with the groups side by side.
2. Perform a Data Analysis using t-Test: Two-Sample Assuming Equal Variances to compare Florida and Indiana sales.
3. Perform a Data Analysis using Anova: Single Factor to compare Florida and Indiana sales.

   You'll find that the two methods give the same p-value, and $t^2 = F$.
4. Save and close the workbook.

6. Exploring Regression

This exercise shows you how to drag points on an XY scatter chart and see the effect on the regression line. In the real world, you would not have the luxury of manipulating your data this way, but it is a very useful tool for learning regression. It is especially useful studying the effect of outliers (data points that don't fit the pattern), since you can easily create and fix outliers by dragging data points.

1. Open the XL3-0514 workbook and save it as **`Challenge6`**.
2. Click cell B32 and type **`156`**.

   Assume the correct value is really 556, but was mistakenly entered as 156. This is called an outlier—a value that is inconsistent with the rest of the data. Outliers are often due to clerical errors, but there could be other reasons. This exercise shows that an outlier can have a substantial impact on an analysis.

3. Re-run the regression and place the results in a new worksheet ply.

   Note the impact of the outlier by comparing the output to the original results. In particular, note the R-Square value. This value can be between 0 and 1—the closer to 1 the better the fit. Also notice the Significance F p-value—the smaller the value, the more significant the result.

   Assuming you determine the correct value really should be 556, you can simply type it in and replace the wrong value, but here is an alternative.

4. Click on the scatter chart to select the data points.
5. Click and hold the left mouse button over the outlier until the cursor changes to a four-tipped arrow. As you drag the point, the current X value will be shown on the screen. Drag it until the value is the original value of 556 or as close as you can get it.
6. Save and close the workbook.

Discovery Zone

Discovery Zone exercises require advanced knowledge of topics presented in *Essentials* lessons, application of skills from multiple lessons, or self-directed learning of new skills. Each exercise is independent of the others, so that you may complete the exercises in any order.

1. Manipulating a Scatter Chart

Open or create a workbook that contains an XY scatter chart (for example, XL3-0506). Right-click the scatter chart to display the shortcut menu, and select Add Trendline; click the Linear box and then click the Options tab. Check the last two boxes to display the equation and R-squared.

Select and drag some of the data points to create outliers, or drag the points closer to the line. You can learn a lot about regression by tinkering with the data points. Just remember that you are doing this in learning mode; you would not have the luxury of modifying data points in real-life situations.

Note that with the options selected, the Trendline output summarizes the most important information of the full regression output.

2. Using Forecasting

Open or create a time-series workbook that includes an XY scatter chart (for example, XL3-0506). Right-click the scatter chart and select Add Trendline from the shortcut menu. On the Type tab, select Linear, but also experiment with other types of lines. On the Options tab, check the last two options. Then, in the Forecast area, use the spin box to forecast three years into the future.

3. Using t-Test and Anova

Use the Data Analysis Tools Random Number Generator to create two groups of normally distributed numbers. First make the groups with nearly the same means and then run the t-Test for two groups as described in Lesson 4. Then, create groups with moderate and large group differences and note the effect on the t-Test.

Do a similar procedure with three or more groups and run the Anova: Single Factor test.

Project 6

Using Goal Seek, Scenarios, Solver, and Auditing Tools

Objectives

In this project, you learn how to

- ➤ Use Auditing Tools to Interpret Error Messages
- ➤ Use Auditing Tools to Check Worksheet Formulas
- ➤ Use Auditing Tools to "Reverse Engineer" a Worksheet
- ➤ Use Goal Seek to Forecast Revenues
- ➤ Perform What-If Analyses with Data Tables
- ➤ Use Scenarios to Perform What-If Analyses
- ➤ Use Solver to Maximize Profits
- ➤ Use Solver to Minimize Costs

Key terms introduced in this project include

- auditing tools
- constraints
- data table
- error value
- Goal Seek
- reverse engineer
- Scenario Manager
- scenarios
- Solver
- what-if analyses

Why Would I Do This?

Due to their ease of use and versatility, spreadsheets are a principal data analysis tool. Data can be changed to reflect different situations, and analyses performed to predict outcomes.

This project uses ***auditing tools*** to examine Excel workbooks and verify the accuracy of your formulas. You learn to use four Excel features—Goal Seek, Data Tables, Scenarios, and Solver to make projections.

Visual Summary

Figure 6.1 shows the summary result of a Scenario analysis that was used to explore various loan payment parameters. Figure 6.1A shows the result of an analysis by the Solver add-in. Solver can be used for many situations. This example shows the minimization of shipping costs when a company has several factories supplying several distribution warehouses.

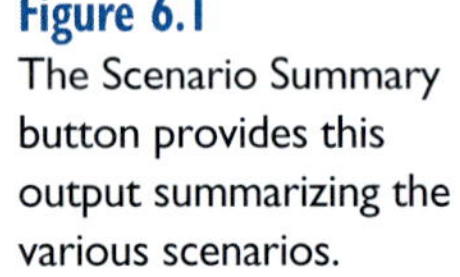

Figure 6.1
The Scenario Summary button provides this output summarizing the various scenarios.

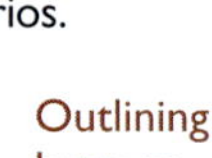

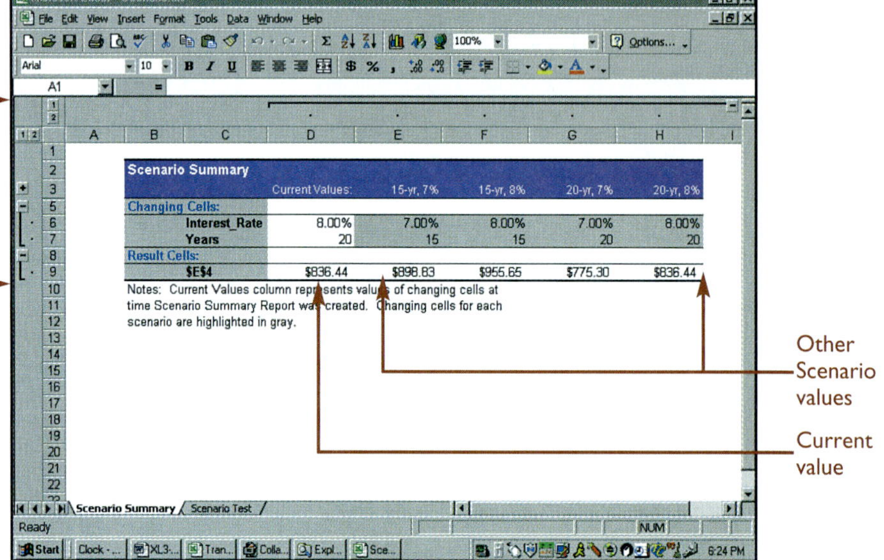

Figure 6.1A
This what-if problem attempts to minimize shipping costs without using Excel's analysis tools. Lesson 8 will use Solver to optimize this data.

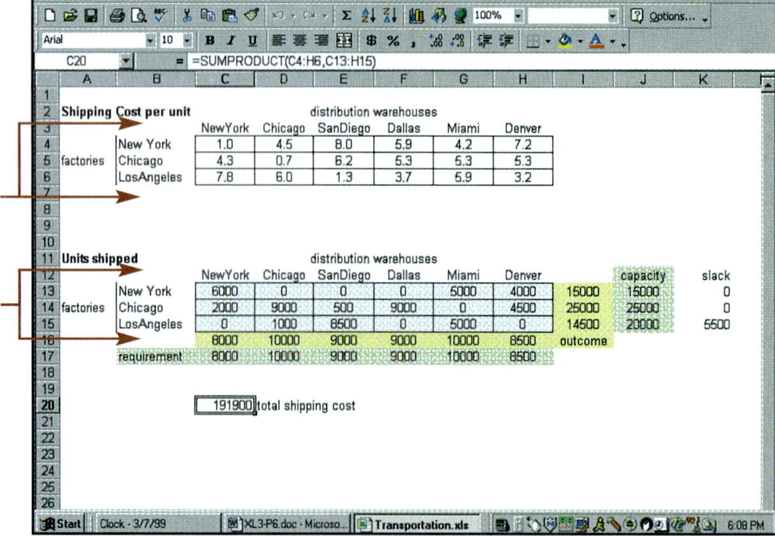

Lesson 1: Using Auditing Tools to Interpret Error Messages

Important decisions can ride on the results of data analysis and projections, so it is critical to verify that your formulas are accurate and your results are valid. The Excel Trace Error auditing tool allows you to find any errors in your worksheet formulas before decisions are made based on the results.

To Use Auditing Tools to Interpret Error Messages

1. **Open the file XL3-0601 and save it as `Welcome Inn Income`.**
   Note that the worksheet is split so that the top and bottom portions of the worksheet can be viewed simultaneously.

2. **Click in cell B11.**

3. **Select Tools, Auditing, Show Auditing Toolbar.**
   See Figure 6.2.

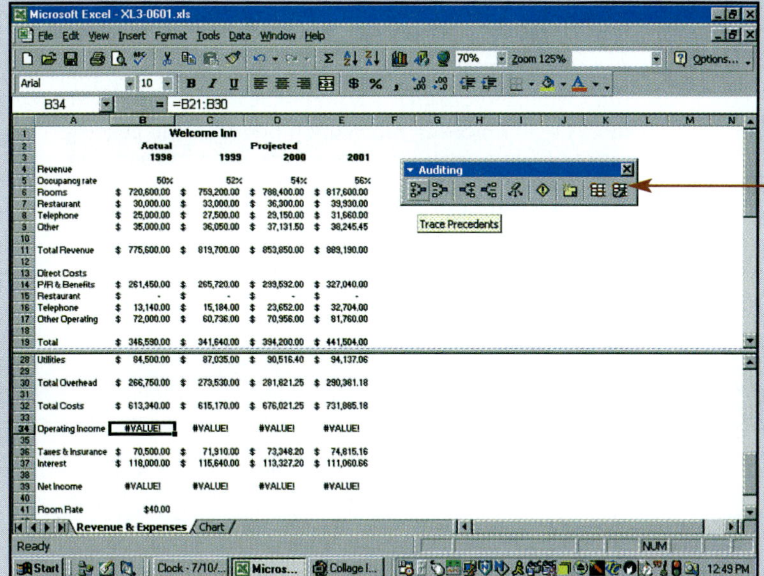

Figure 6.2
The Auditing toolbar provides access to all of the auditing functions.

> The Auditing toolbar may be anchored beneath the Formatting toolbar. To float the Auditing toolbar, place the mouse on the bar-shaped handle along the top or left edge of the toolbar and drag the toolbar onto the worksheet.

4. **Click cell B34.**
   The `#VALUE!` error message is displayed in cells B34:E34 and B39:E39

5. **Click the Trace Error button on the Auditing toolbar.**
   A blue border now surrounds cells B21:B30 that are involved in the error shown in cell B34. You should also see a blue tracer line with an arrow pointing to cell B34 as shown in Figure 6.3.

continues ▶

To Use Auditing Tools to Interpret Error Messages (continued)

Figure 6.3
The Trace Error button generates a trace error line and error dot to identify the cell responsible for the error.

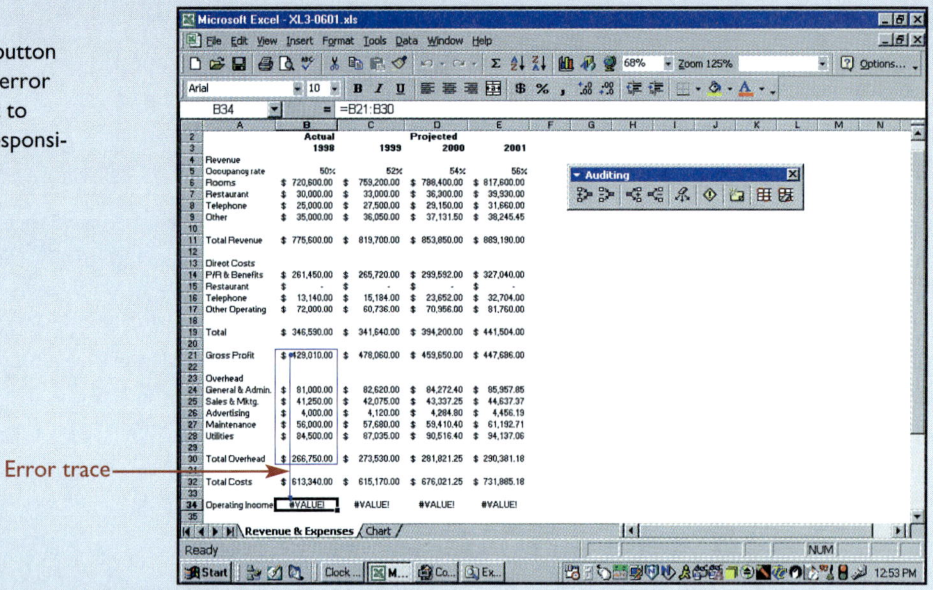

Error trace

A `#VALUE!` error message means that the wrong operand was used in the formula. Note that a colon indicating a range was used, instead of a minus sign indicating subtraction between the cell references.

6 Click the Formula bar; delete the colon and replace it with a minus sign. Press ↵Enter.

7 Copy the formula from cell B34 to cells C34:E34.

You have now corrected the error. Save the changes, and leave the workbook open for the next lesson.

An *error value* is the message code that is displayed to identify a problem in a formula. Review Table 6.1 and then go on to Lesson 2.

Table 6.1 Error Values

Error Value	Description
`#DIV/0!`	The formula is attempting to divide by zero.
`#N/A`	There is no value in the formula.
`#NAME?`	Excel doesn't recognize the name in the formula.
`#NULL!`	An incorrect cell reference or range operator is used in the formula.
`#NUM!`	There is a problem with a number in the formula.
`#REF!`	The formula refers to a cell that is not valid.
`#VALUE!`	The wrong type of operand or argument is used in the formula.

What Does the Red Tracer Line Mean?
Depending on the type of value you are tracing, a red tracer line may appear. A red tracer line points to a formula that is in error rather than to the values involved in the error.

Removing Gridlines
The gridlines can be removed from the worksheet by selecting Tools, Options, and then clicking the View tab. Deselect the Gridlines check box and then click OK to remove the gridlines. This may make it easier to see the arrows and borders as you work through this lesson.

Control Display Size with the Zoom Button
You may want to use the Zoom button on the Standard toolbar to increase the display area. The best zoom factor will depend on your screen size and resolution. Try 70 percent for a start. You can select sizes from the drop-down list or you can type in a value.

Lesson 2: Using Auditing Tools to Check Worksheet Formulas

Trace Precedents and Trace Dependents are auditing tools that enable you to review your worksheets for errors or to help you understand how a worksheet performs its calculations. Trace Precedents shows what cells provide information to the cell and Trace Dependents shows what other cells use the results of the cell.

To Use Auditing Tools to Check Worksheet Formulas

1. **In the Welcome Inn Income workbook, click cell B11.**
   Cell B11 contains the formula you are going to trace.

2. **Click the Trace Precedents button on the Auditing toolbar.**
   A blue tracer line now connects cell B11 to the related cells, as shown in Figure 6.4. By following the tracer line, you can see that cell B9 was erroneously omitted from the SUM function.

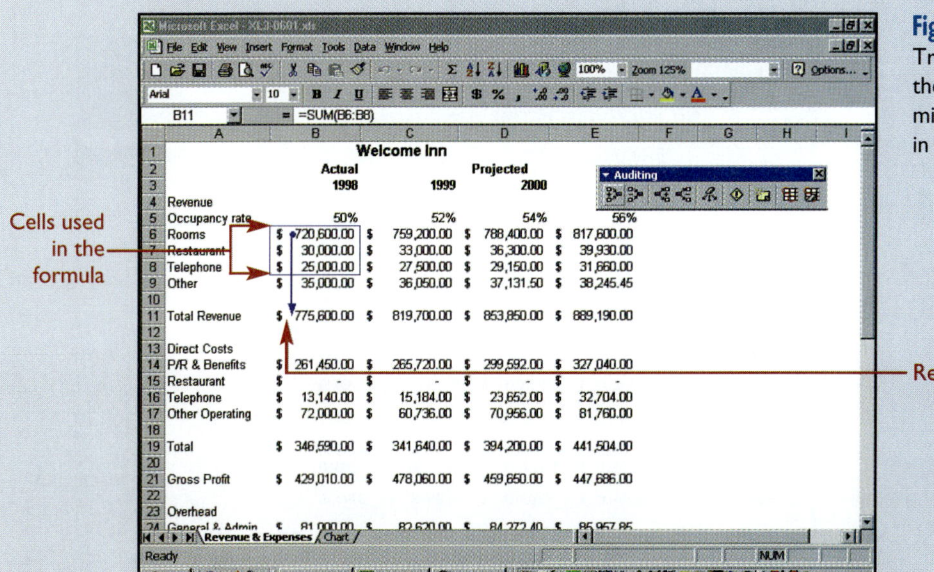

Figure 6.4
Trace Precedents shows the cells used to determine the solution shown in the results cell.

continues ▶

To Use Auditing Tools to Check Worksheet Formulas (continued)

3. **Click cell C11, and click the Trace Precedents button.**
   Note that cell C9 was not included in the total.

4. **Click cell D11, and click the Trace Precedents button.**

5. **Click cell E11, and click the Trace Precedents button.**

> Trace Precedents can trace only one cell at a time. If you select multiple cells, Trace Precedents only traces the first cell chosen. You need to check each cell of a formula. If you create a formula and copy it to other cells, those cells should be checked, too.

6. **Click cell B11. Correct the formula to sum the range B6:B9.**

7. **Copy the formula from cell B11 to cells C11:E11.**

8. **Click cell B32, and click the Trace Precedents button.**
   A blue tracer line points from cell B19 to cell B32. You can see blue dots in cells B19 and B30. These dots indicate that cell B32 uses the values in those cells.

9. **Click the Trace Precedents button again.**
   Each time you click the Trace Precedents button, the trace moves to the next level of cells used by the formula.

10. **Click the Remove All Arrows button on the Auditing toolbar.**
    This action removes all of the tracer lines and arrows.

11. **Click cell B21.**

12. **Click the Trace Dependents button on the Auditing toolbar.**
    This enables you to see which cells reference the formula in cell B21.

13. **Click the Trace Dependents button again to see the next dependent cell.**
    Figure 6.5 shows the results of Trace Dependents.

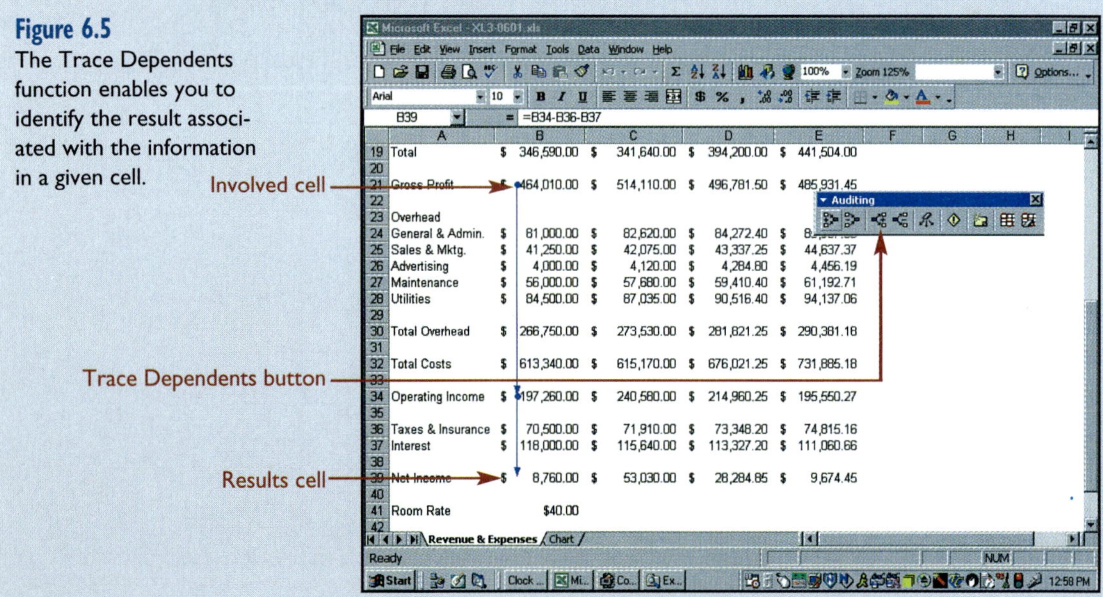

Figure 6.5
The Trace Dependents function enables you to identify the result associated with the information in a given cell.

 ⑭ **Click the Remove All Arrows button.**
Save your changes, and leave the workbook open for Lesson 3.

Disappearing Tracer Lines Do Not Mean the Formula Is Correct
Whenever a change is made to a cell included in a trace, the tracer lines automatically disappear. This does not mean the formula is correct. Retrace the formula to check for accuracy.

Lesson 3: Using Auditing Tools to "Reverse Engineer" a Worksheet

Often you are faced with the task of figuring out how somebody else's worksheet works (or remembering what you did several weeks ago). Determining how somebody else's product works by taking it apart and looking at it is sometimes called ***reverse engineering***.

To Use Auditing Tools to "Reverse Engineer" a Worksheet

① **In the Welcome Inn Income workbook, click in cell C36.**

② **Select Tools, Auditing, Show Auditing Toolbar if it is not already visible.**

③ **Click on the Trace Precedents button.**
This shows that the cell depends on cell B36, but in what way? If you look at the formula bar, you see that cell C36 contains a formula that increases the contents of cell B36 by 2%.

You could do this for every cell, but it would be time-consuming. There is a better way.

④ **Click the drop-down arrow on the Name box, and note any named cells or ranges.**
If you click on the name, the range will be highlighted. If a worksheet utilizes named ranges, it is important to know what cells are being referenced.

⑤ **Choose Tools, Options.**

⑥ **On the View tab, check Formulas under Window options; then click OK.**
This gives a better view of the operations of the worksheet. By using Trace Precedents and Trace Dependents, you can see how a worksheet works. You may need to re-size some columns to see the entire formula.

⑦ **Hold down Ctrl and press ~.**
You will find that you use Ctrl+~ more often than the dialog box method, since you do not have to click through two menu levels to activate it.

Save the changes and leave the workbook open for Lesson 4.

Use Print Preview Setup to Print Cell Formulas
If you want to print cell formulas, go to Print Preview. Then click the Setup button, and select the Sheet tab. Check the Gridlines and Row and Column Headings boxes. Otherwise, you will have cell references but no way of knowing where the cell is. In most worksheets, it is also useful to use Landscape printing for cell formulas.

Lesson 4: Using Goal Seek to Forecast Revenues

Goal Seek is a Microsoft Excel tool that allows you to determine a formula variable when you know the result. A simple example would be determining how many units would have to be sold to gross a given amount when you know the price per unit.

To Use Goal Seek to Forecast Revenues

1. **In the Welcome Inn Income workbook, select cell D6.**
   This cell contains the projected revenue for rooms in the year 2000, based on a 54% occupancy rate.

2. **Select Tools, Goal Seek.**

3. **Click the To value text box and type `800000`.**
   This is the new revenue amount you want to project.

4. **Click the By changing cell text box, and click cell D5 in the worksheet.**
   Cell D5 is the location of the cell that contains the value you want to change. Figure 6.6 shows the Goal Seek dialog box.

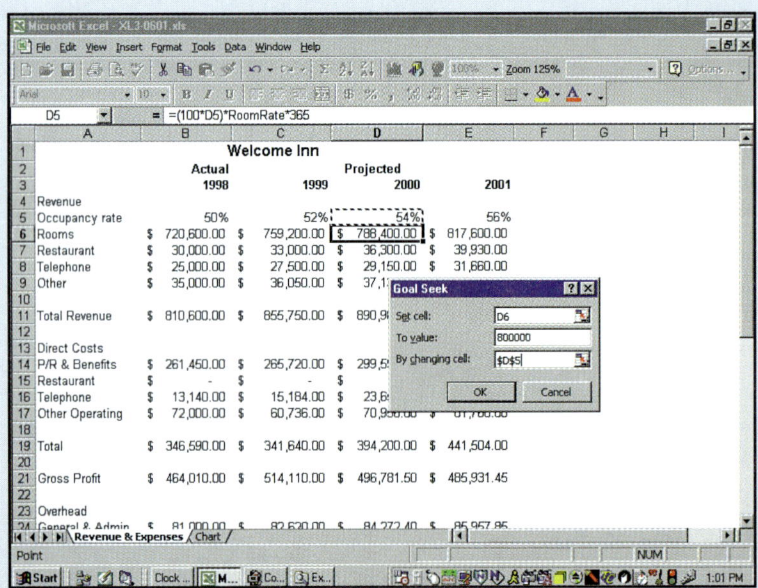

Figure 6.6
Input variables are entered into the Goal Seek dialog box.

5. **Click OK.**
   The Goal Seek Status dialog box indicates when the solution has been reached, as shown in Figure 6.7.

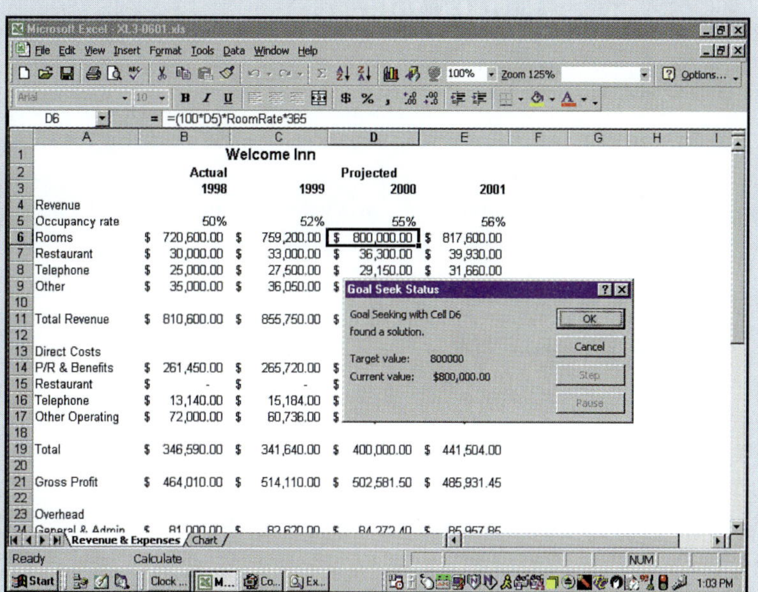

Figure 6.7
Goal Seek results are shown in the Goal Seek Status dialog box.

6 Click OK again.

The Goal Seek Status dialog box closes and the worksheet reflects the new cell values.

7 Click on cell D5, and notice in the formula bar that the answer is actually around 54.79%, not 55% even.

Save the workbook as Welcome Inn Income 2, and close the workbook.

Use a Value for the Changing Cell, Not a Formula

The variable cell you enter in the By changing cell box must be a value. Goal Seek cannot operate correctly if the cell contains a formula. If the cell contains a formula, Goal Seek displays an alert box.

You Can Undo the Goal Seek Operation

To change your worksheet back to the original values before the Goal Seek operation, click the Undo button on the Standard toolbar.

Lesson 5: Performing What-If Analyses with Data Tables

What-if analyses involving several variations on only one or two variables can be accomplished with data tables. A ***data table*** is a range of cells that shows how changing certain values in your formula affects the results of the formula.

In the following example, you explore how the length of the loan affects mortgage loan monthly payments and the total payback over the period of the loan.

To Perform What-If Analyses with Data Tables

1. **Open XL3-0602, and save it as `DataTable`.**
2. **Examine the payment formula in cell B7 and the total payback cells in C7:C10.**

   Examining the contents of a worksheet to understand how it works is what we have described as "reverse engineering" in Lesson 3.
3. **Select cells A7:B10.**
4. **Choose Data, Table.**
5. **The Table dialog box will be visible. Click in the Column input cell box.**
6. **Click on cell A7, and click OK.**

   Figure 6.8 shows the completed Table dialog box.

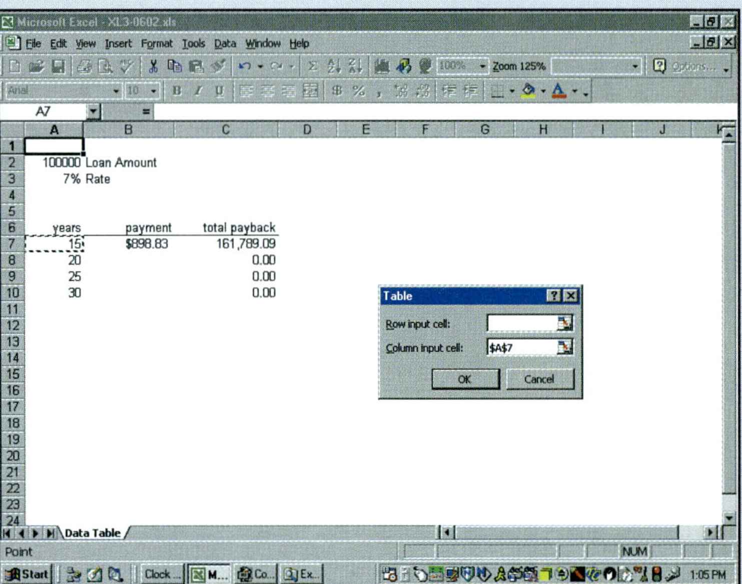

Figure 6.8
Input values are entered into the Table dialog box.

Note that as the length of the loan increases, the payment becomes less, but the total payback increases. As you change the loan amount and interest rate, the table will be updated.

Save the changes, close the workbook, and go on to Lesson 6.

Lesson 6: Using Scenarios to Perform What-If Analyses

Scenario Manager is a means of saving multiple input values and results (*scenarios*). This can be useful when you have several what-if assumptions and want to be able to present the results of all of them on your model. For example, you might want to know the effect of various combinations of interest rates and number of payments on the size of a loan payment. You could certainly type the values in directly; however, the Scenario Manager makes the process easier.

To Use Scenarios to Perform What-If Analyses

1. **Open XL3-0603, and save it as `Scenario`.**

2. **Look at the cell formulas and the named ranges; use Trace Precedents and Trace Dependents for the key cells.**
   In other words, reverse engineer the worksheet as described in Lesson 3 to figure out how it works. Note that there are named cells in the worksheet.

3. **Select Tools, Scenarios.**
   The Scenario Manager dialog box will appear as shown in Figure 6.9.

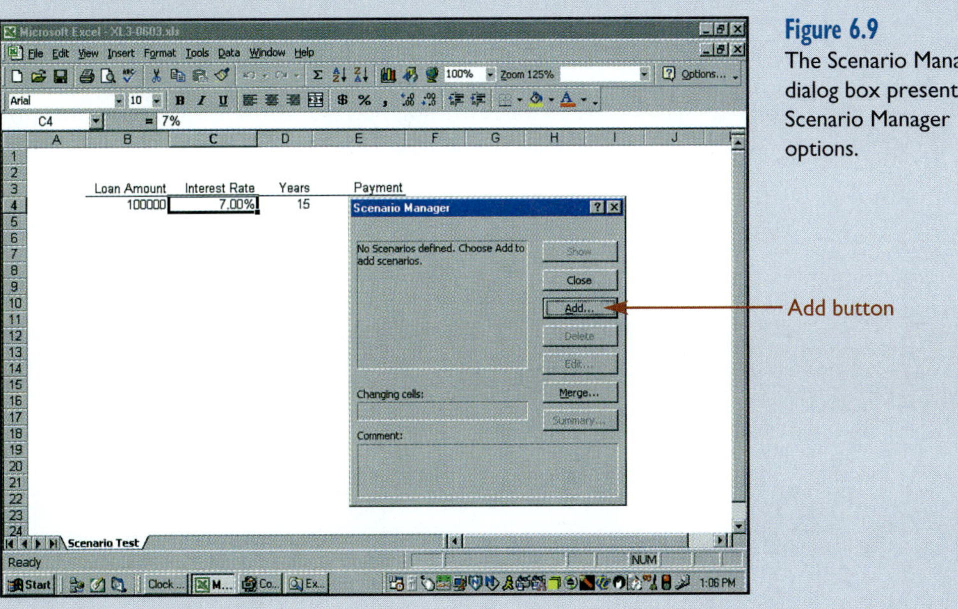

Figure 6.9
The Scenario Manager dialog box presents the Scenario Manager options.

4. **Using the Office Assistant or Excel Help, search for Scenario, and explore the help topics relating to the Scenario Manager.**

5. **Click the Add button in the Scenario Manager dialog box to display the Add Scenario dialog box, and then type `15yr, 7%` in the Scenario Name text box.**
   The Edit Scenario dialog box is displayed, as shown in Figure 6.10.

continues ▶

To Use Scenarios to Perform What-If Analyses (continued)

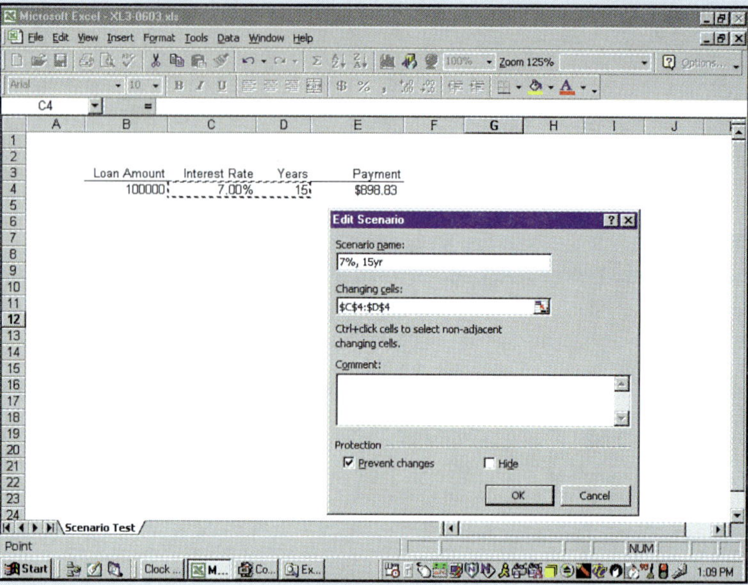

Figure 6.10
Scenario parameters are entered into the Edit Scenario dialog box.

6 Click in the Changing Cells text box, and then select cells C4:D4 and click OK.

The Scenario Values dialog box should be displayed as shown in Figure 6.11 with the appropriate values in place.

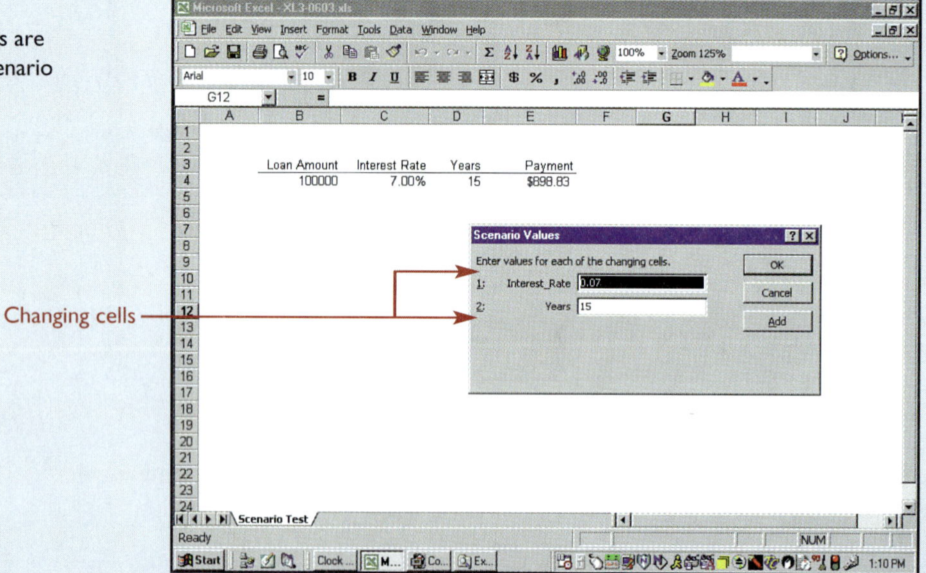

Figure 6.11
Changing cell values are displayed in the Scenario Values dialog box.

7 Click on the Add button, and type `15yr, 8%` in the Scenario Name text box, and click OK.

You have now set up the second scenario.

8 Type `8%` in the Interest Rate text box of the Scenario Values dialog box and type `15` in the years box.

9. **Click on the Add button, and type `20yr, 7%` in the Scenario Name text box, and click OK.**

10. **Type `7%` in the Interest Rate text box of the Scenario Values dialog box, and type `20` in the Years box.**

11. **Click on the Add button, and type `20yr, 8%` in the Scenario Name text box, and click OK.**

12. **Type `8%` in the Interest Rate text box, and type `20` in the Years text box of the Scenario Values dialog box, and click OK.**

    You have now set all four possible scenarios.

13. **Click on `20yr, 8%`; then click the Show button.**

    The results of this scenario are now displayed on your worksheet. To display the results of the other scenarios, click on the scenario name, and then click the Show button.

14. **Click on the Summary button on the Scenario Manager dialog box.**

15. **Click on the Scenario summary option, and in the Result cells box, click on cell E4 to specify the results cell. Then click OK.**

    The Scenario Summary is shown in Figure 6.12. Notice that the summary output includes outlining symbols. Click on them to see how they expand or contract the output.

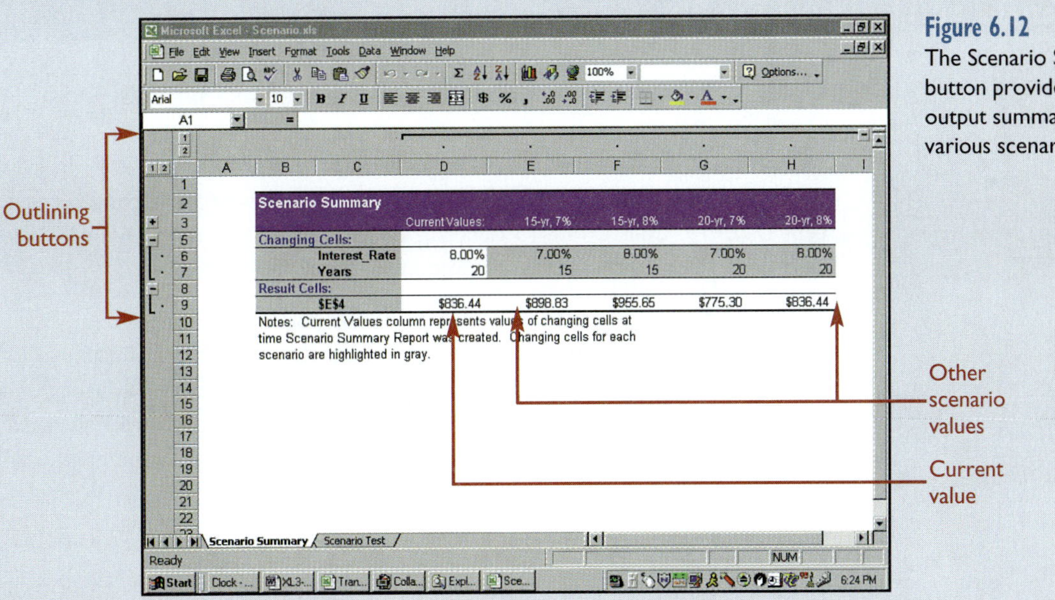

Figure 6.12
The Scenario Summary button provides this output summarizing the various scenarios.

Save the changes and close the workbook.

If you are thinking that data tables in Lesson 5 and scenarios in Lesson 6 do pretty much the same thing, you are correct. Data tables are easier to use, but scenarios have the advantage of being able to view different possible outcomes and add other possibilities.

Lesson 7: Using Solver to Maximize Profits

Solver, like Goal Seek, enables you to manipulate variables to achieve a known result. The difference is that Solver enables you to do much more complex problem solving, because you can alter multiple variables and apply ***constraints*** to the changes. A constraint reflects the fact that all resources are limited. We never have an infinite amount of time, raw materials, labor, and so on, nor can we sell an infinite amount of what we produce. Also, constraints can reflect that we may have to have a certain amount of specific ingredients in a product or that we have sales commitments for a certain number of items. Constraints are usually stated as "less than" or "greater than" but we can also have "equal to" constraints.

Assume a factory produces two models of their product: Standard and Deluxe. The Standard and Deluxe models respectively contribute $19 and $24 to profit. How many of each should we produce each month to maximize profit? Obviously we cannot produce and sell an infinite amount of each—the world has constraints on how much we can produce and sell.

The product has two manufacturing operations, machining and assembly. Each month we have 2,500 machining hours available and 800 assembly hours. Each Standard model requires 4 hours machining and 2.5 hours assembly; the Deluxe model requires 9 hours machining and 2 hours assembly. The following exercise shows you how to use Solver to maximize profits in this example.

To Use Solver to Maximize Profits

1. **Open XL3-0604 and save it as `Solver`, and then examine its contents.**
   The purpose of this workbook is to determine the production levels in cells B5:C5 that will maximize the revenue in cell D8, subject to the constraints in cells D12:F15. Cells D14:D15 calculate the machining and assembly hours and cells F14:F15 show the maximum amount of hours available.

2. **Enter some values in cells B5:C5 to see if you can find the combination that will give the largest possible profit in cell D8.**
   If the value you enter is too large, the "hrs. used" cells will be highlighted with Conditional Formatting to indicate that the constraint has been violated. If one of the "slack" values is positive, it means that there is under-utilized capacity.

   Even if you are persistent enough to find what you think is the correct answer, how could you be sure it was really the best combination? As you have probably guessed, Excel has a better way to find the answer.

3. **Select Tools, Solver.**
   Figure 6.13 shows the Solver Properties dialog box.

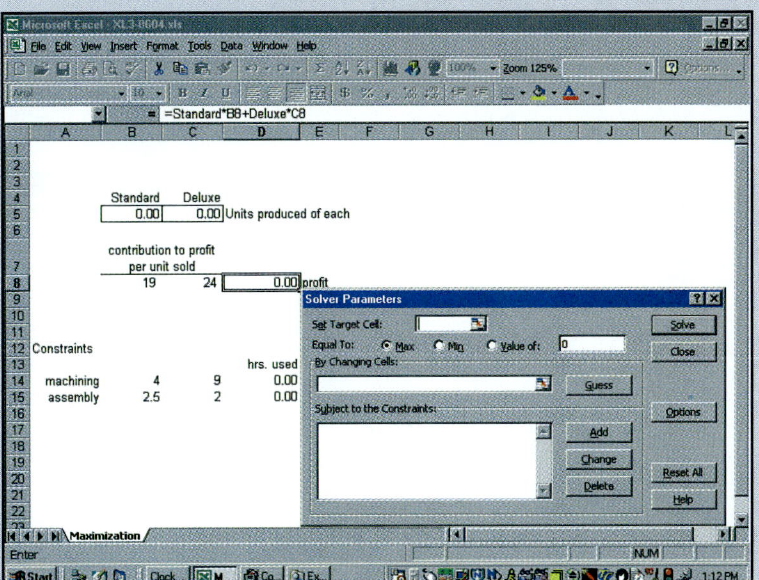

Figure 6.13
Problem parameters are set in the Solver Properties dialog box.

Solver is not an intrinsic part of Microsoft Excel—it is an add-in. If your Tools menu does not include Solver, you need to install it. Select Tools, Add-Ins. Scroll down the list box until you find Solver Add-in and then click on it, and click OK. If Excel asks if you want to install, click Yes. You will probably need your Microsoft Office CD.

All of the input boxes in the Solver Parameters dialog box should be blank. If not, click the Reset All button, and click OK in the resulting message box.

4. **Click the Help button in the dialog box, and explore the help topics related to Solver.**

5. **Click in the Set Target Cell box, and then click cell D8.**
   Cell D8 calculates the revenue. This is the value we want to maximize. The official name for this cell is the "objective function."

6. **Beside Equal To, click the Max option button.**

7. **Click in the By Changing Cells box and then select cells B5:C5.**
   These cells contain the number of units produced of the Standard and Deluxe models.

8. **Click in the Subject to the Constraints box, and then click Add to display the Add Constraint dialog box.**

9. **Click in the Cell Reference box, and then click cell D14.**

10. **In the operator box in the middle of the dialog box, select the "<=" operator if it is not already visible.**

11. **Click in the Constraint box, and then click cell F14.**
    This is the constraint for machining hours as shown in Figure 6.14.

continues ▶

To Use Solver to Maximize Profits (continued)

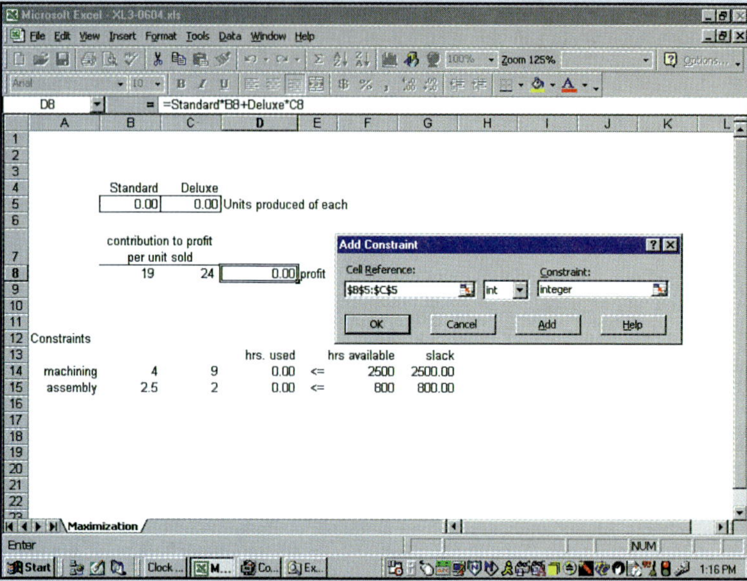

Figure 6.14
Problem constraints are entered into the Add Constraint dialog box.

12 Click the Add button, and then create another constraint that says D15 <= F15 ; then click Add.

This is the constraint for assembly hours.

13 Click the Cell Reference box, and select cells B5:C5.

14 Click the drop-down arrow for type of constraint, click on int, and then click OK.

This constraint forces the answer to be an integer, because we cannot produce fractional units.

As long as you are adding constraints, click Add; when you have added the last constraint, click OK. After you click OK, your screen should look like Figure 6.15.

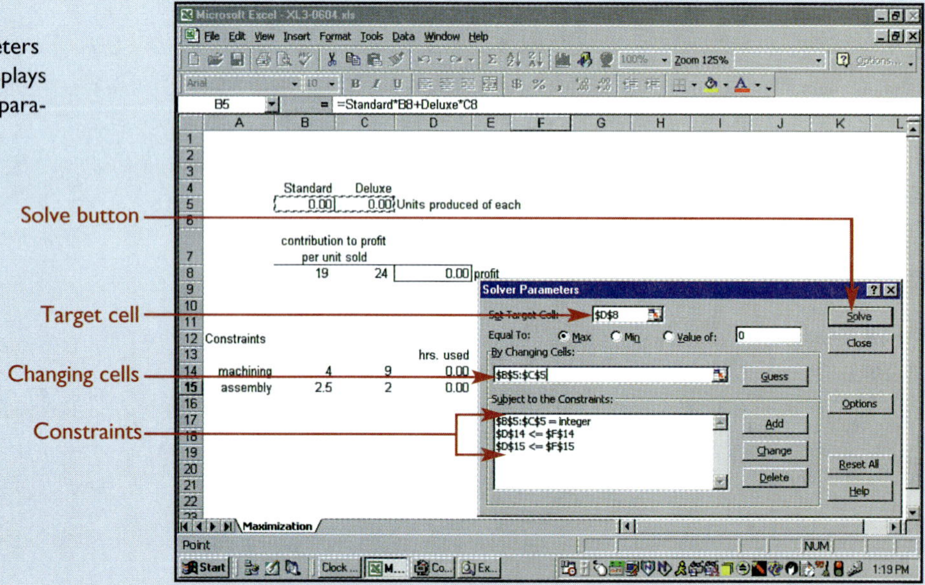

Figure 6.15
The Solver Parameters dialog box now displays all of the problem parameters.

15 **Click the Solve button to calculate the solution.**

Figure 6.16 shows the Solver Results dialog box.

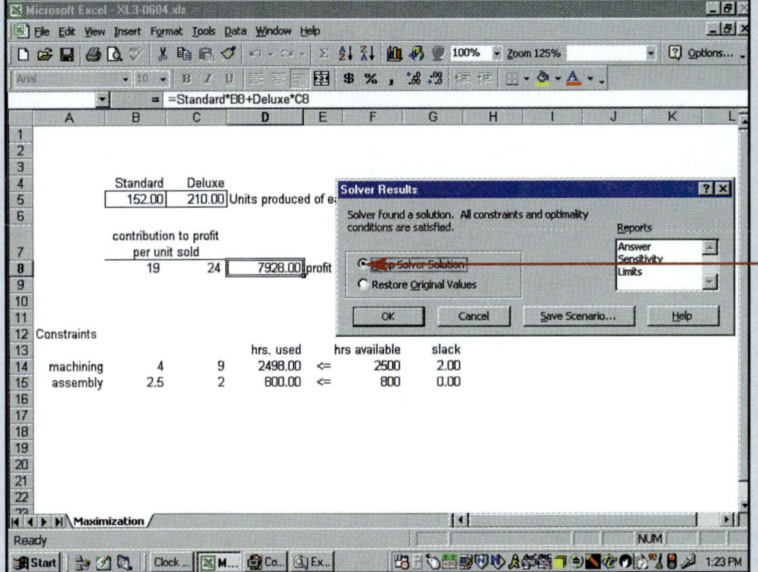

Figure 6.16
The Solver Results dialog box provides options for keeping the worksheet changes.

16 **Click the Keep Solver Solution option button, and click OK.**

Make note of the maximum profit and then try some other values in cells B5:C5 to convince yourself that the Solver values are indeed the optimum values.

Save the workbook, and close it.

Solver Solutions Cannot Be Undone

The Keep Solver Solution option in the Solver Results dialog box is the default option. If you choose to keep the solution, you should know that the change is permanent and cannot be undone. It is a good idea to make a backup copy of your original worksheet to retain it for future use.

Solver Values Are Saved with the Workbook

Solver results and parameters remain even after the workbook is saved and closed, so you can access your scenario when the workbook is reopened.

Lesson 8: Using Solver to Minimize Costs

Solver can also be used to minimize costs. One common application is known as the transportation model. If a company has several factories and several warehouses, what is the best way to ship items to the warehouses in order to minimize shipping cost?

To Use Solver to Minimize Costs

1 Open XL3-0605, and save it as `Transportation`.

2 Examine the worksheet's contents.

The Transportation workbook shows an initial allocation of shipments from the factories to the warehouses (refer to Figure 6.1A in the Visual Summary); however, we do not know whether this is the best solution.

- Cells C4:H6 show the cost per unit of shipping one unit from any factory to any warehouse.
- Cells C13:H15 show the units shipped.
- Cell C20 uses a SUMPRODUCT function to calculate the total shipping cost by multiplying shipping cost times units shipped. This is the objective function that we want to maximize.
- The cells shown in green indicate the capacity of each factory and the requirements of each warehouse. Note that the total capacity is larger than the total warehouse requirement, so the final solution will show some slack.
- The cells shown in yellow represent the actual amount produced/shipped.

Assume you are the shipping manager without the benefit of using Excel's Solver.

3 Enter some values in cells C13:H15 to see if you can minimize cost while getting the correct number of units to the warehouses without exceeding factory capacity.

You would ship as much as you could to the lowest cost warehouses that are near the factories, but after that it becomes challenging. It is fairly easy to get a solution that is feasible, but you don't know if it is optimal. Make note of your best solution, and see how it compares to the Solver solution.

4 Select Tools, Solver.

All of the input boxes should be blank. Otherwise, click the Reset All button.

5 Make your Solver Parameters dialog box look like the one in Figure 6.17.

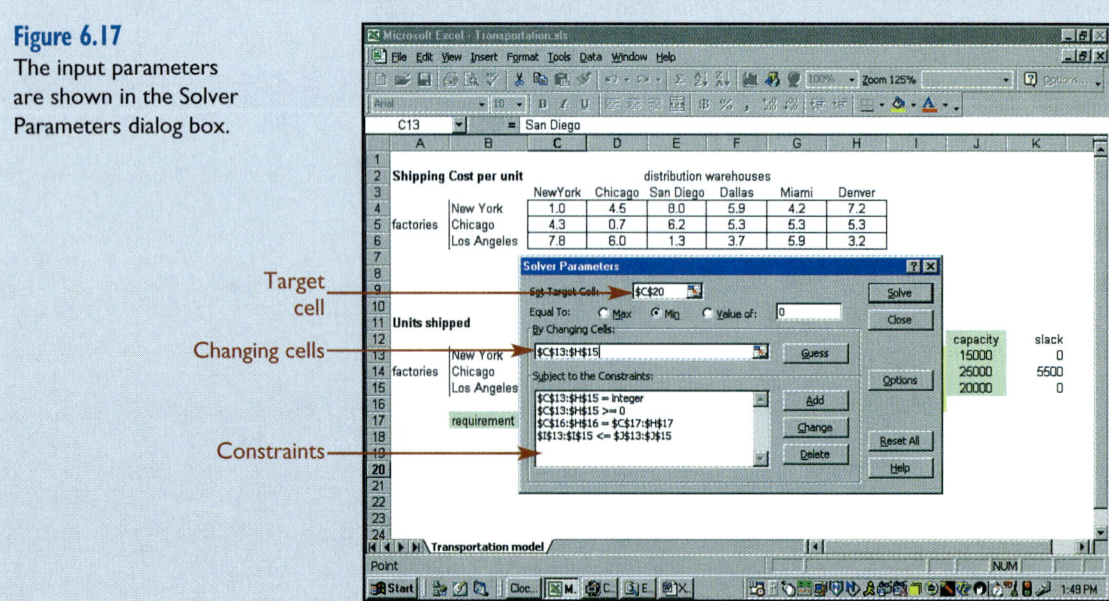

Figure 6.17
The input parameters are shown in the Solver Parameters dialog box.

Select the appropriate cell ranges—don't just type them in. As you are creating the constraints, note their purpose: The first one makes the quantities integers, and the second one forces non-negative answers. The third constraint sets the warehouse requirements. It could have been entered as five separate constraints but it works to enter ranges. The last constraint is for factory capacity.

6. **Click the Solve button.**

7. **Click the Keep Solver Solution option, and click OK.**
   Figure 6.18 shows the final Solver solution output.

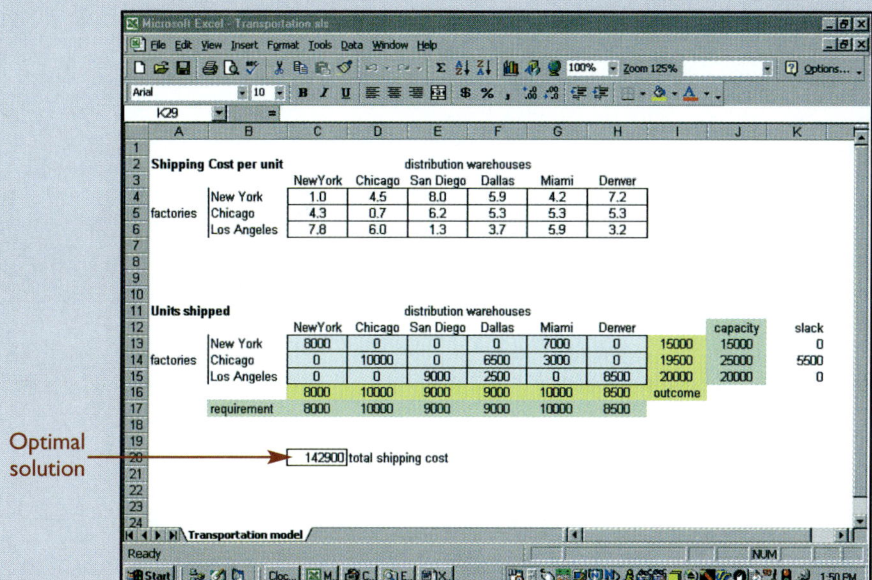

Figure 6.18
Final Solver solution for the problem shown in Figure 6.17.

Save the changes, and close the workbook.

Summary

In this project, you have learned how to use Excel's auditing tools to verify the accuracy of your worksheet formulas. You have also seen four Microsoft Excel tools for doing what-if analysis. Data tables are appropriate in instances where you are trying multiple versions of just one or two variables. You would use Goal Seek when you know the result you want and are looking for the variables to achieve that result. Solver is similar to Goal Seek in that it is used when the result is known, but Solver can work with several variables and apply constraints to those variables. Scenario Manager enables you to set up several variable situations and save them for later use.

You can explore your knowledge of these topics by exploring Help topics; however, to get in-depth knowledge of Solver topics you would need to read a book on linear programming and/or operations management; or, if you are really serious about it, take a course in operations management.

Checking Concepts and Terms 

True/False

For each of the following, check *T* or *F* to indicate whether the statement is true or false.

__T __F **1.** The Trace Dependents tool is used to show the cells to which a formula refers. [L1]

__T __F **2.** $C$4 is an error value. [L1]

__T __F **3.** Goal Seek is used when the result is known. [L4]

__T __F **4.** You can enter multiple cell references in a Solver text box by separating them with a comma. [L7]

__T __F **5.** Solutions found through Solver cannot be saved for future use. [L7]

__T __F **6.** In auditing tools, the blue tracer arrow points to a value error. [L1]

__T __F **7.** You may trace precedents for multiple cells by highlighting them all at once. [L2]

__T __F **8.** If you select the Keep Solver Solution option, the changes in the worksheet will be permanent. [L7]

__T __F **9.** In the Scenario dialog box, the Add button enables you to enter additional scenarios. [L6]

__T __F **10.** A data table enables you to test several options for a single variable. [L5]

Multiple Choice

Circle the letter of the correct answer for each of the following.

1. When the Trace Precedents tool is used, a red tracer line shows [L1]

a. the cells being referred to in the active cell formula

b. the cells with formulas that reference the active cell

c. the errors in the formula in the active cell

d. none of the above

2. Which error value suggests that the wrong kind of operand or argument is used in the formula? [L1]

a. `#NAME?`

b. `#REF!`

c. `#VALUE!`

d. `#N/A`

3. Use the Auditing toolbar to access which of the following auditing options? [L1]

a. Trace Precedents

b. Trace Dependents

c. Remove All Arrows

d. all of the above

4. When a solution is found with Solver, [L7]

a. the worksheet is automatically updated with the designated changes

b. you can keep the Solver solution or restore the original values

c. you can specify Solver reports

d. both B and C are correct

5. Which of the following is an operand? [L1]

a. `$D$5`

b. `#NULL!`

c. `+`

d. `<:>`

6. Constraints can be applied to a variable in [L7]

a. Data Tables

b. Goal Seek

c. Solver

d. Scenario Manager

7. Which of the following is a Microsoft Excel add-in? [L7]
   a. Scenario Manager
   b. Solver
   c. Goal Seek
   d. none of the above
8. "Reverse Engineering" is a term used in the context of Excel to mean [L2]
   a. doing what-if analyses when the expected outcome is known
   b. "taking apart" and examining a worksheet
   c. doing Goal Seek analysis
   d. doing Solver analysis
9. Microsoft Excel's Auditing tools are used for [Why]
   a. accounting scenarios
   b. validating outcomes
   c. financial functions
   d. none of the above

Discussion Questions

1. You work for a manufacturing company that is considering the purchase of new equipment to increase its productivity. Assuming that you know the cost of the new equipment, what analysis tool would you use to determine the parameters that would make the new equipment profitable?
2. Your company has decided to obtain the equipment but now must decide whether to purchase or lease. How can analysis tools help make this decision?
3. A competitor is offering free shipping. What analysis tools would you use to help determine how to respond?

Skill Drill

Skill Drill exercises reinforce project skills. Each skill reinforced is the same, or nearly the same, as a skill presented in the project. Detailed instructions are provided in a step-by-step format.

1. Using Auditing Tools

In this exercise, you use Auditing tools to find a formula error.

1. Open XL3-0606, and save it as `Exercise1`.
2. Click cell B39.
3. Choose Tools, Auditing, Trace Error.
4. Click in cell B11.
5. Fix the error. It should read `=SUM(B6:B9)`.
6. Choose Tools, Auditing, Remove All Arrows.
7. Save the changes and keep the workbook open for the next exercise.

2. Using Goal Seek

This exercise uses Goal Seek to forecast revenues.

1. Save the Exercise1 workbook as `Exercise2`.
2. Click cell D39.
3. Select Tools, Goal Seek.
4. Click the To value text box and type `50000`.
5. Click the By changing cell text box and click cell D5 in the worksheet.
6. Click OK.

   After reviewing the results, you decide that $50,000 is not the goal you want to use.
7. Save and close the workbook.

3. Using Solver to Maximize Portfolio Investment

An investment portfolio manager has to allocate funds between safe, moderate, and risky investments given certain constraints imposed by the company.

1. Open XL3-0607 and save it as `Exercise3`.
2. Examine the worksheet to determine how it works.
3. Choose Tools, Solver and click the Reset All button if the cells are not empty.
4. Set the options to maximize cell C3 by changing cells C7:E7.
5. Add the constraints listed in rows 11 through 15.
6. Add a constraint to force cells C7:E7 to be non-negative.
7. Click the Solve button.

   The optimal amount should be $8,200.
8. Save and close the workbook.

4. Using Solver to Minimize Transportation Cost

A company imports products from three ports (New York, Miami, and San Francisco) and sends them to four distribution centers (Chicago, Dallas, Denver, and Los Angeles). The company wants to minimize shipping costs from the ports to the distribution centers.

1. Open XL3-0608, and save it as `Exercise4`.
2. Examine the workbook, and determine how it works.
3. Enter values in cells C13:F15 to see if you can find a combination that you think minimizes cost while satisfying the constraints.
4. Choose Tools, Solver, and click the Reset All button if the cells are not empty.
5. Set the options to minimize cell C20 by changing cells C13:F15.
6. Add the constraints for distribution center requirements and the port capacity.
7. Add a constraint to force cells C13:F15 to be non-negative and integers.
8. Click the Solve button. (The minimum cost should be $184,600.)
9. Save and close the workbook.

5. Using Data Tables

In this exercise you will use Data Tables to examine the total amount of loan payback based on various loan parameters.

1. Open XL3-0609, and save it as `Exercise5`.
2. Examine the worksheet to see how it works.

   In particular, examine the formulas in cell A7, cells A8:A18, and cells H8:K18.

   In this worksheet you want to vary the interest rate and the number of years to see the impact on the payment and total payback. The payment table on the left will calculate the payments, and the total payback table on the right will use the results to calculate the total payback.
3. Select cells A7:E18.
4. Choose Data, Table.
5. Click cell A4 for the Row input cell, and click cell A3 for the Column input cell. Click OK.

   Note the effect of the interest rate and number of years.

   Experiment with different values for the loan amount and interest rate.
6. Save and close the workbook.

6. Using Scenario Manager

In this exercise you are going to use Scenario Manager to evaluate mortgage options. The house costs $285,000 and your variables are the amount you will mortgage and the term of the mortgage.

1. Open a new workbook, and name it `Exercise6`.
2. Type `250000` in cell B4. Type `Loan Amount` in cell C4.
3. Type `6.25%` in cell B5. Type `Interest Rate` in cell C5.
4. Type `15` in cell B6. Type `Term` in cell C6.
5. Type `Payment` in cell C8.
6. Name cells B4:B6 "Amount," "Rate," and "Term" respectively, using the Name box.
7. Enter `=PMT(Rate/12,Term*12,-Amount)` in cell B8.
8. Select Tools, Scenarios.
9. Click the Add button, and type `230K, 15-yr` in the Scenario Name text box.
10. Click in the Changing Cells text box, and then select cells B4:B6 and click OK.
11. Click on the Add button, type `230K, 30-yr` in the Scenario Name text box, and click OK.
12. Now create scenarios for 250K at 15 years, and 250K at 30 years by following the steps outlined for the previous scenarios.
13. Click OK.

    You have now set all four possible scenarios.
14. Click on 230K,15-yr in the Scenarios list; then click the Show button.
15. Check the results of each scenario and click the Summary button to summarize the scenarios.
16. Save and close the workbook.

Challenge 

Challenge exercises expand on or are somewhat related to skills presented in the lessons. Each exercise provides a brief narrative introduction followed by instructions in a numbered step format that are not as detailed as those in the Skill Drill section.

Each exercise is independent of the others, so that you may complete the exercises in any order. Be sure to save the workbook after completing each exercise. If you need a paper copy of the completed exercise, enter your name centered in a header before printing.

1. Updating a Chart with Goal Seek

Goal Seek can also be used to forecast results to a chart. In this exercise you forecast revenues with Goal Seek and post the results to a chart.

1. Open XL3-0610, and save it as `Challenge1`. Click the Chart sheet tab.

    The Revenue data in this chart is reflected in the column bars.
2. Click the Revenue & Expenses tab and select cell D6.

    This cell contains the projected revenue for rooms in the year 2000, based on 54% occupancy.
3. Select Tools, Goal Seek.
4. Click the To value text box, and type `850000`.
5. Click the By changing cell text box, and click cell D5 in the worksheet. Click OK.
6. Click on the Chart sheet tab.

    The chart should reflect the changes.
7. Save the changes and keep the workbook open for the next exercise.

2. Activating Goal Seek from a Chart

Use the following steps to do a projection for 2001.

1. Open the Challenge1 workbook if it is not open from the previous lesson. Save the workbook as `Challenge2`, and then click the Chart sheet.

2. Click the last column of the chart, which represents 2001.
3. Click the last Revenue column marker again.
4. Drag the handle at the top of the column to the $970,000 mark.

   You return to the Revenue & Expenses worksheet and the Goal Seek dialog box is displayed. The Set cell text box reads E11 and the To value text box should read 970,000. If these values are not in the text boxes, click Cancel and readjust the column marker or type in the number.
5. Type `E5` in the By changing cell text box, and click OK.

   Both the worksheet and the chart should reflect the solution.
6. Click OK, save the changes, and close the workbook.

A Chart Must Be Linked in Order to Perform Goal Seek
Goal Seek can only be activated from a chart when the data series that you are importing is linked to a formula cell in the worksheet.

3. Additional Options with Solver

In this exercise you are going to generate a Solver Answer report.

1. Open XL3-0611, and save it as `Challenge3`.

   This workbook is the completed Solver exercise from Lesson 7.
2. Select Tools, Solver.
3. Click the Solve button.
4. In the Solver Results box, click Answer in the Reports list box.
5. Click OK. A new worksheet tab is created.
6. Open the new worksheet and examine the contents.
7. Save and close the workbook.

4. Saving Solver Models

When you go to the trouble of creating a Solver model you may want to save the values so you can run it again later, perhaps making some changes to the model or the input data.

1. Open XL3-0612 and save it as `Challenge4`.
2. Select Tools, Solver.
3. Click the Options button.
4. Click the Save Model button.
5. In the Select Model Area box, click on cell J20. Click OK.
6. In the Solver Options dialog box, click Cancel. In the Solver Parameters dialog box, click the Reset All button and then click OK.
7. Click the Options button, and then click the Load Model button.
8. Enter J20 in the Load Model dialog box and click OK to restore the Solver options. Click Cancel, and then Close to close the dialog boxes.
9. Save and close the workbook.

5. Adding Solver Constraints

If new constraints become necessary, they can be added to the existing solver model.

1. Open Challenge3 (or XL3-0611) and save it as `Challenge5`.
2. Open Solver, and note the current constraints.
3. Add constraints as described below.

   Assume that the sales department says we have to produce at least 170 Standard items in order to meet sales commitments, and we cannot sell more than 200 units of the Deluxe model.
4. Click the Solve button.
5. Add a constraint to say that we must produce 500 units of the Deluxe model.
6. Click the Solve button.

   There is not enough capacity to produce this many Deluxe units, so you see how Solver responds with a non-feasible constraint.
7. Experiment with some other constraints.
8. Save and close the workbook.

Discovery Zone 

Discovery Zone exercises require advanced knowledge of topics presented in *Essentials* lessons, application of skills from multiple lessons, or self-directed learning of new skills. Each exercise is independent of the others, so that you may complete the exercises in any order.

1. Using Solver with Linear Programming Examples

Find an Operations Management or Linear Programming textbook and look for some linear programming examples. Most introductory business mathematics and quantitative methods textbooks would also have chapters on linear programming. Attempt to solve the examples using Solver.

2. Using Goal Seek to Shop for Interest Rates

Use Goal Seek to determine what interest rate would be needed in order to have the payment be $350 for a loan of $15,000 for 48 months.

Integrating Applications with OLE

Objectives

In this project, you learn how to

- **Link Excel Data to a Word Document**
- **Edit Linked Data**
- **Examine and Edit a Link**
- **Embed Excel Data in a Word Document**
- **Edit Embedded Data**
- **Insert an Excel File in a Word Document**
- **Link Excel Data to a PowerPoint Slide**
- **Link an Excel Chart to a PowerPoint Slide**

Key terms introduced in this project include

- compound documents
- destination file
- embedded
- linked
- object
- OLE (Object Linking and Embedding)
- source file

Why Would I Do This?

One of the advantages of using Office as an integrated set of programs is that any of the programs can refer to data generated by another program. For example, you can insert an Excel workbook in a Word document but still use Excel to edit and update the workbook. In other words, you create ***compound documents*** that contain more than one type of data.

This method of sharing data is called ***Object Linking and Embedding (OLE)***. In computer jargon, an ***object*** is anything that has properties and can be referenced and used by another program. An object can be as large as an entire workbook or as small as a worksheet cell. If an object is ***linked*** to another file, it is not actually a part of the file, but there is just a link to the ***source file*** (such as a Windows shortcut). If an object is ***embedded,*** the entire file is contained inside the parent file. The file that contains a link or embedded data is called the ***destination file***. There are advantages and disadvantages to each method, as we discuss in this project.

The following lessons primarily work with placing Excel data in a Word document or a PowerPoint slide; however, the procedures are basically the same no matter what objects or programs you use. For example, you can embed a Word document in an Excel workbook or link a PowerPoint slide to Excel. Indeed, you can even link and embed non-Microsoft objects if they are OLE-compatible.

Visual Summary

The Word document shown on the right side of Figure 7.1 is an example of a compound document. Although the table in the Word document looks like a Word table, it is actually a linked Excel workbook and can be edited with Excel. Figure 7.2 shows an embedded Excel table that actually looks like a small Excel workbook inside a Word document when it is edited.

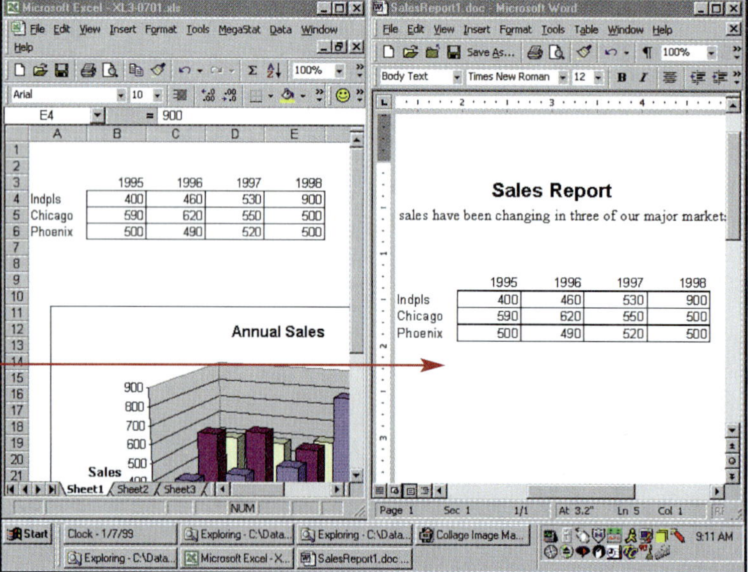

Figure 7.1
The compound document on the right side of this screen combines Word and Excel data.

Excel data within a Word document

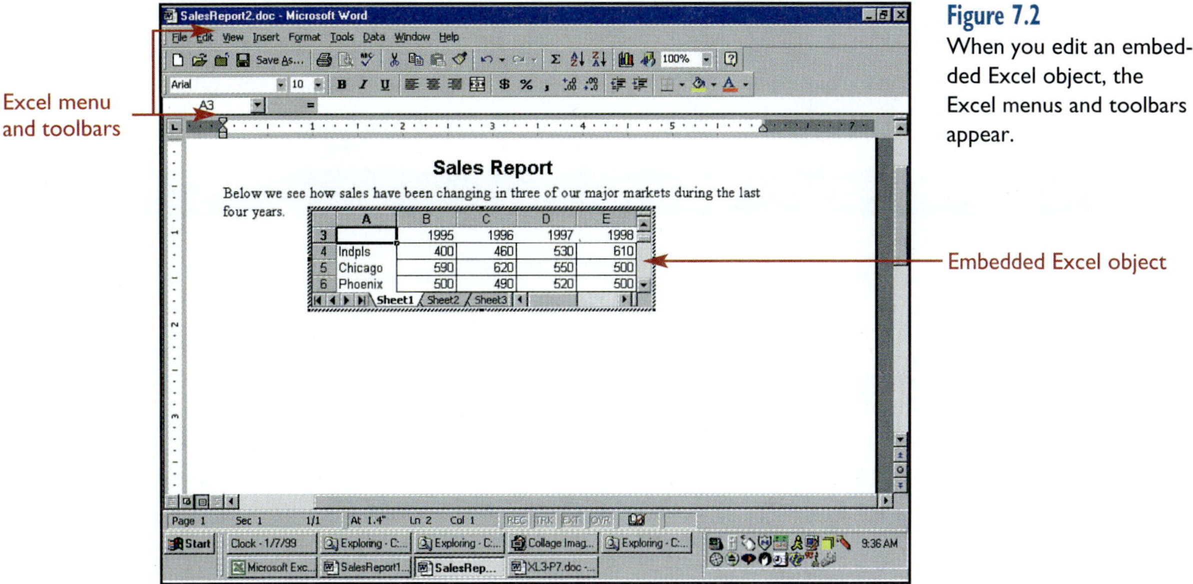

Figure 7.2
When you edit an embedded Excel object, the Excel menus and toolbars appear.

Figure 7.3 shows another type of compound document, an Excel chart within a PowerPoint slide. This type of linking enables a PowerPoint presentation to display data from an active workbook and can reflect changes that are made in the workbook and chart.

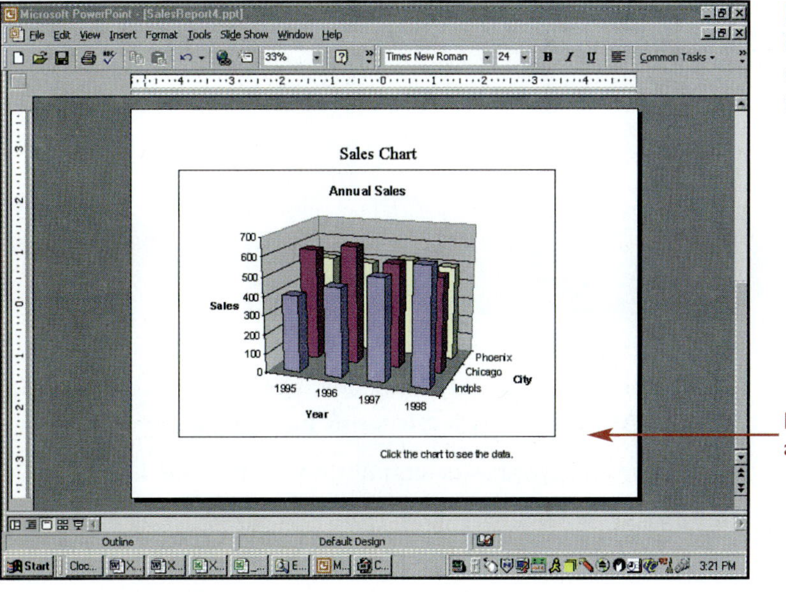

Figure 7.3
PowerPoint presentations can be enhanced by linking Excel charts.

PowerPoint slide with a linked Excel chart

Lesson 1: Linking Excel Data to a Word Document

Assume you are writing a sales report in Word, and you want to refer to data stored in an Excel workbook. When you link an object, you are just inserting a picture of the object with a shortcut (that is, *link*) to the source file. The advantage of this is that even though the Excel data appears in the Word document, the document is only a few bytes larger than it would have been without the Excel data. Also, when the Excel workbook is changed, the changes will automatically appear when the Word document is opened.

The disadvantage of a link is that a link will be broken if either of the linked files is moved to a different drive. If the files are moved to a different computer, you need to make sure they are in folders with the same name as the original computer. Otherwise, you'll need to create the link again.

To Link Excel Data to a Word Document

1. **Open the file XL3-0701.xls, and save it as `SalesData1.xls`.**
   This file contains the worksheet data that we want to include in the Word document. It also contains a chart that is used in a later lesson.

2. **Using the Office Assistant or the Help Answer Wizard, search for `overview of linked and embedded objects`. Display and read the Help topic and related topics.**

3. **Select cells A3:E6, and then choose Edit, Copy.**

4. **Start Microsoft Word, open the file XL3-0702.doc, and save it as `SalesReport1.doc`.**
   This file contains the start of a sales report.

5. **Place the insertion point at the end of the file, and choose Edit, Paste Special.**
   Figure 7.4 shows the Paste Special dialog box.

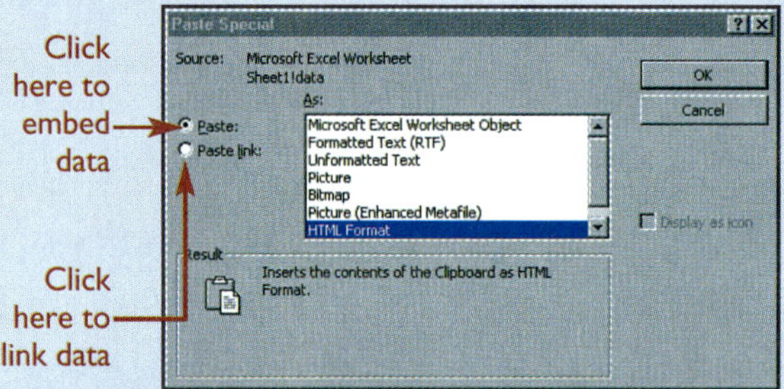

Figure 7.4
Use the Paste Special dialog box to link and embed data.

6. **In the Paste Special dialog box, click the Paste link option, and in the As list box, click Microsoft Excel Worksheet Object.**

7. **Leave the Display as icon option unchecked, and click OK.**

8. **Choose Format, Object; then click the Layout tab in the Format Object dialog box, and click the Center option button. Click OK.**
   The inserted cells are now centered horizontally.

   Save the Word document, and keep it open for the next lesson. Close Excel.

Lesson 2: Editing Linked Data

The advantage of a compound document is that you can edit one type of data from within a different type of document. In this lesson, you will see how to edit linked Excel data from within a Word document.

To Edit Linked Data

1. **In the open SalesReport1.doc document in Microsoft Word, click once on the Excel object to select it.**

2. **Choose Edit, Linked Worksheet Object, Edit Link. (You could also double-click the Excel object.)**
   This opens Excel with the linked workbook just as if you had opened the file directly with Excel.

3. **Resize the Word and Excel windows such that you can see the Excel table in both windows.**
   Figure 7.5 shows both the Word and Excel windows.

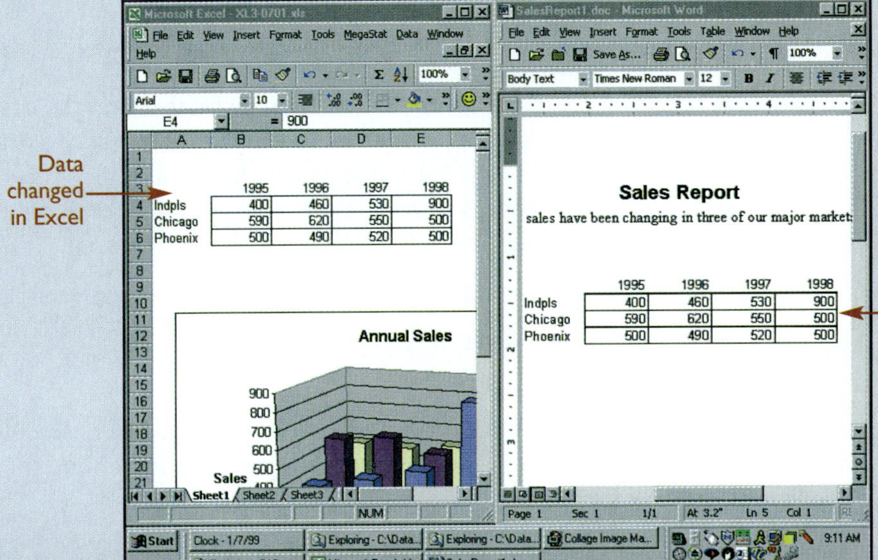

Figure 7.5
Note that when data is changed in the Excel document, it is automatically changed in the Word document.

4. **In the Excel window, click on cell E4, and change it to `900`.**
   You see the change immediately reflected in the Word window.

   Save the workbook, and exit Excel. Save the Word document, and leave it open for the next lesson.

Lesson 3: Examining and Editing a Link

When a file contains links, you may want to check what files are being linked, or you may want to edit the links. Although this lesson uses Microsoft Word, the procedure would be the same in any Microsoft Office program.

To Examine and Edit a Link

1 In Microsoft Word, open the SalesReport1.doc document.

2 Choose Edit, Links.
The Links dialog box will be displayed as shown in Figure 7.6.

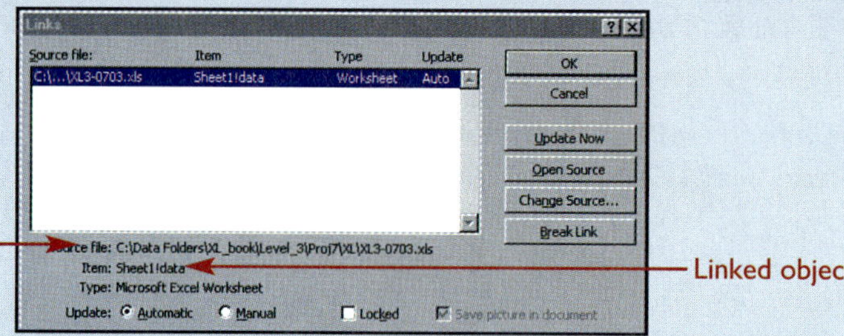

Figure 7.6
The Links dialog box provides information about the linked object.

Near the bottom of the dialog box, you see the source file that gives the exact location of the linked file. (The folder location on your computer may not be the same as shown in Figure 7.6.) The linked item is also listed. In this instance, it is `Sheet1!data`, where 'data' is a named range referring to the linked cells. If you did not use a named range, the cell references would be shown.

You can also change whether the links are updated automatically or manually.

3 Click the Manual option button, and then click OK.
The dialog box disappears, and you see the Word document.

4 Edit the data by double-clicking the table, which will activate Excel. Change cell E4 to 500, and then switch to the Word document.
Notice that the value in the Word document has not been changed.

5 Choose Edit, Links. Click Update Now, and then click OK.
The value is now updated.

In general, you want to use automatic updating unless you are making many changes in a large workbook that takes a long time to recalculate.

Close the Word document and Excel workbook without saving your changes.

Using the Change Source Button
You would use the Change Source button in the Links dialog box if you moved the file to a different folder on a different computer, or to a different drive.

Lesson 4: Embedding Excel Data in a Word Document

As noted in Lesson 1, data can be either linked or embedded. The advantage of embedded data is that it actually becomes a part of the Word document as opposed to being a separate file. This means you do not have to be concerned about breaking links if a source file gets moved or renamed. This would be especially important if you were going to send the file(s) to someone else.

To Embed Excel Data in a Word Document

1. **Open the file XL3-0703.xls.**
   This file contains the worksheet cells that we want to embed in the Word document.

2. **Using the Office Assistant or the Help Answer Wizard, search for "embedded objects." Display and read the Help topic and related topics.**

3. **Select cells A3:E6, and choose Edit, Copy.**

4. **In Microsoft Word, open the file XL3-0704.doc, and save it as `SalesReport2.doc`.**
   This file contains the start of a sales report.

5. **Place the insertion point at the end of the file, and choose Edit, Paste Special.**

6. **In the Paste Special dialog box, click the Paste option; in the As list box, click Microsoft Excel Worksheet Object.**

7. **Leave the Display as icon option unchecked, and click OK.**
   Figure 7.7 shows the inserted cells. Note that the entire contents of the Excel workbook are embedded in the Word document even though only the selected cells are visible.

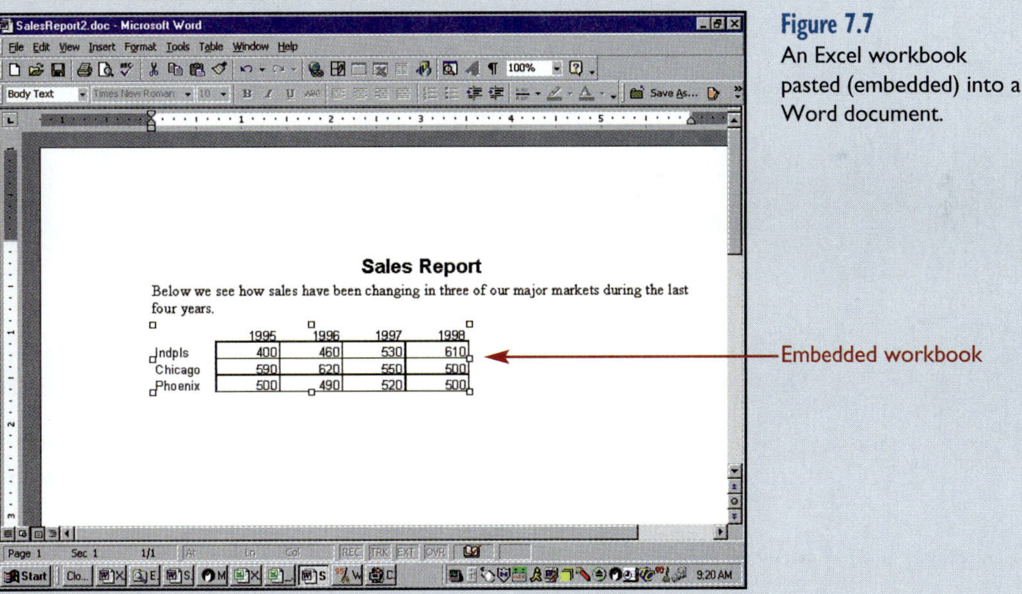

Figure 7.7
An Excel workbook pasted (embedded) into a Word document.

8. **Choose Format, Object; then click the Layout tab, and click the Center option button. Click OK.**
   Close the Excel workbook. Save the Word document, and keep it open for the next lesson.

Lesson 5: Editing Embedded Data

When an Excel workbook is embedded in a Word document, there is no separate .xls file—the entire workbook is contained within the Word document and must be edited from the Word document.

To Edit Embedded Data

1. **In Microsoft Word, open SalesReport2.doc (if it is not already open from the previous lesson).**
2. **Click once on the Excel cells to select them.**
3. **Double-click the cells to edit them.**
   The cells resemble a small worksheet, and Word menus and toolbars are temporarily replaced with Excel's menus and toolbars (see Figure 7.8).

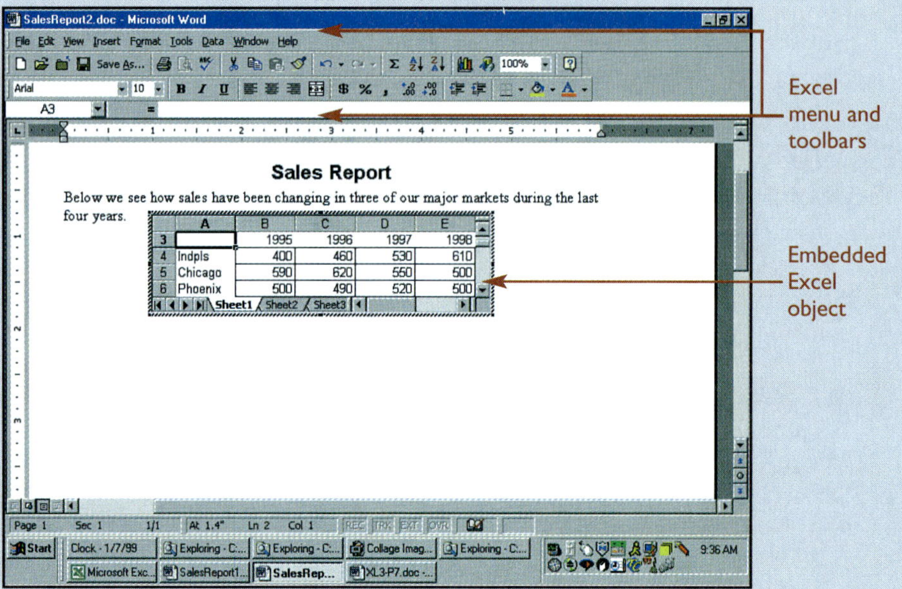

Figure 7.8
When you edit an embedded Excel object, the Excel menu and toolbars appear.

4. **In the Excel window, click on cell E4, and change it to `800`.**
5. **Click somewhere in the Word text, outside the Excel window.**
   The object is deselected, and Word's menus and toolbars reappear.

   Save and close the Word document.

Lesson 6: Inserting an Excel File in a Word Document

It is traditional to think of files according to the program that created them, that is, Excel workbooks or Word documents. However, with OLE you should think about compound documents that are a combination of types. In the previous lessons we have created compound documents by linking or embedding existing files. In this lesson a new Excel workbook is inserted within a Word document.

To Insert an Excel File in a Word Document

1. **In Microsoft Word, open the XL3-0705.doc file, and save it as `SalesReport3.doc`.**
   This file contains the start of a sales report.

2. **Place the insertion point at the end of the file, and choose Insert, Object.**
   The Object dialog box will be displayed as shown in Figure 7.9.

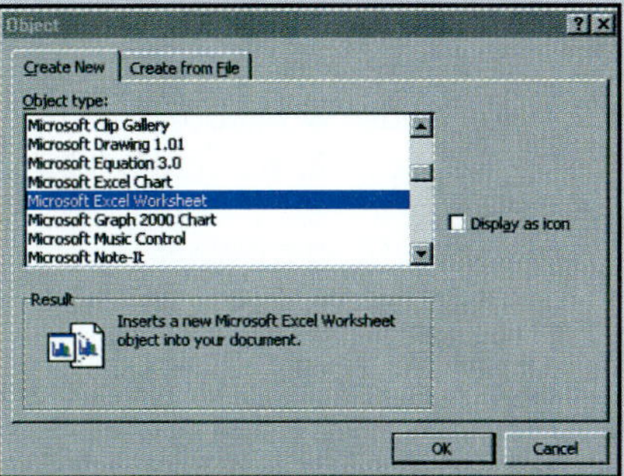

Figure 7.9
Objects are inserted from the Object dialog box.

3. **Click the Create New tab if it is not already selected.**

4. **In the Object type list, scroll down and select the Microsoft Excel Worksheet option. Leave the Display as icon option unchecked, and click OK.**
   A new workbook is now visible and ready for editing, as shown in Figure 7.10.

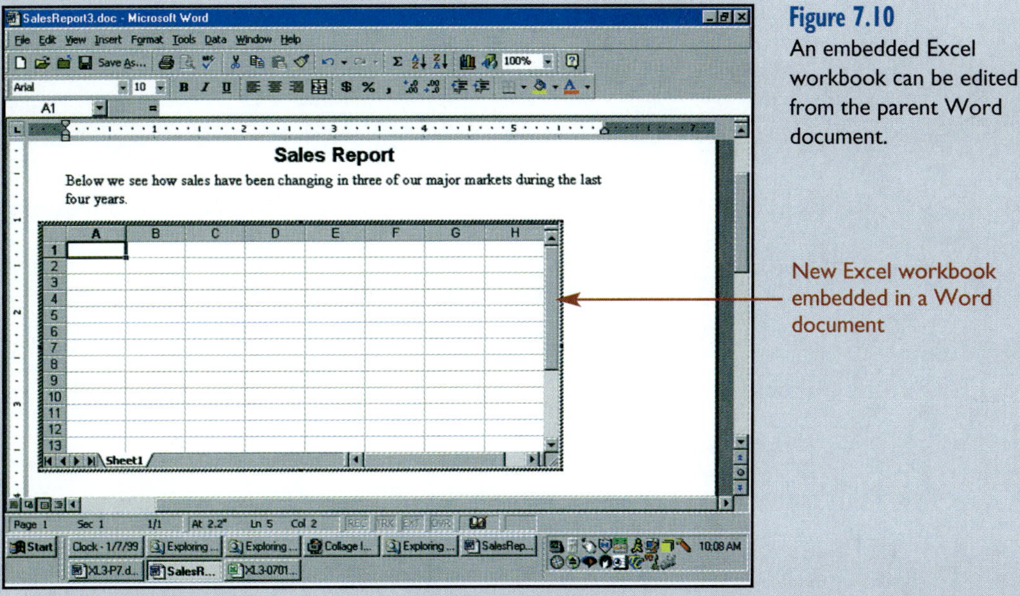

Figure 7.10
An embedded Excel workbook can be edited from the parent Word document.

New Excel workbook embedded in a Word document

5. **Click on the sizing handles, and change the size of the worksheet to match the width of the page margins.**

continues ▶

To Insert an Excel File in a Word Document (continued)

6 Experiment with entering some data and formulas in the cells.
Note that if you scroll through the worksheet, only the last visible cells will be shown in the Word document when you click outside the worksheet.

Save the document, and then exit Word.

An Embedded Workbook Can Contain Multiple Worksheets
You may right-click the Sheet1 tab and insert more than one worksheet in the embedded workbook. You may switch among the worksheets; however, only the last sheet selected will be visible in the Word document.

Lesson 7: Linking Excel Data to a PowerPoint Slide

When creating a PowerPoint presentation, you may want to present the contents of an active workbook. It is more efficient to refer to the actual worksheet or chart than to create a slide that looks like the chart. More importantly, if the data in the workbook changes, those changes will be shown the next time you give the presentation.

To Link Excel Data to a PowerPoint Slide

1 Open the file XL3-0706.xls, and save it as `SalesData2.xls`.
This file contains the worksheet cells that we want to display in the PowerPoint presentation.

2 Select cells A3:E6, and choose Edit, Copy.

3 Open the file XL3-0707.ppt with Microsoft PowerPoint, and save it as `SalesReport4.ppt`.
This file contains the two slides that are the start of a sales report presentation.

4 Select the first slide, and choose Edit, Paste Special.

5 In the Paste Special dialog box, click Paste link; in the As list box, select Microsoft Excel Worksheet Object; click OK.
The cells will appear in the slide, but they will probably be too small.

6 Click on one of the corner sizing handles, and hold down the Shift key while resizing the object.
Holding the Shift key maintains the object's proportions while resizing. Figure 7.11 shows the completed slide.

To edit the linked data, use the procedure described in Lesson 2. Note that the data cannot be edited while in Slide Show presentation mode.

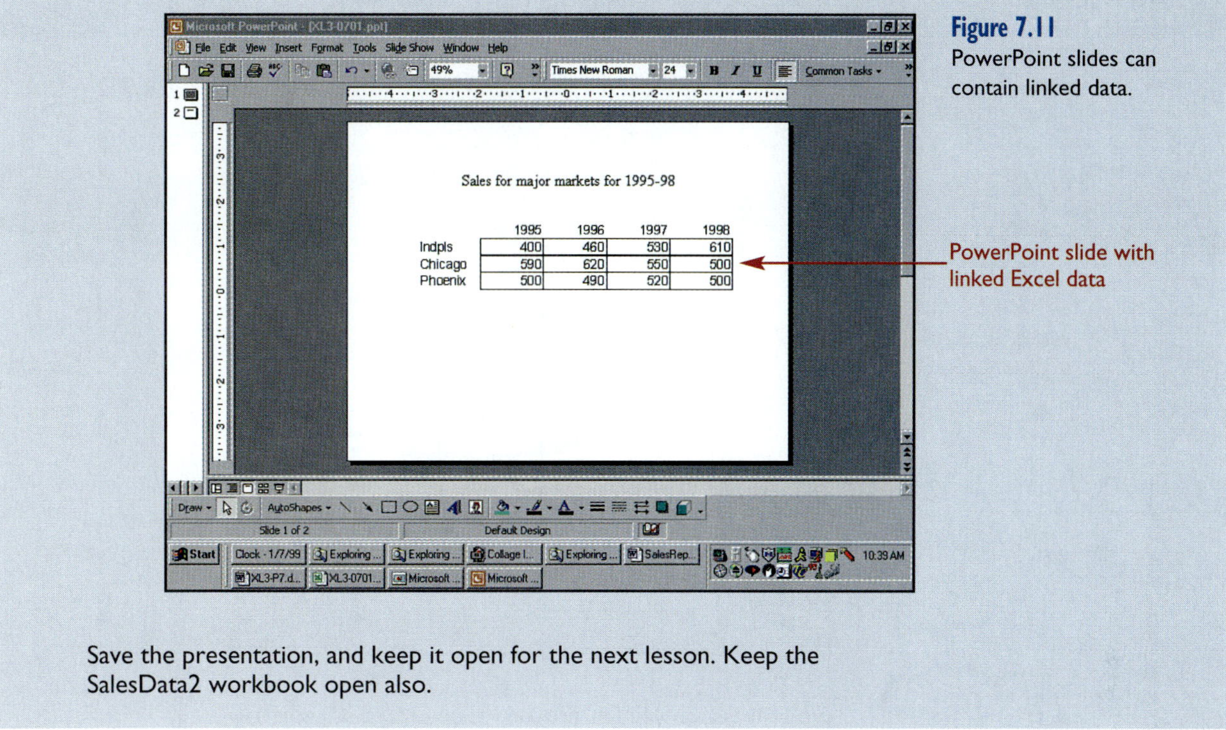

Figure 7.11
PowerPoint slides can contain linked data.

Save the presentation, and keep it open for the next lesson. Keep the SalesData2 workbook open also.

Lesson 8: Linking an Excel Chart to a PowerPoint Slide

Charts and graphics can greatly enhance a presentation. Although you can create charts within PowerPoint, you may already have a chart within an existing Excel workbook. In this lesson, an Excel chart is linked to a PowerPoint slide.

To Link an Excel Chart to a PowerPoint Slide

1. **Open the SalesData2.xls workbook (if it is not already open from the previous lesson).**
   This file contains the chart that you want to appear in the PowerPoint presentation, and also the range that you already linked.
2. **Click on the chart to select it, and then choose Edit, Copy.**
3. **Open the SalesReport4.ppt presentation (if it is not already open from the previous lesson).**
   This file contains the two slides that are the start of a sales report presentation.
4. **Press PgDn to display Slide 2, and then choose Edit, Paste Special.**
5. **In the Paste Special dialog box, click Paste link; in the As list box, select Microsoft Excel Worksheet Object; click OK.**
   The chart appears in the slide as shown in Figure 7.12.

continues ▶

To Link an Excel Chart to a PowerPoint Slide (continued)

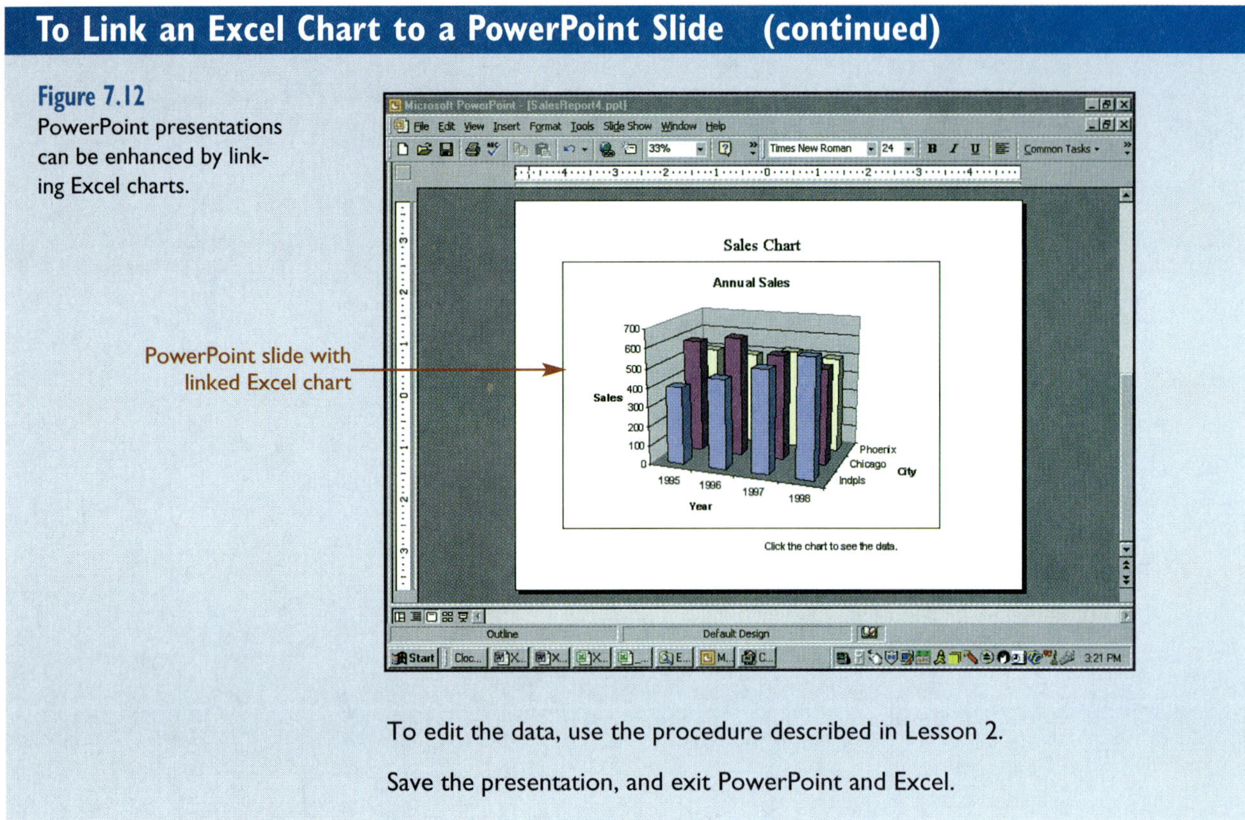

Figure 7.12
PowerPoint presentations can be enhanced by linking Excel charts.

To edit the data, use the procedure described in Lesson 2.

Save the presentation, and exit PowerPoint and Excel.

Summary

In this project you learned how to use Object Linking and Embedding to create compound documents. We used only two types of objects in the examples, but you could use several types of objects in a file. Indeed, each linked or embedded object itself can contain other objects.

Although linked and embedded objects look and act the same, they are stored quite differently. Linked objects contain only a link (that is, shortcut or pointer) to another file, whereas an embedded object is entirely contained within the parent document.

You can expand your knowledge of linking and embedding by using the Office Assistant or the Help Answer Wizard, and searching for "overview of linked and embedded objects." By reading this topic and clicking on the associated links, you can increase your knowledge of OLE.

Checking Concepts and Terms 

True/False

For each of the following, check *T* or *F* to indicate whether the statement is true or false.

__T __F **1.** An embedded Microsoft Excel object cannot be larger than one worksheet. [Why]

__T __F **2.** If an object is linked to a file, it is not actually a part of the file. [L1]

__T __F **3.** A Microsoft Excel worksheet can be embedded in a Microsoft Word document. [L4]

__T __F **4.** A link can only be edited in its own application. [L2]

__T __F **5.** Only embedded objects can be edited. [L2]

Multiple Choice

Circle the letter of the correct answer for each of the following.

1. Microsoft Excel data can be linked to which of the following? [L4]
   a. Word documents
   b. another Excel workbook
   c. PowerPoint slides
   d. all of the above

2. An object is [Why]
   a. only a text file
   b. anything that has properties and can be referenced by another program
   c. only a Microsoft application file
   d. an ASCII file

3. If an object is embedded, [L4]
   a. it cannot be edited
   b. it can only be edited from its own application
   c. it is contained within the parent file
   d. it continues to exist as a separate file within its own application

4. A link is [Why]
   a. like a shortcut to another file
   b. a macro
   c. a connection between files on different drives
   d. none of the above

5. A compound document is a document with [Why]
   a. a link
   b. embedded data
   c. either A or B
   d. none of the above

Discussion Questions

1. If you are going to create a compound document using Word and Excel, how would you decide which should be the parent document and which should be the linked or embedded object? In other words, which should be the source and which should be the destination?

2. Discuss the situations when linking would be preferable and when embedding would be preferable.

3. If you inserted a Word object in Excel, it would appear the same as a text box that you would create with the Drawing tools. What are the similarities or differences and advantages or disadvantages of a Word object versus a text box?

Skill Drill

Skill Drill exercises reinforce project skills. Each skill reinforced is the same, or nearly the same, as a skill presented in the project. Detailed instructions are provided in a step-by-step format.

1. Linking Data

Assume you are writing a report that describes how to create a centered moving average. This exercise links the Excel data to the Word document.

1. In Excel, open XL3-0708.xls, and save it as `Exercise1.xls`.
2. Select cells A1:D30.
3. Choose Edit, Copy.
4. In Word, open XL3-0709.doc, and save it as `Link.doc`.
5. Place the cursor at the end of the document, and choose Edit, Paste Special.

6. In the Paste Special dialog box, click Paste link, select Microsoft Excel Worksheet Object, and leave Display as icon unchecked. Click OK.
7. Click on the inserted cells, and drag them to the center of the document.
8. Save and close both files.

2. Locating the Source of Linked Documents

Assume you want to copy the linked files to another computer. This exercise shows how to determine where the linked files are stored.

1. In Word, open Link.doc.
2. Choose Edit, Links.
3. Click on each of the links in the Links dialog box, and note the filename and folder of the linked file.
4. Close the Link.doc file.

3. Embedding Data

In this exercise, Excel data is embedded in a Word file.

1. In Excel, open XL3-0708.xls.
2. Select cells A1:D30.
3. Choose Edit, Copy.
4. In Word, open XL3-0709.doc, and save it as `Embed.doc`.
5. Place the cursor at the end of the document and click Edit, Paste Special.
6. In the Paste Special dialog box, click Paste, select Microsoft Excel Worksheet Object, and leave Display as icon unchecked. Click OK.
7. Click on the inserted cells, and drag them to the center of the document.
8. Save the Embed.doc file, and keep it open for the next exercise. Close the Excel file.

4. Editing Embedded Data

In this exercise, you edit the data you embedded in the previous exercise.

1. In the Embed.doc file from the previous exercise, click on the worksheet object to select it.
2. Choose Edit, Worksheet Object, Edit. (You could also double-click the cells to edit them.)
3. Click on some of the formulas in column D to see how they work.
4. Change the value in cell C11 from **`5057`** to **`5000`**, and note which cells are affected.
5. Change the value in cell C11 back to **`5057`**.
6. Save and close the file.

5. Linking an Excel Chart

In this exercise, an Excel chart is linked in a Word document.

1. Open Link.doc that you saved from Exercise 1.
2. Place the insertion point at the end of the document, and insert a page break.
3. Type the following text at the top of the new page: `Below is a chart of the original data and the centered moving average.`
4. In Excel, open Exercise1.xls that you saved from Exercise 1.
5. Click on the chart to select it, and then choose Edit, Copy.
6. Switch to Word, click at the end of the Word document, and choose Edit, Paste Special.
7. In the Paste Special dialog box, click Paste link, select Microsoft Excel Chart Object, and leave Display as icon unchecked. Click OK.
8. Edit one of the data values in column C from the linked data on page 1 of the document, and note the change in the chart.
9. Close the document without saving your changes, and exit Word. Close Exercise1.xls, and leave Excel open.

6. Linking a Chart in a PowerPoint Slide

In this exercise, a new slide is created and an Excel chart is inserted.

1. In Excel, open XL3-0708.xls, and save it as `Exercise6.xls`.
2. Click on the chart to select it, and then choose Edit, Copy.
3. Open a new presentation in PowerPoint.
4. Choose Format, Slide Layout. Select the Title Only layout, and click Apply.
5. Click on the title box, and type `Centered Moving Average`. Then click outside the title box.
6. Choose Edit, Paste Special.
7. In the Paste Special dialog box, click Paste link, select Microsoft Excel Chart Object, and leave Display as icon unchecked. Click OK.
8. Click the Slide Show button to see what the slide would look like in presentation mode.
9. Save the presentation as `SalesReport5.ppt`, and then exit PowerPoint and Excel.

Challenge 

Challenge exercises expand on or are somewhat related to skills presented in the lessons. Each exercise provides a brief narrative introduction followed by instructions in a numbered step format that are not as detailed as those in the Skill Drill section.

Each exercise is independent of the others, so that you may complete the exercises in any order. Be sure to save the workbook after completing each exercise. If you need a paper copy of the completed exercise, enter your name centered in a header before printing.

1. Opening an Embedded Object

You want to edit cells of an embedded worksheet which are not visible.

1. Open Embed.doc.
2. Click on the worksheet object to select it.
3. Choose Edit, Worksheet Object, Open.

   This opens the workbook for editing with Excel, even though it is not a linked object.
4. Close Word and Excel without saving.

2. Fixing a Broken Link

The Link.doc file created in Lesson 1 contains links to Exercise1.xls. In this exercise the name of the linked file is changed so the parent file can no longer find it.

1. Use Windows Explorer to change the name of Exercise1.xls to `Exercise1.XXX`. Respond Yes to the dialog box that asks if you're sure you want to rename the file.
2. Open Link.doc, and attempt to edit the worksheet object.

   An error box appears, stating that it cannot find the linked file.
3. Use Windows Explorer to change Exercise1.XXX back to `Exercise1.xls`.
4. Check to make sure the link works again. Keep the file open for the next exercise.

3. Changing a Link

If a linked file is moved or renamed, you will need to edit the link. You will also need to edit the link if you want to link to a different file.

1. Use Windows Explorer to change the name of Exercise1.xls to `MyLink.xls`.
2. In the Link.doc file, attempt to edit the worksheet object again.

   An error message may appear, as in the previous exercise; if Link.doc was open when you renamed the linked data file, the link in the document will update automatically to use the new filename.
3. Choose Edit, Links.
4. Select each of the links in the Source file list box, and click on Change Source. In the Change Source dialog box, select MyLink.xls, and click Open.

   This step is not necessary if your link updated automatically.
5. Click OK. Check to make sure the links work.
6. Save and close the file.

4. Copying Linked Files to a New Drive

When copying or moving files containing links, you must be sure to copy or move the linked files also. If the linked files are in the same folder as the parent file, there should be no problem; however, if the linked files are moved to a different relative folder than where they were established, you would need to use the Change Source option to re-establish the links.

1. Use Windows Explorer to copy Link.doc and MyLink.xls to a different drive (a floppy disk, Zip drive, or network drive).
2. Open Link.doc from the new location.
3. Check to make sure the links still work. If not, use the Change Source button in the Edit Links dialog box to attempt to make the links work again.
4. Save and close the file, and then exit all open applications.

Discovery Zone

Discovery Zone exercises require advanced knowledge of topics presented in *Essentials* lessons, application of skills from multiple lessons, or self-directed learning of new skills. Each exercise is independent of the others, so that you may complete the exercises in any order.

1. Checking Sizes of Linked Versus Embedded Files

In Lesson 1 you created SalesReport1.doc that had a linked file. In Lesson 4 you created SalesReport2.doc that was identical except that the data object was embedded. Use Windows Explorer to find the sizes of these two files. You should find that SalesReport1.doc is smaller than SalesReport2.doc, because it contains only the link, not the actual worksheet data.

2. Inserting a Non-Microsoft Office Object

Open a new Word document, and choose Insert, Object. Scroll through the object types, and experiment with inserting some object other than from Excel, Word, or PowerPoint. The list will vary, depending on what is installed on your computer. For a start, see if there is an object called Microsoft Note-It or Microsoft Drawing.

Project 8

Collaborative Tools and Hyperlinks

Objectives

In this project, you learn how to

- **Track Changes in a Workbook**
- **Accept or Reject Changes**
- **Share a Workbook**
- **Use Hyperlinks Within a Workbook**
- **Use a Hyperlink in a Word Document to Reference Excel Data**
- **Use a Hyperlink in a PowerPoint Slide to Reference Excel Data**
- **Convert an Excel Workbook into a Web Page**
- **View and Edit an Excel Web Document**
- **Email an Excel Workbook**

Key terms introduced in this project include

- hyperlinks
- share
- tracking changes
- Web pages

Why Would I Do This?

Excel has the capability of ***tracking changes*** to each cell made since the last time the workbook was saved. While you may occasionally want to see what you have changed during a session, tracking changes is especially useful when two or more users are sharing or collaborating on a workbook.

With the advent of Internet Web browsers, we have become accustomed to ***hyperlinks***: underlined text that you click to jump to another location. Typically these links are in ***Web pages*** and refer to other Web pages; however, these links can also be in Microsoft Office documents and refer to other documents or locations within any Microsoft Office document as well as Internet links.

You can also create Web documents from Excel so that Internet users can not only see the document, they can also interact with it.

Visual Summary

Figure 8.1 shows an example of a shared workbook. Another user has made a change and the current user is deciding whether to accept the change.

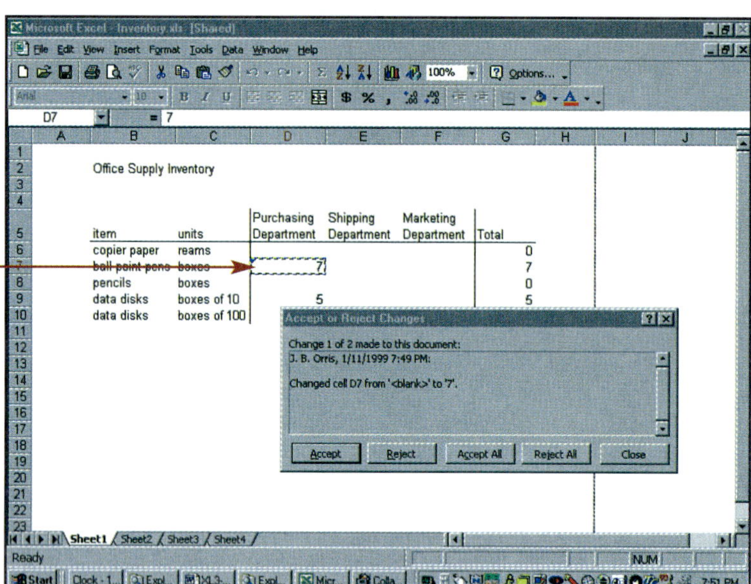

Figure 8.1
When more than one person makes changes in a workbook, someone has to decide whether or not to accept the changes.

Figure 8.2 shows an example of an interactive Excel chart saved as a Web page. At first glance it appears to be an Excel worksheet; however, it is being viewed as a Web page with Explorer. Unlike a static Web page, the viewer can change the data in the cells and see the change on the chart.

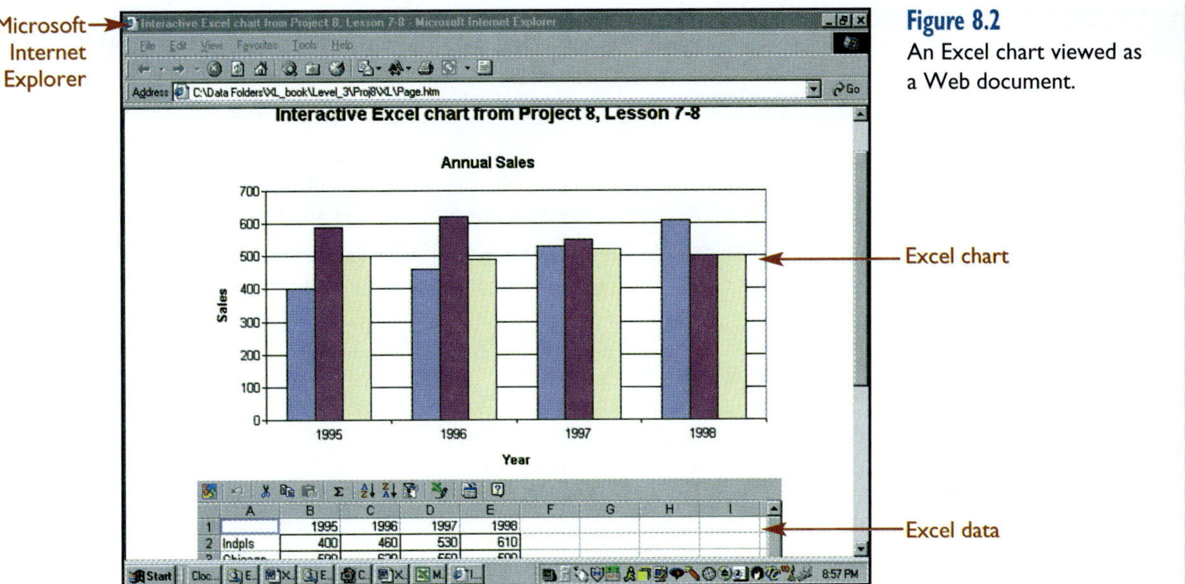

Figure 8.2
An Excel chart viewed as a Web document.

Lesson 1: Tracking Changes in a Workbook

This lesson explains how to set up a workbook to track changes. The most common use of this feature is when two or more people are collaborating on a workbook and each user needs to know what changes the other users have made. The changes could be part of developing a workbook or the changes could be limited to entering data into an existing workbook.

The workbook could be on a network where the users have access to it or it could be passed among the users via email or a disk.

To Track Changes in a Workbook

1. **Open the file XL3-0801.xls and save it as `Inventory.xls`.**
   This file will be used by different departments to monitor items they use from a central supply area.
2. **Choose Tools, Track Changes, Highlight Changes.**
   You now see the Highlight Changes dialog box as shown in Figure 8.3.

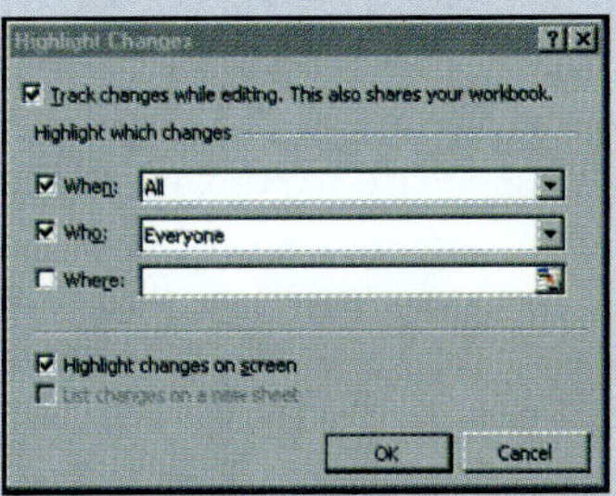

Figure 8.3
Parameters for tracking changes are set from the Highlight Changes dialog box.

3. **Check the Track changes while editing check box.**

continues ▶

To Track Changes in a Workbook (continued)

4 Check the When check box, and then select All from the drop-down list.

As the name implies, the When check box determines when changes will be tracked. "All" means all changes will be tracked; this is the default choice. You can specify "Since I last saved" or "Not yet reviewed." You could also specify "Since date," and Excel will prompt you for a date.

5 Check the Who check box, and then select Everyone from the drop-down list.

Who can be "Everyone" or "Everyone but me." The latter might be used if you were a supervisor or wanted to monitor changes other people in your workgroup made to the workbook.

Leave the Where check box unchecked. (If you check Where, you can select specific cells to be monitored.)

6 Check the Highlight changes on screen check box, if necessary.

This creates a cell comment for every cell that is changed.

7 Click OK. If a message box appears asking if you want to save the file, click OK.

Note in the Excel title bar that tracking changes automatically shares the workbook even though you may not actually be sharing with anyone yet (the word `Shared` appears in the title bar). While in shared mode, certain operations are not available. For example, you cannot delete a worksheet while a workbook is shared.

Save the file and leave it open for the next lesson.

Lesson 2: Accepting or Rejecting Changes

Typically one person would be in charge of the content of a workbook and after tracking changes, he or she would accept or reject the changes made to the workbook. It is a good idea to do this on a regular basis. If you have several people making changes, eventually they will be changing the changes, and it can become complicated.

To Accept or Reject Changes

1 In the Inventory.xls file from the previous lesson, click in cell D7 and enter the number 7.

Note that a border is placed around the cell, and a comment indicator tells you that a comment has been added. Also, the row heading number and column heading letter change color.

2 Place the mouse pointer over the cell to view the comment.

The comment indicates the change in the cell as shown in Figure 8.4.

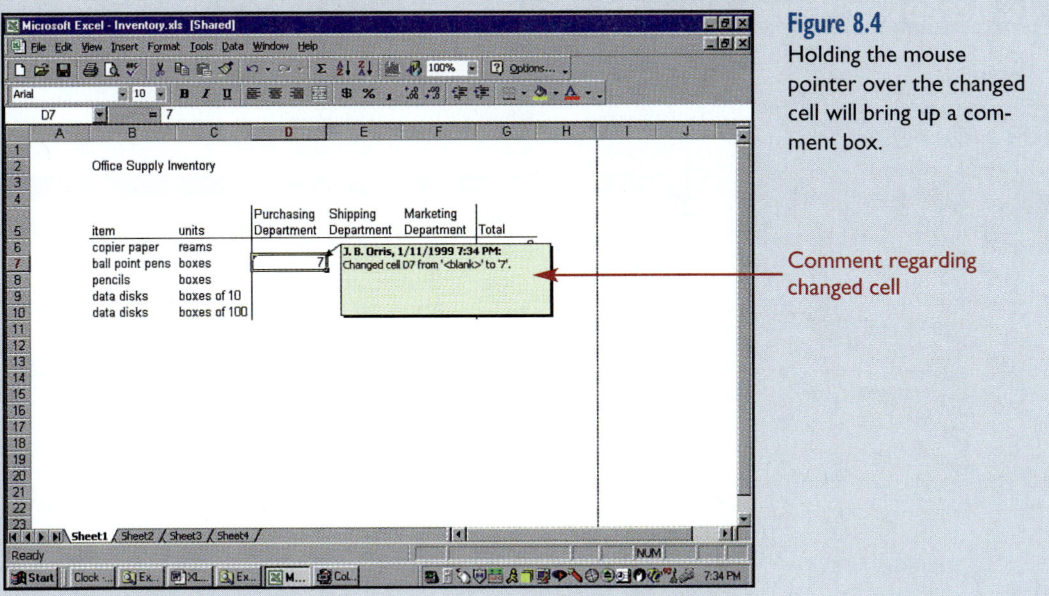

Figure 8.4
Holding the mouse pointer over the changed cell will bring up a comment box.

3 **Click in cell D9 and enter the number 5.**

4 **Choose Tools, Track Changes, Accept or Reject Changes.**

A message box appears with the following text: `This action will now save the workbook. Do you want to continue?`

5 **Click OK.**

The Select Changes to Accept or Reject dialog box appears, as shown in Figure 8.5.

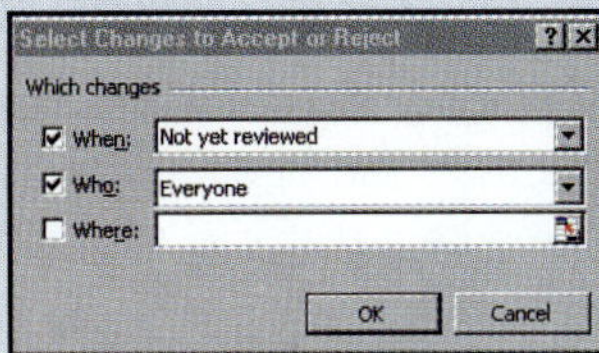

Figure 8.5
Changes to be accepted or rejected are identified in this dialog box.

6 **Check the When box, and select Not yet reviewed from the drop-down list (if necessary).**

7 **Check the Who box, and select Everyone from the drop-down list (if necessary).**

Leave the Where box unchecked.

8 **Click OK.**

The Accept or Reject Changes dialog box appears as shown in Figure 8.6.

continues ▶

To Accept or Reject Changes (continued)

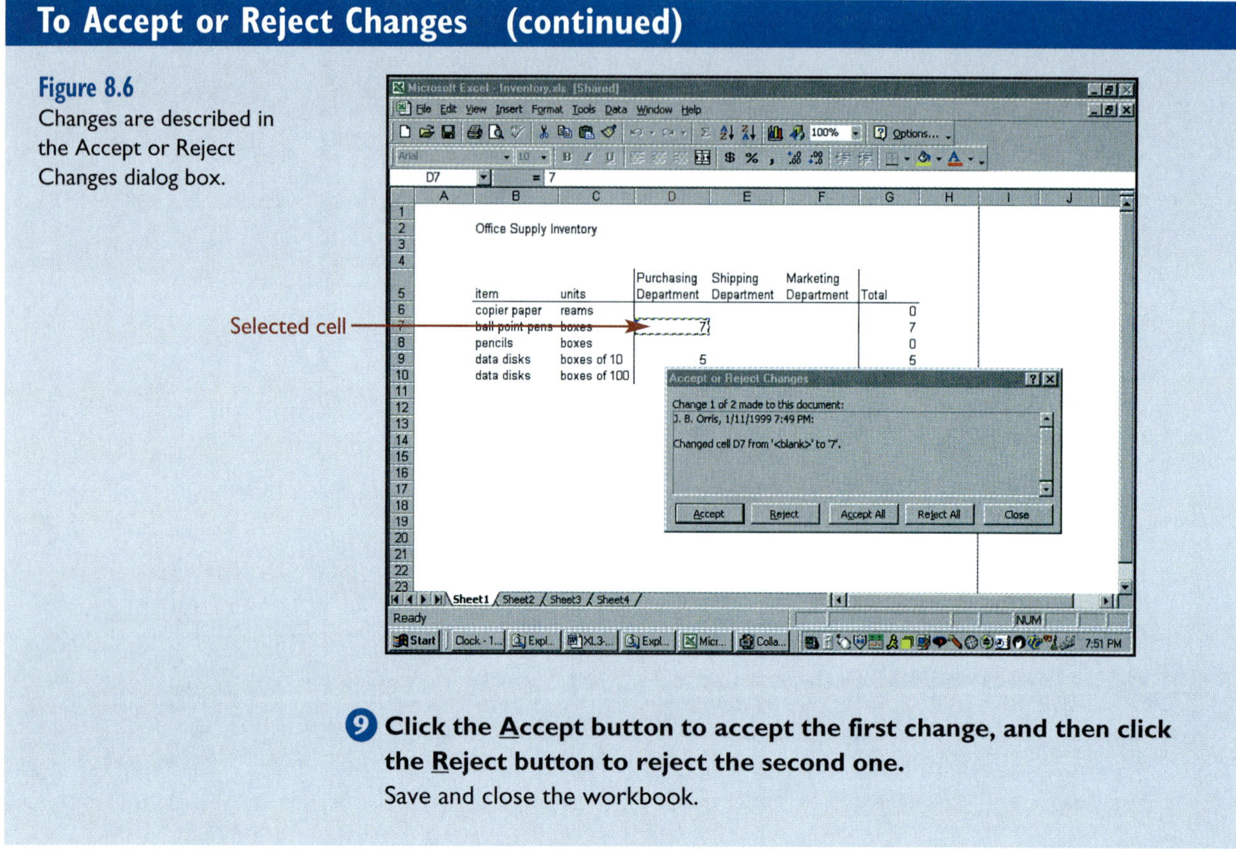

Figure 8.6
Changes are described in the Accept or Reject Changes dialog box.

9. **Click the Accept button to accept the first change, and then click the Reject button to reject the second one.**
   Save and close the workbook.

Lesson 3: Sharing a Workbook

A primary use of tracking changes is when two or more users ***share*** a workbook, that is, the users can open it from a common location. This lesson is to be completed with two computers that can access the file via a network. If you have any questions, ask your instructor.

If You Do Not Have a Network...
If you do not have access to networked computers, you can do this exercise by copying the file to another computer with a floppy disk (or email) after the first person works on it. Or, have another user use the same computer but change the username (by choosing Tools, Options, and making the change on the General tab).

To Share a Workbook

1. **Open the Inventory.xls file. Make sure it is still shared.**
   If the file is shared, `[Shared]` will appear after the filename in the title bar.
2. **Use the Excel Help Answer Wizard or the Office Assistant to search for `How do I share a workbook?`. Display the relevant topics.**
3. **Choose Tools, Options; then click the General tab and change the User name to `Purchasing`. Click OK.**

4 **Open the same Inventory.xls file from another computer.**

5 **Choose Tools, Options; then click the General tab and change the User name to `Shipping`. Click OK.**

6 **Enter the number `10` in cell E7.**

7 **Save the file.**
Changes made on another computer cannot be detected until the file is saved.

On the first computer:

8 **Choose Tools, Track Changes, Accept or Reject Changes.**
The Accept or Reject Changes dialog box appears as shown in Figure 8.7.

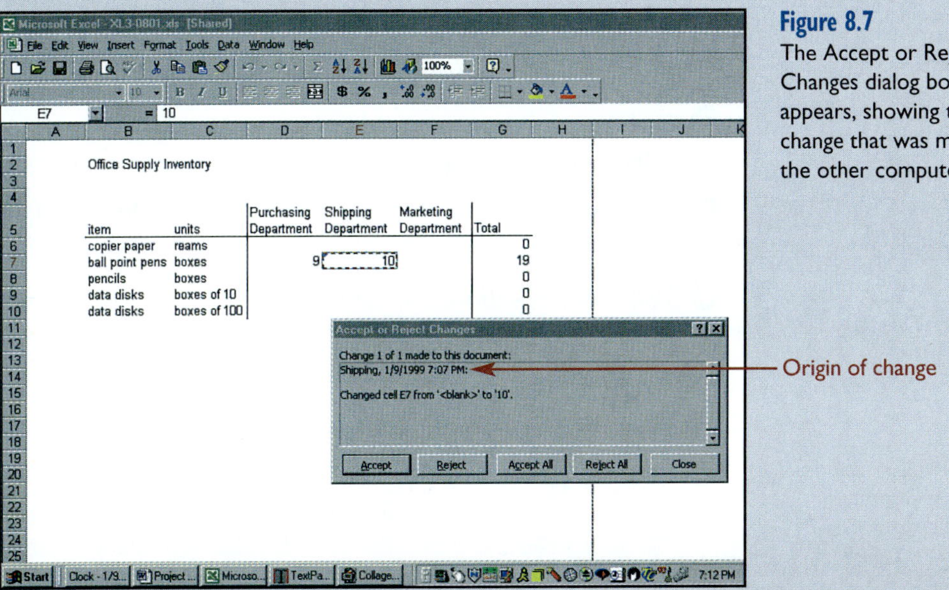

Figure 8.7
The Accept or Reject Changes dialog box appears, showing the change that was made on the other computer.

9 **Check the When box (if necessary), and select Not yet reviewed from the drop-down list.**

10 **Check the Who box (if necessary), and select Everyone from the drop-down list.**
Leave the Where box unchecked.

11 **Click OK.**
If you didn't check for changes, Excel would automatically check when you saved the file.

12 **Click Close.**
The Accept or Reject Changes dialog box closes without accepting or rejecting the change.

13 **On both computers: Choose Tools, Options; then click the General tab and change the Username options to what they were previously. Click OK.**
Save the file as `Inventory2.xls` and close the files on both computers.

Lesson 4: Using Hyperlinks Within a Workbook

One handy use of hyperlinks is to jump to specific locations within a workbook (or any Office file). In this lesson, you create a Table of Contents for a workbook that includes hyperlinks to various sections.

To Use a Hyperlink Within a Workbook

1. **Open XL3-0802.xls and save it as `BalanceSheet.xls`.**
   This file contains the beginnings of an annual report workbook. The first worksheet is the Table of Contents page. Create a hyperlink to jump to the start of the Balance Sheet and another link to jump back to the top of the workbook.

2. **Use the Excel Help Answer Wizard or the Office Assistant to search for "Create a hyperlink." Display the relevant topics.**

3. **Click in cell A1 of the Table of Contents page and name the cell `Top`.**
   Although you can jump to specific cells, it is easier to jump to named cells.

4. **Click on cell A45 of the Balance Sheet worksheet and name the cell `BalSheet`.**

5. **Click on cell C10 of the Table of Contents worksheet, and then choose Insert, Hyperlink.**
   The Insert Hyperlink dialog box appears, as shown in Figure 8.8.

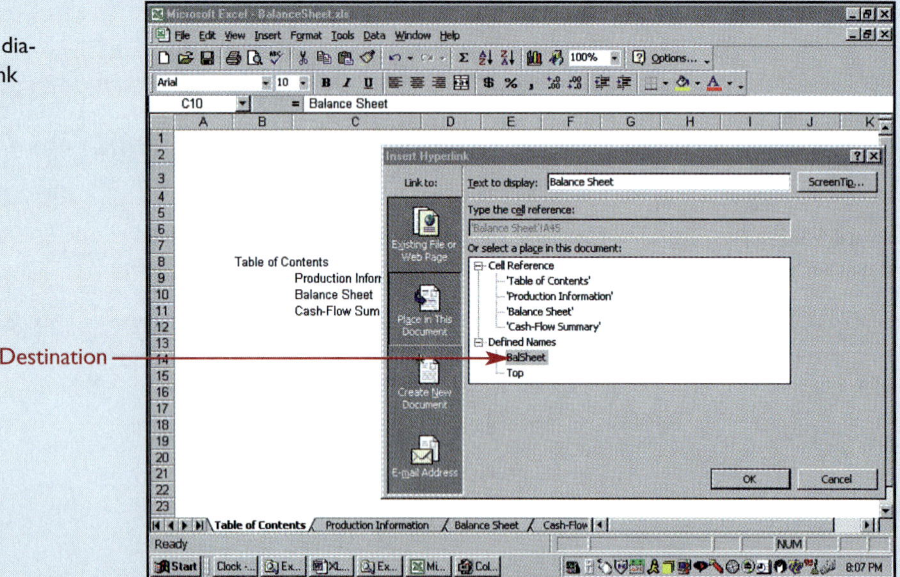

Figure 8.8
The Insert Hyperlink dialog box defines the link cell and destination.

6. **In the Link to area on the left side of the dialog box, click Place in this Document.**

7. **Click on BalSheet in the center of the dialog box.**
   If you do not see BalSheet, you may need to expand the Defined Names item by clicking the '+' next to it.

8. **Click the ScreenTip button, and type: `Click here to see the Balance Sheet` in the text box.**

9. **Click OK to close the Set Hyperlink ScreenTip dialog box, and then click OK again to close the Insert Hyperlink dialog box.**
   `Balance Sheet` in the worksheet now appears as a hyperlink (blue and underlined).

10. **Click on the hyperlink in cell C10.**
    Excel jumps to the destination for the hyperlink, on the Balance Sheet worksheet.

11. **Click on cell H72 and make it a hyperlink to the cell named Top.**
    Save and close the workbook.

Changing the Appearance of Hyperlinks

Hyperlinks are initially shown in blue, underlined text. In most cases it would be best to leave them this way, because we are becoming accustomed to associating blue underlining with hyperlinks. However, the appearance of the hyperlink is entirely under your control and you can apply any formatting (font, color, size, shading, and so on) to it. There may even be situations where you want to make the hyperlink invisible by making it look the same as surrounding text.

To change the formatting of a hyperlink, right-click the hyperlink and choose Format Cells from the shortcut menu. Make your desired selections from the Format Cells dialog box, and click OK.

Lesson 5: Using a Hyperlink in a Word Document to Reference Excel Data

Assume you are writing a sales report and you want to be able to have readers jump to an Excel worksheet if they want to see some supporting data.

To Use a Hyperlink Between Excel and Word

1. **In Word, open XL3-0803.doc and save it as `DataLink.doc`.**
   The document is part of a sales report and you want the reader to be able to see the Excel worksheet supporting the report.

2. **Select the phrase `Click here to see the Excel data`.**
   This phrase will be the hyperlink to the Excel document.

3. **Choose Insert, Hyperlink.**

4. **In the Link to area on the left side of the dialog box, click Existing File or Web Page.**

5. **Click the Browse for File button, select XL3-0805.xls, and click OK.**

6. **Click the ScreenTip button and type: `This link will open the Excel file` in the text box. Click OK to close the Set Hyperlink ScreenTip dialog box.**

continues ▶

To Use a Hyperlink Between Excel and Word (continued)

7. **Click OK again to close the Insert Hyperlink dialog box.**

8. **Click the hyperlink to open the Excel file.**
   If Excel is accessed from a hyperlink, the Web toolbar will be visible as shown in Figure 8.9.

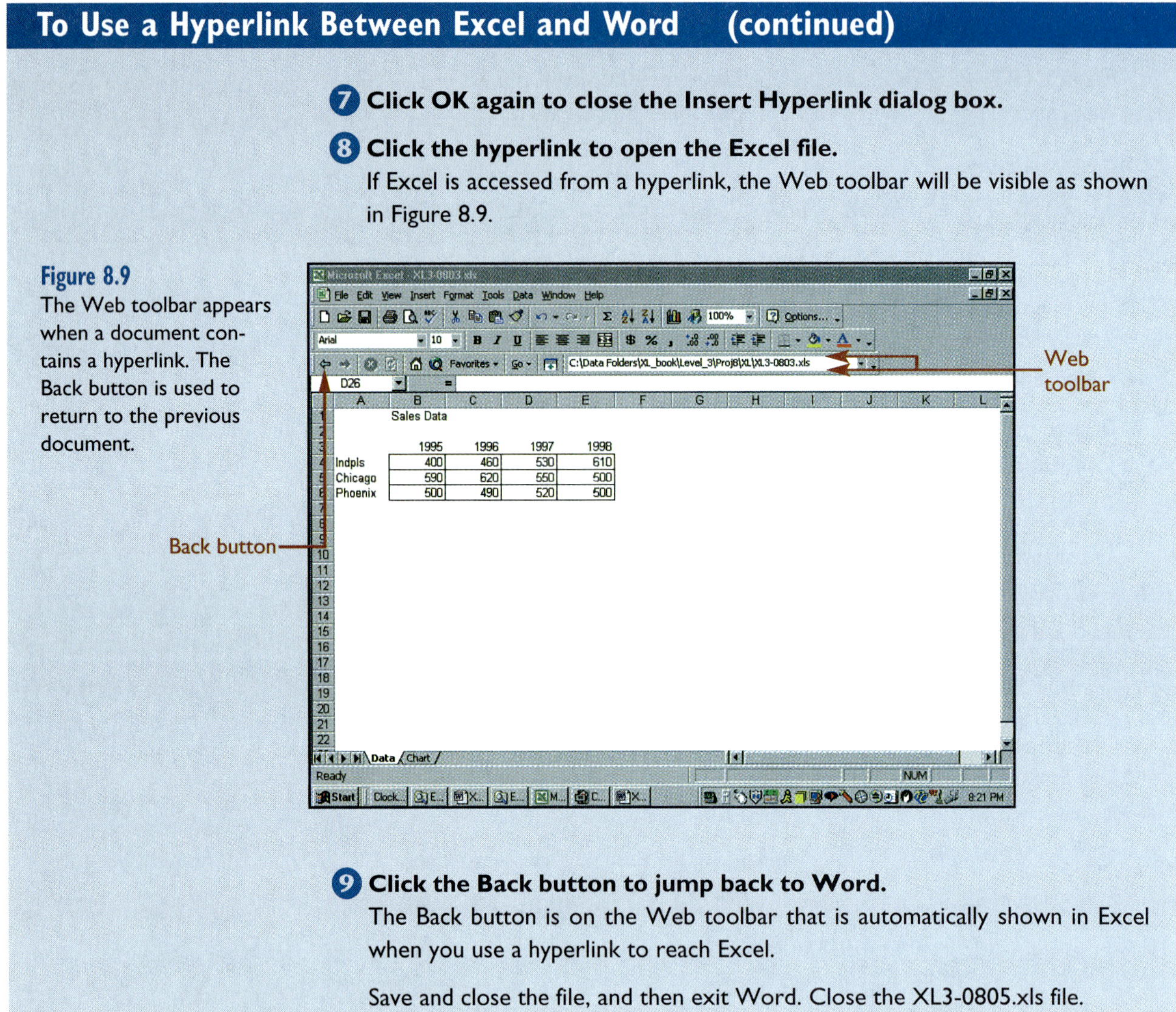

Figure 8.9
The Web toolbar appears when a document contains a hyperlink. The Back button is used to return to the previous document.

9. **Click the Back button to jump back to Word.**
   The Back button is on the Web toolbar that is automatically shown in Excel when you use a hyperlink to reach Excel.

   Save and close the file, and then exit Word. Close the XL3-0805.xls file.

Lesson 6: Using a Hyperlink in a PowerPoint Slide to Reference Excel Data

A hyperlink in a PowerPoint presentation enables you to reference Excel data without making it a primary focus of a slide. The data would not be visible on the slide, but there would be a hyperlink you could click during the presentation that would load Excel with the appropriate worksheet.

To Use a Hyperlink Between Excel and PowerPoint

1. **In PowerPoint, open XL3-0804.ppt and save it as `PowerPointLink.ppt`.**

2. **Click the chart to select it, and choose Insert, Hyperlink.**

3. **In the Link to area on the left side of the dialog box, click Existing File or Web Page.**
4. **Click the Browse for File button and select XL3-0805.xls and click OK.**
5. **Click the ScreenTip button and type:** `Click the chart to see the data.`
6. **Click OK to close the Set Hyperlink ScreenTip dialog box, and then click OK to close the Insert Hyperlink dialog box.**
7. **Click the Slide Show button, and then click on the chart in the slide.**

   This opens the file in Excel.
8. **Use the Back button on the Web toolbar to jump back to the presentation.**
9. **End the presentation, and then save and close the file.**
   Exit PowerPoint, and close the XL3-0805.xls file.

Hyperlinks Are Active During a Presentation
Unlike OLE links, hyperlinks are active during a presentation; however, any changes made in the worksheet are not reflected in the PowerPoint slide during the presentation.

Lesson 7: Converting an Excel Workbook into a Web Page

You can display worksheet data, such as the result of a survey or research paper, on a Web page. With Excel 2000, you can not only save workbooks as Web pages, but the Web pages can have some spreadsheet functionality. This is useful if you have a worksheet that performs some computations that you want to make available to users via a Web page. For example, you could have a worksheet that calculated loan payments or created a loan amortization table.

If you are working in a lab or on a commercial network, consult your instructor before proceeding with this lesson because you will need to publish your workbook to a Web server to test it.

To Convert an Excel Workbook into a Web Page

1. **In Excel, open XL3-0805.xls. Click the Chart worksheet.**
2. **Use the Excel Help Answer Wizard or the Office Assistant to search for "Put a worksheet on a Web page." Display the relevant topics.**
3. **Choose File, Save as Web Page.**
   The Save As dialog box is shown in Figure 8.10.

continues ▶

To Convert an Excel Workbook into a Web Page (continued)

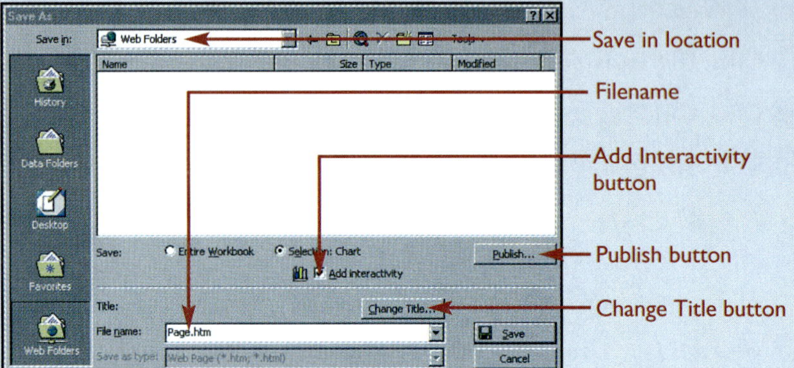

Figure 8.10
Providing the information requested in the Save As dialog box is the first step in publishing an Excel document as a Web page.

4. **Select a file location in the Save in drop-down list and then specify `WebChart.htm` as the File name.**

5. **Click the Selection: Chart option button.**

6. **Check the Add Interactivity check box, if necessary.**

   This specifies that the Web page will be created to enable the user to interact with it almost as if it were a worksheet.

7. **Click the Change Title button and type a title, for example: `Interactive Excel Web Chart`. Click OK.**

   This is the name that will appear in the title bar of the Web browser.

8. **Click the Publish button.**

   The Publish as Web Page dialog box appears as shown in Figure 8.11.

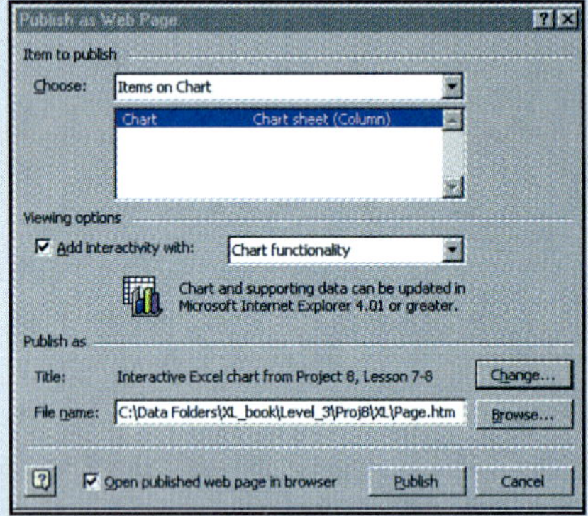

Figure 8.11
Information is verified in the Publish as Web Page dialog box. This is the final step in publishing an Excel document as a Web page.

9. **Check the Open published Web page in browser box.**

10. **Click the Publish button.**

    If you have Microsoft Internet Explorer 4.01 or 5.0 set as your default browser, the document will appear in the browser. (The interactive features will not work with other browsers.)

    Leave the file open for Lesson 8.

Lesson 8: Viewing and Editing an Excel Web Document

Once an Excel worksheet is saved as an interactive Web page, you will want to view it and make changes. While a Web worksheet does not have as much functionality as an actual Excel worksheet, you can still perform a substantial amount of work with it.

To View and Edit an Excel Web Document

1 The interactive Excel Web page should still be active from Lesson 7. If not, open WebChart.htm by choosing File, Open in Internet Explorer.

Figure 8.12 shows the interactive Excel Web document.

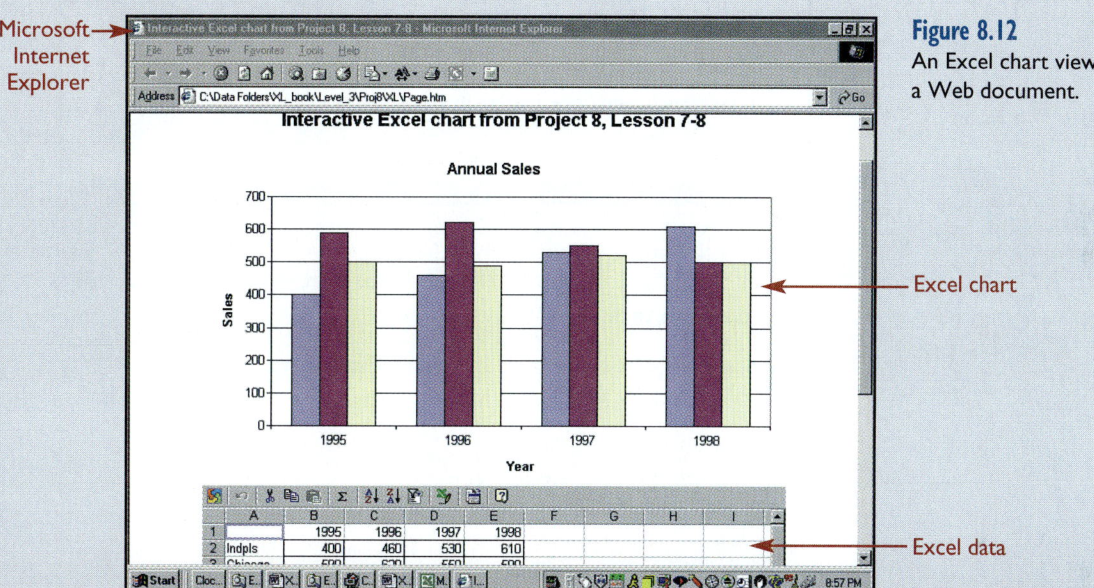

Figure 8.12
An Excel chart viewed as a Web document.

Note that the three-dimensional chart became a two-dimensional chart. Below the chart is the Web version of the worksheet.

2 Double-click cell E2 and change the value to `900`.

Note that the chart immediately reflects the change.

3 Change the value in cell E2 back to `610`.

4 Select cells B2:F4 and click the AutoSum button.

5 In cell C7, type `=SQRT(C4)` and press Enter.

6 Select cell C7 and then click the Property Toolbox toolbar button.

Figure 8.13 shows the Spreadsheet Property Toolbox.

continues ▶

To View and Edit an Excel Web Document (continued)

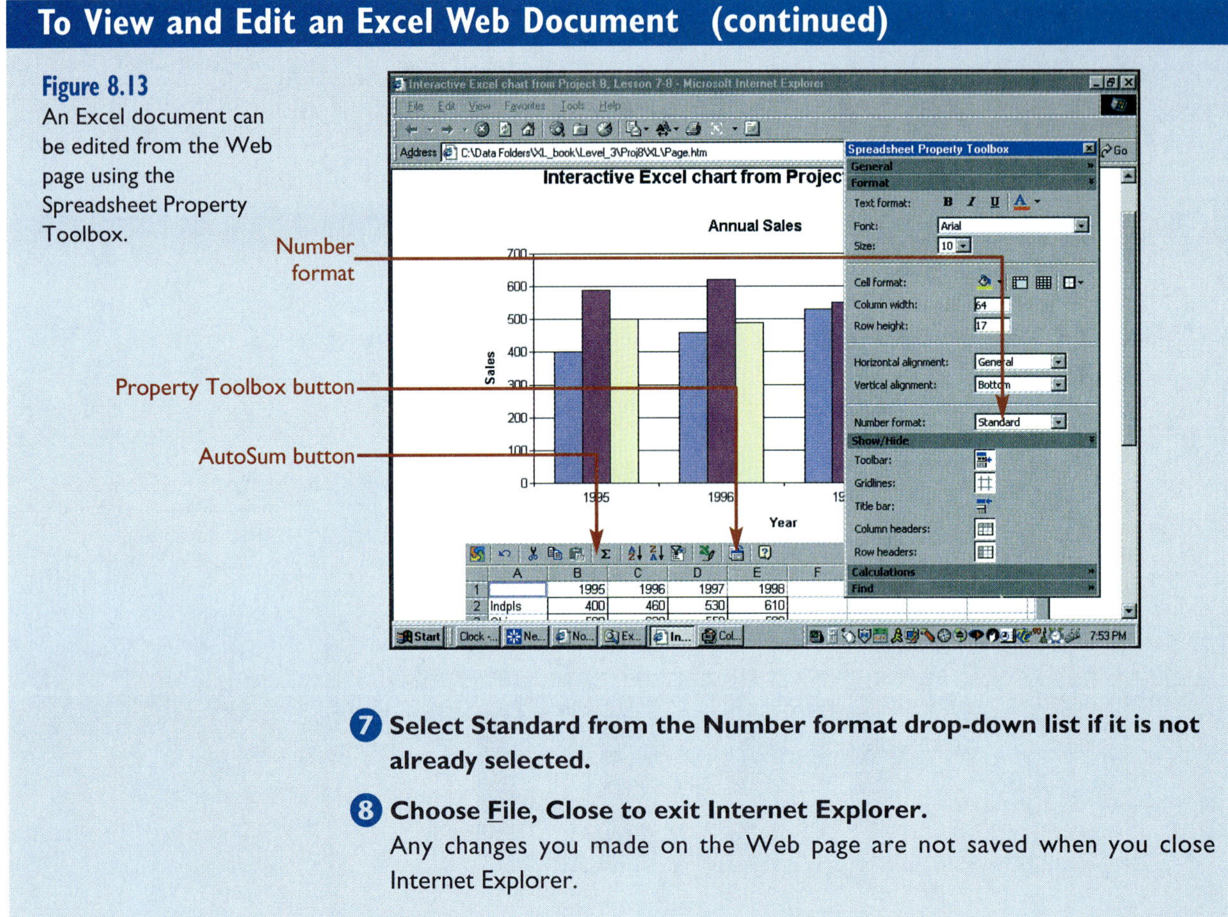

Figure 8.13 An Excel document can be edited from the Web page using the Spreadsheet Property Toolbox.

7 **Select Standard from the Number format drop-down list if it is not already selected.**

8 **Choose File, Close to exit Internet Explorer.**

Any changes you made on the Web page are not saved when you close Internet Explorer.

Close the workbook without saving.

Lesson 9: Emailing an Excel Workbook

If you have Internet access and have an email program that is MAPI-(Messaging Application Programming Interface) compliant (such as Outlook, Outlook Express, and most Windows-based email programs) you can email a workbook directly from Excel. If your computer uses a modem to send and retrieve email, connect to your ISP (Internet service provider) for this lesson.

To Email a Workbook

1 **Open XL3-0806.xls.**

2 **Choose File, Send To, Mail Recipient or click the Email button on the Standard toolbar.**

This will make Excel look like Figure 8.14.

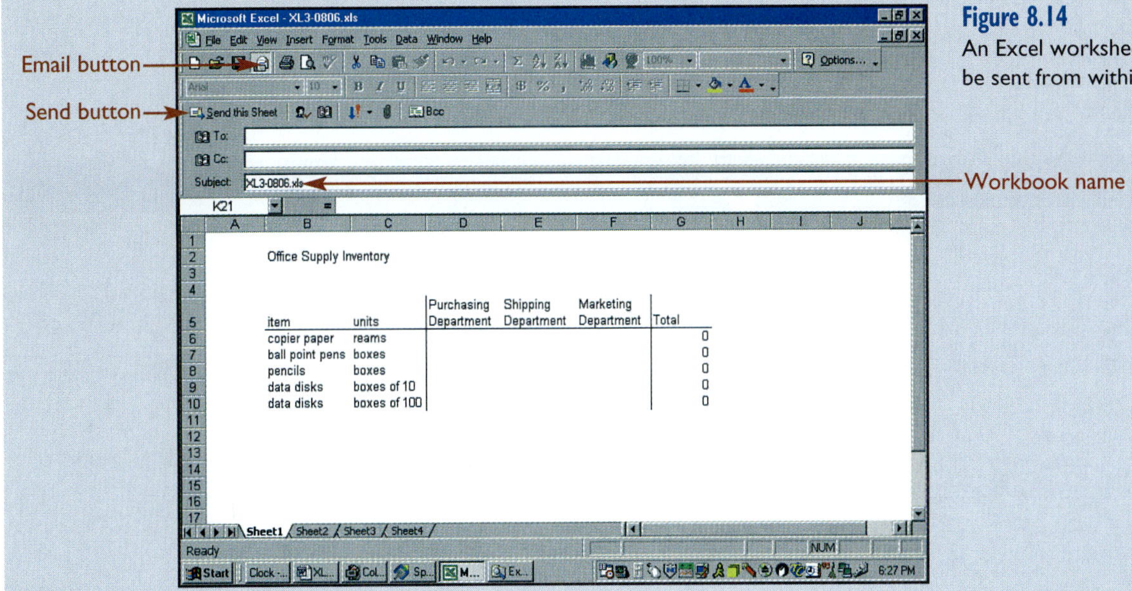

Email button

Send button

Workbook name

Figure 8.14
An Excel worksheet can be sent from within Excel.

3 **Specify yourself as the recipient and send the message by clicking Send this Sheet.**

4 **Switch back to Excel and close XL3-0806.xls.**

5 **Open your email program and retrieve the message.**

6 **Close all open applications.**

Two Ways to Send Excel Worksheets
If you choose File, Send To, Mail Recipient, the active worksheet will be inserted as text in an email message. This works best if the content of the worksheet is simple and the worksheet is small.

If you choose File, Send To, Mail Recipient (as Attachment), the entire workbook is sent as an attached file. This method is preferable if you want the recipient to be able to see all of the worksheets and be able to work with the workbook.

Summary

In this project you have seen how to share a workbook and monitor changes. This can be useful if you are developing a workbook jointly and you want to see what the other person has done. It is also useful if two or more users update information in a workbook.

Hyperlinks were shown to be a handy way of jumping between files and locations within files. In a large workbook, it is handy to have a table of contents that jumps the user to specific locations within the workbook.

Saving workbooks in HTML format is as easy as using the Save As command, but we also saw how you can save a workbook in interactive format so that Web users can actually work with it without downloading it.

You can gain knowledge about collaboration, hyperlinks, and Web pages by searching the Help system, but the best way to learn about these topics is to use them on a regular basis and experiment with the various features.

Checking Concepts and Terms 

True/False

For each of the following, check *T* or *F* to indicate whether the statement is true or false.

__T __F **1.** The Tracking Changes feature will show the changes that were made the last time a workbook was used. [L1]

__T __F **2.** Web documents created from Excel can be interactive. [L7]

__T __F **3.** A worksheet cannot be deleted while the workbook is in shared mode. [L1]

__T __F **4.** Workbook sharing can only be done on a network. [L1]

__T __F **5.** A hyperlink can only link to named cells. [L4]

Multiple Choice

Circle the letter of the correct answer for each of the following.

1. A hyperlink can be a link to [L4]

a. a Web page

b. another document

c. a location within another document

d. all of the above

2. During a PowerPoint presentation, hyperlinks are [L6]

a. like OLE links

b. active

c. inactive

d. both a and b

3. An example of an interactive Excel Web page might be [L7]

a. an order form

b. a rate table

c. a price list

d. none of the above

4. In order to email a worksheet directly from Excel, your email program must be [L9]

a. Microsoft Explorer

b. PINE

c. EUDORA

d. MAPI-compliant

5. An interactive document must be saved in [L7]

a. HTML format

b. interactive format

c. XLS format

d. none of the above

Discussion Questions

1. You work for a mortgage company that has decided to post a Web site. What Excel documents might you want to use and which would be interactive?

2. You work in the accounting department and you are giving a PowerPoint presentation in conjunction with the annual report. What types of Excel documents might you want to include, and which type of link would be appropriate for each document?

3. You and a co-worker in another branch office have been assigned to work on a project together. You will be sharing an Excel workbook. What factors should you consider, and how will you set up the sharing and tracking functions?

Skill Drill

Skill Drill exercises reinforce project skills. Each skill reinforced is the same, or nearly the same, as a skill presented in the project. Detailed instructions are provided in a step-by-step format.

1. Tracking Changes in a Shared Workbook

When you are tracking changes and make several changes to the same cell, does Excel remember all of the changes or just the last one? In this exercise you will discover the answer.

1. Open XL3-0807.xls and save it as `Exercise1.xls`.
2. Choose Tools, Track Changes, Highlight Changes.
3. Check the When check box and select All from the drop-down list.
4. Check the Who check box and select Everyone from the drop-down list.
5. Check the Highlight changes on screen check box and then click OK.
6. Enter `11` in cell D9.
7. Enter `19` in cell D9 to replace the previous value.
8. Enter `40` in cell D9 to replace the previous value.
9. Choose Tools, Track Changes, Accept or Reject Changes.

   The only change shown is the last one—going from a blank cell to 40.
10. Close the dialog box without accepting or rejecting the change.
11. Save the workbook and close it.

Only the Last Cell Change Is Tracked
Intermediate changes are not tracked. The only way intermediate changes would be tracked is if you saved the file after each change.

2. Sharing a Workbook via Email

If you decide to send an Excel sheet to someone, you can do it directly from Excel.

1. Open XL3-0808.xls and save it as `Exercise2.xls`.
2. Choose File, Send To, Mail Recipient (as Attachment).
3. Send the workbook to yourself as an attachment.
4. Close the workbook.
5. Open your email program and open the attached workbook.
6. Choose Tools, Track Changes, Accept or Reject Changes.
7. Accept all of the changes.
8. Save and close the workbook.

3. Using Hyperlinks Within a Document

Hyperlinks make it easy to jump to locations within a document. This document associates hyperlinks with values within cells.

1. Open XL3-0809.xls and save it as `Exercise3`.
2. In cells B3:B7, create hyperlinks to each of the worksheets named Level 1 through Level 5.

   You'll be able to see the worksheet names when you click '+' to expand the Cell References in the center of the dialog box.
3. Click on the ScreenTips button and type an appropriate label. Do this for each link.
4. In cell A1 of worksheets Level 1 through Level 5, make a hyperlink back to the Top sheet. In the Text to display box, type `Top`.

   Hint: Once you create the first hyperlink, you can copy or paste it into cell A1 of the other worksheets.
5. Click on the ScreenTips button and type an appropriate label.
6. Test the links to make sure they work.
7. Save and close the workbook.

4. Hyperlinking to a Word Document from Excel

If you have a complex worksheet, you might want a link to detailed instructions in a Word document.

1. Open XL3-0810.xls and save it as `Exercise4`.
2. In cell A16, type: `Click here for detailed instructions`.
3. With cell A16 selected, choose Insert, Hyperlink.
4. Create a hyperlink to XL3-0811.doc; include an appropriate ScreenTip.

   This is the file that would contain the instructions.
5. Test the link and return to the Excel document using the Back button.

   If a file contains hyperlinks, the Web toolbar is automatically visible.

   Also note in the Excel document that the text in cell A16 overflows into adjacent cells, but only the part in cell A16 activates the link.
6. Save and close the Exercise4 file. Then exit Word without saving the XL3-0811.doc file.

5. Editing a Hyperlink

It is possible to change hyperlinks after they have been created.

1. Open XL3-0812.xls and save it as `Exercise5`.
2. Right-click cell A16.
3. From the shortcut menu, select Hyperlink, Edit Hyperlink.
4. Change the ScreenTip to: `Make sure you click in cell A16`. Then click OK.
5. Verify that the change worked.
6. Save and close the file.

6. Removing a Hyperlink

If you no longer need a hyperlink, they are easy to remove.

1. Open XL3-0813.xls and save it as `Exercise6`.
2. Right-click cell A16.
3. From the shortcut menu, choose Hyperlink, Remove Hyperlink.
4. Verify that the link has been removed.
5. Save and close the file.

Another Method for Removing a Hyperlink
You can also remove an existing hyperlink by clicking the Remove Link button in the Edit Hyperlink dialog box.

7. Creating an Interactive Excel Web Page

This exercise creates a Web page that enables users to calculate a loan amortization table.

1. Open XL3-0814.xls.
2. Note that the workbook is protected, except for the input cells for amount, rate, and date. The panes are frozen so the input information at the top stays visible while scrolling through the document. Also note that there are two hyperlinks.
3. Choose File, Save as Web Page.
4. In the Save As dialog box, name the Web page `Exercise7.htm`, click Publish, and then check the Add interactivity box.
5. Check that you want to open the Web page with the browser.
6. Leave the page open for the next exercise.

8. Working with an Interactive Excel Web Page

The purpose of having an interactive Web page is so that users can use it. In this exercise, you will use the Web page to calculate a loan payment.

1. With the interactive Web page from the previous exercise visible in Internet Explorer, enter a loan of $120,000 in cell F3, with 8% (cell F4) interest starting on March 5, 1999 (cells C4:C6).
2. Click the View summary hyperlink and note the total principal paid back after 30 years is indeed $120,000, and that the total amount of interest is more than the amount of the loan.
3. Click the View Summary and Go to Top links at the top and bottom of the worksheet.
4. Click the Property Toolbox button on the toolbar.
5. Hide the gridlines using the Show/Hide option.
6. Click on Calculations in the Spreadsheet Property Toolbox and click on different cells to view the cell formulas.
7. Exit Internet Explorer.

Challenge

Challenge exercises expand on or are somewhat related to skills presented in the lessons. Each exercise provides a brief narrative introduction followed by instructions in a numbered step format that are not as detailed as those in the Skill Drill section.

Each exercise is independent of the others, so that you may complete the exercises in any order. Be sure to save the workbook after completing each exercise. If you need a paper copy of the completed exercise, enter your name centered in a header before printing.

1. Automatically Updating Shared Files

Instead of checking for changes when a file is saved, you can have Excel automatically check every few minutes. This exercise will require that you have a partner or are able to access two computers yourself.

1. Open XL3-0815.xls and save it as `Challenge1`.
2. Have a partner open the same file on another computer.
3. On both computers, choose Tools, Share Workbook; then select the Advanced tab.
4. In the Update Changes area, select Automatically every 5 minutes.

   Five minutes is the shortest interval allowed.
5. Make some changes (such as entering different cell values), and then wait five minutes and see what happens.
6. Save the changes and keep the files open for the next exercise.

2. Handling Conflicting Changes

What happens if two users sharing a workbook place different values in the same cell? With the workbooks open from the previous exercise, try it. As with Exercise 1, this exercise requires a partner or access to two computers simultaneously.

1. Open both files created in Challenge Exercise 1, if necessary.
2. On one system, enter **12** in cell D6.
3. On the other system, enter **33** in cell D6.
4. Save both workbooks, or wait for an automatic check within 5 minutes.

   A Resolve Conflicts dialog box appears and you can determine which value wins.
5. Close the files.

3. Listing Changes

Sometimes you may want to see a detailed list of changes since the last time a file was saved.

1. Open the Challenge1.xls file from the previous exercise and make some more cell entries. Also, enter some cell formulas.
2. Save the workbook.
3. Choose Tools, Track Changes, Highlight Changes.
4. Check the When box and select Not yet reviewed from the drop-down list.
5. In the Highlight Changes dialog box, check List changes on a new sheet. Click OK.
6. Accept or reject each change as desired.

   There is now a new sheet called History, detailing all of the changes since the last save.
7. Save and close the workbook.

4. Saving a File as a Web Page

In Skill Drill Exercise 7, you created an interactive Excel Web document. In this exercise, you simply save a document as an HTML Web page.

1. Open XL3-0805.xls and click the Chart sheet tab.
2. Choose File, Save As.
3. In the Save as type box, select Web Page from the drop-down list.
4. In the File name box, enter `Challenge4.htm`.
5. Click the Change Title button, add an appropriate title, and click OK.
6. Click the Save button, and close the file.
7. In Windows Explorer, double-click the Challenge4.htm file to open it with your default browser.
8. Note how the page is different from the interactive version.

5. Creating a Hyperlink to an Internet Site in Excel

As more and more users have Internet access, it becomes feasible to have Internet links within documents.

1. Open XL3-0805.xls and save it as `Challenge5`.
2. Click in cell C9 in the Data sheet, and then choose Insert, Hyperlink.
3. Select Existing File or Web Page.
4. In the Type the file or Web page name box, type the name of a Web site or select one from the Browsed Pages or Inserted Links box. Click OK after you have selected a page.

   If you cannot find any links, you can use `http://www.microsoft.com`.
5. If you are connected to the Internet, try clicking the link.
6. Use the Back button in your browser to get back to Excel.

6. Creating an Email Hyperlink in Excel

Hyperlinks can also include email addresses. If you find you are frequently sending email while working on a workbook, you can put an email link in the workbook.

1. Open XL3-0815.xls and save it as `Challenge6`.
2. Click in cell C12, and choose Insert, Hyperlink.
3. Select E-mail address in the Link to box.
4. Type in your email address.
5. Type in appropriate Text to display and a ScreenTip.

   If you type in a Subject line, it will always be inserted in your email, although it can be changed within the email message.
6. If you are connected to the Internet, try clicking the link and send yourself a message. The default mail program will be loaded.

Discovery Zone

Discovery Zone exercises require advanced knowledge of topics presented in *Essentials* lessons, application of skills from multiple lessons, or self-directed learning of new skills. Each exercise is independent of the others, so that you may complete the exercises in any order.

1. Placing an Excel Web Page on the Server and Creating a Link

If you have your own Web site, place an Excel Web page on your Web server and make a link to it from your Web page.

If you do not have a Web site, ask your instructor how you could create a site. If you have access to the Internet, it is very likely you can also create your own page. Microsoft FrontPage and FrontPage Express make it very easy to create Web sites.

2. Using Hyperlinks

Hyperlinks are easy to use and have many purposes. When you create new documents, think "hyperlinks." Review some Word, Excel, and PowerPoint files that you use frequently and see if you can find a use for hyperlinks. Add one or more hyperlinks to your documents and then test them. Edit the hyperlinks as necessary.

Task Guide

A book in the *Essentials* series is designed to be kept as a handy reference beside your computer, even after you have completed all the projects and exercises. Any time you have difficulty recalling the sequence of steps or a shortcut needed to achieve a result, look up the general category in the alphabetized listing below, and then quickly home in on your task at hand. For your convenience, some tasks have been duplicated under more than one category. If you have difficulty performing a task, turn to the page number listed in the third column to locate the step-by-step exercise or other detailed description. For the greatest efficiency in using this Task Guide, take a few minutes to familiarize yourself with the main categories and keywords before you begin your search.

To Do This	Use This Command	Page Number
Analysis ToolPak		
Comparison: multiple group means	Choose Tools, Data Analysis; select Anova: Single Factor; click OK. Click Input Range text box; select range. Select grouping by Columns or Rows; enter an Alpha level. Select Output Range; select the range of the current worksheet, or select New Worksheet in Ply or New Workbook to place the output in a new worksheet or workbook. Click OK.	96-97
Comparison: paired Two Sample for Means	Choose Tools, Data Analysis; select t-Test: Paired Two Sample for Means; click OK. In the Input area, select the two variable ranges; enter a number for Hypothesized Mean Difference and Alpha level. Select Output Range; select the range in the current worksheet, or select New Worksheet Ply or New Workbook to place the output in a new worksheet or workbook. Click OK.	95
Comparison: two independent group means	Choose Tools, Data Analysis; select t-Test: Two-Sample Assuming Equal Variances; click OK. In the Input area, select the two variable ranges; enter a number for Hypothesized Mean Difference and Alpha level. Select Output Range; select the range in the current worksheet, or select New Worksheet Ply or New Workbook to place the output in a new worksheet or workbook. Click OK.	93-94
Moving average, create	Choose Tools, Data Analysis; select Moving Average; click OK. Click Input Range text box; select range. Enter the number of values in the Interval box. Select Output Range; select the range where output will be placed. Click OK.	91-92

continues ▶

To Do This	Use This Command	Page Number
Analysis ToolPak		
Random numbers, generate	Choose Tools, Data Analysis; select Random Number Generation; click OK. In the Number of Variables text box, type the number of columns of random numbers. In the Number of Random Numbers text box, type the number of random numbers in each column. In the Distribution drop-down list, choose a distribution method. Enter value(s) in the Parameters area. Select Output Range; select the range in the current worksheet, or select New Worksheet Ply or New Workbook to place the output in a new worksheet or workbook. Click OK.	87-88
Random sample, create	Choose Tools, Data Analysis; select Sampling; click OK. Click Input Range text box; select the range of data that contains the population of values to sample. In the Sampling Method area, select Random and then type a number in the Number of Samples text box; or select Periodic and then type the periodic interval of the sampling.	90
Regression, examine relationships between variables	Choose Tools, Data Analysis; select Regression; click OK. Enter the Input Y Range for dependent data and the Input X Range for independent data. Select Labels if the first row or column of input ranges contains labels. Select Output Range; select the range in the current worksheet, or select New Worksheet Ply or New Workbook to place the output in a new worksheet or workbook. Click OK.	98
Auditing Tools		
Auditing arrows, remove	Choose Tools, Auditing, Remove All Arrows.	114
Auditing toolbar, display	Choose Tools, Auditing, Show Auditing Toolbar.	115
Dependents, view cells affected by a cell	Select a cell; choose Tools, Auditing, Trace Dependents.	114
Error messages, trace	Select a cell that contains an error message; choose Tools, Auditing, Trace Error.	111
Precedents, view cells that affect a cell	Select a cell; choose Tools, Auditing, Trace Precedents.	113-114
Forms		
Align object to cell border	Hold down Alt while drawing, moving, or sizing an object.	3
Check box, add to worksheet	Click the Check Box button on Forms toolbar; click on worksheet, or drag to draw the box the desired size.	3
Combo box, add to worksheet	Click the Combo Box button on Forms toolbar, click on the worksheet, or drag to draw the box the desired size.	6-7
Combo box, link to a list	Hold down Ctrl and click the combo box. Click the Control Properties button on the Forms toolbar; select the Control tab; click in the Input range text box, and select the cells to be linked. Click OK.	6-7

To Do This	Use This Command	Page Number
Forms		
Delete form object	Hold down Ctrl and click the object. Press Del to delete the object.	4
Move form object	Hold down Ctrl and click the object. Drag the border to move the object.	4
Option button, add to worksheet	Click the Option Box button on Forms toolbar; click on the worksheet or drag to draw the box the desired size.	5
Resize form object	Hold down Ctrl and click the object. Drag handles to resize the object.	4
Template, create new form using	Choose File, New; select the template from the list. Click OK.	13
Template, save form as	Choose File, Save As; in the Save as type drop-down list box, and select Template (*.xlt). Click Save.	13
Functions		
Formula palette, use	Click '=' in the formula bar; from the list of the 10 most recently used functions select More Functions; click on a Function category; select a Function name; click OK. Enter function arguments; click OK.	45
User-defined function, examine	Choose Tools, Macro, Visual Basic Editor; select the function on the Project Explorer.	51
Hyperlinks, Web Pages, and Email		
Hyperlink: insert from outside a workbook	Select the cell that will contain the hyperlink; choose Insert, Hyperlink; in the Link to area, click Existing File or Web Page. In the Type the file or Web page name text box, specify the file or Web page to be linked; click the Screen Tip button to enter a screen tip.	161
Hyperlink: insert within a workbook	Select the cell that will contain the hyperlink; choose Insert, Hyperlink; in the Link to area, click Place in This Document. In the Type the cell reference text box, specify the cell reference or worksheet to be linked, and click the Screen Tip button to enter a screen tip.	160
Workbook: email a workbook	Choose File, Send To, Mail Recipient; in the To text box, specify a recipient; in the Subject text box, type a subject; click the Send this Sheet button.	166-167
Workbook: email a workbook as an attachment	Choose File, Send To, Mail Recipient (as Attachment); the email program launches. In the To text box, specify the recipient; type a subject line in the Subject text box and type a message in the message box. Click the email program's Send button.	167
Workbook: save as interactive Web page	Choose File, Save as Web Page; specify a filename; click Selection: Sheet; check the Add Interactivity check box; click Publish. In the Choose drop-down list, choose the item to publish; click Publish.	163-164
Workbook: save as static Web page	Choose File, Save as; select Web page (*.htm;*.html) from the Save as type drop-down list. Click Save.	

continues ▶

To Do This	Use This Command	Page Number
Macros		
Macro button: add to toolbar	Choose View, Toolbars, Customize; click the Commands tab, scroll the Categories list and select Macros; drag an icon from the Commands box to an existing toolbar; right-click the button on the toolbar, choose Assign Macro from shortcut menu, and select a macro. Click OK; click Close.	35-36
Macro button: create	Draw a button using the Forms toolbar; right-click the new button; choose Assign Macro from the shortcut menu. Select a macro name in the Macro name list box; click OK.	34
Macro: play	Select Tools, Macro, Macros; select the macro from the list; click Run.	28
Macro: record	Select Tools, Macro, Record New Macro; specify macro name in the Macro name text box; in the Store macro in drop-down list, select where the macro is to be saved; click OK; select commands to be recorded; click the Stop Recording button.	27
Personal Macro Workbook, unhide	Choose Window, Unhide; click Personal from the Unhide workbook list, and then click OK.	31
Object Linking and Embedding		
Edit embedded object	Double-click the object; edit the object in its source application; click outside the object.	142
Edit linked object	Select the object; choose Edit, Linked Worksheet Object, Edit Link, or double-click the object. Edit the worksheet object; save the worksheet.	139
Embed an object	Select an object; choose Edit, Copy; in another application choose Edit, Paste Special. In the Paste Special dialog box, click Paste; in the As list box, select the object type; click OK.	141
Link an object	Select an object; choose Edit, Copy; in another application choose Edit, Paste Special; in the Paste Special dialog box click Paste link; in the As list box, select the object type; click OK.	138
Link: examine and/or edit	Choose Edit, Links. To edit the link, click the Change Source button; select the file to link; click OK.	140
Protection		
Protect a workbook	Select any cells that are not to be protected; choose Format, Cells, and then click the Protection tab; deselect the Locked check box; click OK. Select Tools, Protection, Protect Sheet. Type a password (optional); click OK.	11-12
Simulation		
Chi-square goodness of fit, simulate	Use the CHITEST function.	76
Discrete values, simulate	Use an IF(RAND()) function.	71
Distribution of discrete values, generate	Use a nested IF() function.	73

To Do This	Use This Command	Page Number
Simulation		
Random integers, create	Use the RANDBETWEEN function.	75
Random number, create	Use the RAND() function.	67
Random numbers, recalculate	Press F9.	67
Text Operations		
Numeric value to text, convert	Use the TEXT function.	57-58
Strings of text, combine	Use the concatenation operator "&" between the two text strings or use the CONCATENATE function.	52
Substring, extract from text	Use the MID function.	55
Symbol, create special	Use the CHAR() function.	53
Tools: Goal Seek, Data Tables, Scenarios, and Solver		
Goal Seek: calculate a value	Select a cell; choose Tools, Goal Seek; enter values for To value and By changing cell. Click OK.	116
Scenario: create summary	Choose Tools, Scenarios; select a scenario from the Scenarios list; click Summary. Enter the range of the Result cells; click OK. Click Close.	121
Scenario: create	Choose Tools, Scenarios; select Add; specify a Scenario name and enter the Changing cells; click OK; enter the values for the changing cells; click Add.	119
Scenario: edit existing	Choose Tools, Scenarios; select a scenario from the Scenarios list; click Edit. Edit the scenario; click OK. Click Close.	119-120
Scenario: use existing	Choose Tools, Scenarios; select a scenario from the Scenarios list; click Show. Click Close.	121
Solver: maximize or minimize costs	Choose Tools, Solver; in the Set Target Cell text box, select the target cell; in the By Changing Cells text box, select cells to be changed. Click Add to enter constraints; enter the constraint and click Add; repeat for additional constraints. Click Solve.	122-127
What-if analysis, perform with Data Table	Choose Data, Table; enter Row input cell and Column input cell. Click OK.	118
Tracking Changes		
Accept or reject changes	Choose Tools, Track Changes, Accept or Reject Changes. Select When, Who, and Where check boxes, and select which changes to check. Click OK. Click Accept or Reject for each change found. Click Close.	157-158
Share a workbook	Set the workbook to track changes, and it will be set as shared.	158-159
Track changes	Choose Tools, Track Changes, Highlight Changes; check the Track changes while editing check box. Click OK.	155-156

Glossary

All key terms appearing in this book (in bold italic) are listed alphabetically in this Glossary for easy reference. If you want to learn more about a feature or concept, turn to the page reference shown after its definition. You can also use the Index to find the term's other significant occurrences.

Analysis ToolPak An Excel add-in that performs various statistical tests. [pg. 86]

Anova Analysis of Variance. A statistical test for comparing the means of two or more groups. [pg. 96]

ANSI codes American National Standards Institute. Character codes used by most Windows applications. [pg. 55]

ASCII codes American Standards Committee for Information Interchange. These character codes were used for pre-Windows applications. [pg. 55]

auditing tools Excel menu and toolbar items that allow you to verify cell formulas and trace errors. [pg. 110]

check box A box on a form that can be clicked to select an option. [pg. 3]

chi-square A statistical distribution that is used for goodness of fit tests and other procedures. [pg. 75]

combo box A form item that allows the user to select from a list or to type in a value. [pg. 6]

compound document A Microsoft Office document that is made up of more than one application, for example, an Excel workbook embedded in a Word document. [pg. 136]

concatenation The process of linking together text strings using the "&" operator. [pg. 52]

conditional formatting Making the appearance of a cell different depending on the contents of the cell. [pg. 70]

constraints Mathematical expressions that express limitations. [pg. 122]

controls Any form object, such as a button or a check box, that allows user interaction. [pg. 2]

data table An Excel procedure that calculates multiple results from a formula that contains one or two variables. [pg. 117]

destination file A file that contains linked or embedded data. [pg. 136]

embedded A file contained entirely within another file. [pg. 136]

error value The message code that is displayed in an Excel cell to identify a problem in a formula. [pg. 112]

expected value The long-term average outcome that is calculated from a probability distribution. [pg. 71]

Formula palette Formerly known as the Function Wizard, the Formula palette presents a list of functions and prompts for the appropriate inputs. [pg. 45]

future value The amount of money at the end of a time period, when money is invested over a period of time. [pg. 46]

Goal Seek A Microsoft Excel tool that allows you to determine a value of a formula variable that would be required to yield a given result. [pg. 116]

hyperlinks Underlined text that is clicked to jump to another location. [pg. 154]

linked An object is linked if it is referenced from another location. [pg. 136]

linked object An object that is referenced from another location. [pg. 6]

macro Multiple commands or keystrokes that are executed as a single operation. [pg. 24]

macro button A button that executes a macro when it is clicked. [pg. 33]

moving average A statistical procedure to smooth time series data by averaging several periods of data at a time. [pg. 91]

normal distribution A probability distribution that approximates many situations. Sometimes called the "bell" curve because of its shape. [pg. 77]

object Anything that has properties and can be referenced and used by another program. An object may be as small as a character or as large as an Excel workbook. [pg. 136]

OLE (Object Linking and Embedding) The process of creating compound files by referencing other files (linking) or inserting files (embedding). [pg. 136]

onscreen form A computer form that resembles a paper form. [pg. 2]

option button Two or more buttons, of which only one can be selected to specify an option. [pg. 4]

Personal Macro Workbook A Microsoft Excel file designed to contain macros which are available to all workbooks. [pg. 29]

present value The amount of money at the beginning of a period, when money is invested over time. [pg. 48]

p-value A statistical calculation that gives the probability of getting a result by chance alone. If the value is small, (usually under .05) then it is assumed that the result is not merely by chance, that is, is statistically significant. [pg. 76]

RAND An Excel function that generates random numbers between 0.0 and 1.0. [pg. 66]

RANDBETWEEN An Excel function that generates random integers between two specified values. [pg. 75]

RANDNORM A user-defined function that generates normally distributed random numbers with a specified mean and standard deviation. [pg. 77]

random data sets Sets of data created with a random generator function. [pg. 66]

random sample A sample selected from a population where every item in the population has an equally likely chance of being selected. [pg. 89]

regression analysis A statistical procedure that examines the relationship between variables with the goal of predicting one variable from another. [pg. 97]

regression line The best-fitting straight line that is fit to a scatter chart of two variables. [pg. 99]

reverse engineer An informal expression that refers to determining how something works by taking it apart. In a computer context, it refers to examining worksheet formulas to see how a spreadsheet works. [pg. 115]

Scenario Manager An Excel procedure for saving multiple input values and results. [pg. 119]

scenarios Multiple sets of input values that are used for "what-if" analyses. [pg. 119]

share Two or more users having simultaneous access to a workbook. [pg. 158]

simulation The process of having Excel create many random input values and studying the effect on certain cells. [pg. 66]

Solver An Excel add-in designed to handle complex problem-solving with mathematical models and constraints. [pg. 122]

source file When a file has a link to another file, the linked file is called the source file. [pg. 136]

spinner A control that is used to increase or decrease the numerical amount that can be placed in a linked cell. The spinner control resembles a two-headed arrow. [pg. 8]

substring Text is sometimes referred to as a string. A portion of the text is called a substring. [pg. 55]

template A document with features such as boilerplate text, styles, and Form controls that will be applied to any document created from the template. [pg. 12]

tracking changes The capability of Excel to "remember" a series of changes so they can be reviewed. [pg. 154]

t-Test analysis A statistical procedure for determining whether two groups are different. [pg. 92]

uniform distribution A probability distribution where every value is equally likely to occur. [pg. 77]

user-defined function A macro written by a user or programmer that works like an Excel function. [pg. 50]

Visual Basic Editor The Excel method of creating and modifying macros using the VBA language. [pg. 24]

Visual Basic for Applications (VBA) A programming language that is built into Microsoft Office applications. Recorded macros can create VBA programming code or procedures can be written directly using VBA. [pg. 24]

Web pages A unit of information displayed on a Web site. [pg. 154]

what-if analysis The process of changing one or more cells in a worksheet and studying the impact on other cells. When this process is automated, it is called simulation. [pg. 117]

Index

F

G

H

I-J

K-L

M

N

O

P

Q-R

U

V

W-Z